ILLNESS AS

PITTSBURGH SERIES IN COMPOSITION, LITERACY,
AND CULTURE
David Bartholomae and Jean Ferguson Carr, Editors

AS NARRATIVE

Ann Jurecic

University of Pittsburgh Press

Published by the University of Pittsburgh Press, Pittsburgh, Pa., 15260
Copyright © 2012, University of Pittsburgh Press
Manufactured in the United States of America
Printed on acid-free paper
10 9 8 7 6 5 4 3 2

Library of Congress Cataloging-in-Publication Data

Jurecic, Ann, 1962–
    Illness as narrative / Ann Jurecic.
        p.   cm. — (Pittsburgh series in composition, literacy, and culture)
    Includes bibliographical references and index.
    ISBN 978-0-8229-6190-1 (pbk. : acid-free paper)
        1. American literature—20th century—History and criticism.   2. Diseases in literature.
3. Autobiography—Authorship.   I. Title.
    PS228.D57J87 2012
    810.9'3561—dc23   2011048866

for my teachers

CONTENTS

ACKNOWLEDGMENTS

This project found me. The ideas for *Illness as Narrative* emerged after my husband was diagnosed with cancer for the first time. They began to evolve with a recurrence of that cancer, the diagnosis of a second kind of cancer, and yet another recurrence. The experience of four surgeries and three trips through chemotherapy was his. My experience was defined by all that happened around his diagnoses, treatments, and recoveries, which included listening to stories that people told me just because I'd become a marginal member of the cancer club. Over time, I would find myself in a crowded lecture hall, a grocery store, or the audience of a school play, and I'd be able to connect many of the faces there to stories of suffering. I became conscious of a new, previously invisible dimension of my workplace and my community, which has never faded from view.

I want to take a moment to say a bit more about the origins of my project because my acknowledgments of the many people who supported me as I wrote *Illness as Narrative* are best understood within that context. As a scholar in writing studies, I've long been interested in the intersection of literature and literacies, where the aesthetic and rhetorical merge. As stories about illness accumulated around me, I used my training to study their history, politics, and form and thus to connect two parts of my life that otherwise felt intolerably separate. I had my professional life, thinking and writing about how meaning gets made with language, and I had my life in the waiting room, where I heard the stories of the ill, their caregivers, and their loved ones. The task of connecting scholarship to everyday matters of concern became an even more compelling challenge when I realized that the critical practices I'd acquired through years of training weren't the right tools for the job of interpreting illness memoirs. Critique is all well and good, but I wanted to more fully understand the various functions that narratives about illness perform for writers and readers, speakers and listeners. In order to comprehend the possibilities as well as the limits of writing and reading about illness, I needed either to look somewhere other than the familiar sources or to see those sources from a different perspective. My goal became to find and develop practices that would allow for critical *and* compassionate analysis.

Given the provenance and aims of my project, I first want to express my deep gratitude to those friends and extended family members whose kindness and compassion made it possible for my family to survive the rough years. While there are many people who helped in countless ways, I'd like to express special thanks to those who helped me make time to think, write, and sleep in the midst of it all: the late Jo Kessel Buyske, Ellen Goellner, Anne Caswell Klein, Kathy Pasewark and the Pasewark family, Zori Stern, Lee Talley, and Amanda Irwin Wilkins. Ellen, Anne, Lee, and Amanda did double duty by offering an essential intellectual as well as personal support network.

The Department of English at Rutgers University is so large that I can't thank everyone by name, so I extend my collective gratitude to the faculty and staff for their constant support and optimism. I owe special thanks to my colleague Kurt Spellmeyer for his encouragement and guidance, as well as for demonstrating that it is possible to be a dedicated scholar, writer, and teacher, all at once. I'd also like to thank my students in general and three students in particular. I'm lucky to have had the chance to work with Zeynep Uzumcu, poet, chemist, and researcher extraordinaire, who showed up at exactly the right moment and helped me with the historical research for the first chapter about the rise of the illness memoir as a genre. I'm fortunate, as well, to have had years of good conversations about literature and medicine with my former student Dr. Daniel Marchalik, who is going to find a way to survive his residency *and* read literature. I am also thankful for Sarah Goldfarb's essential assistance as I prepared the final manuscript.

While working on this book, I had the good fortune to be able to participate in four interdisciplinary working groups, three of which were at Rutgers. Historians Keith Wailoo and Julie Livingston generously invited me to join their group on the history of pain when I was working on the pain chapter. I benefited enormously from conversations about their work, and the research techniques I developed that year contributed a great deal to the first chapter's account of the historical origins of the illness memoir. I offer my thanks, as well, to the members of the year-long seminar on "Health and Body" sponsored by the Institute for Research about Women (IRW). This welcoming community of scholars offered helpful feedback on material that became part of chapter 5.

I am especially grateful to Susan Sidlauskas, whom I met at the IRW and who has continued to sustain me with conversation and friendship. I am thankful, as well, for my fellowship at the Center for Cultural Analysis at Rutgers and to the members of the working group on "Mind and Culture." Our discussions about the intersection of cultural and scientific theory introduced me to a set of debates that helped me to situate my project in a broader scholarly conversation. I also want to express my heartfelt thanks and appreciation to my Fetzer collaborators, Rita Charon, BJ Miller, Peter Schneider, and Kat Vlahos, as well as Louise Aronson, who keep me grounded and inspired. In addition, I'd like to thank the National Council of Teachers of English for permission to reprint in chapters 5 and 6 passages from "Empathy and the Critic," which appeared in *College English* 74 (Sept. 2011): 10–27 (copyright by the National Council of Teachers of English; reprinted with permission).

While I've been supported by many people as I've worked on *Illness as Narrative*, there are a few individuals whose contributions to my thoughts, writing, career, and life have been so essential that this book would not exist without them.

I worked with Kerry Walk for three formative years at the Princeton Writing Program and, following her advice and example, I developed a deeper understanding of scholarly writing, especially how to define my intellectual motives with strength and clarity. I also learned to revise like never before. Kerry's influence on my prose is present from the first articulation of the project to the last clear and coherent sentence.

Many years ago at the Conference on College Composition and Communication (CCCC), I met Charles M. Anderson, who was then the book review editor for *Literature and Medicine*. He encouraged me to write an article for the journal and, in case I had any doubts about his sincerity, he convinced me by handing me his business card even as elevator doors threatened to close on his arm. Years after I wrote that article, Chuck assumed the position of executive editor at *Literature and Medicine* and asked me to succeed him as the book review editor. His invitation to join the board and his mentorship have been enormous gifts.

Everyone who works in the medical humanities knows and admires Rita Charon's book *Narrative Medicine* and the Program in Narrative Medicine she founded at Columbia University College of Physicians and Surgeons. But there's no experience quite like being in her electrifying presence and seeing her mind and pedagogical principles at work. At one of her workshops, I finally figured out how to articulate my sense that the suspicious practices of contemporary criticism were poorly suited to the work of interpreting narratives about illness.

Through the years, I've been lucky to have many chances to talk, present, and collaborate with Rita. My work has benefited from her honest feedback and I've been buoyed on many occasions by her warmth and encouragement.

No one has done more to help me bring *Illness as Narrative* into being than Richard E. Miller. More than a decade ago, reading "The Nervous System" showed me how I might imagine a career in writing studies. Since I arrived at Rutgers, he has listened with care, finding value in my ideas that I sometimes couldn't see myself. More recently, he read every word of the draft of this book and gave me extensive feedback. I've never before received such insightful, attentive, generous advice, focused so completely on helping me find my own way to make my work better. I'm aware there were many occasions in the past six years that he devoted hours to my project when there were many other pressing demands on his time. I'm grateful beyond words for all he has done and all I have learned. Onward!

To my family, Steve, Quinta, and Jack, what can I say? I appreciate your patience, understanding, and good humor. I'll never be able to express my gratitude adequately on this, or any, page, so for now I'll just say, thanks for the chocolate.

ILLNESS AS NARRATIVE

Illness Narratives and the
Challenge to Criticism

FROM THE WINTER OF 1918 until the spring of 1919, an influenza out-break swept the globe, killing fifty to a hundred million people, as much as 5 percent of the world's population (Barry 397). Despite the flu's ferocity, for much of the twentieth century this pandemic nearly vanished from popular consciousness. Although more United States soldiers died from the flu than from combat during World War I, it has rarely been given a significant place in American histories of the war.[1] Even though, according to historian John M. Barry, it "killed more people in a year than the Black Death of the Middle Ages killed in a century" (5), the pandemic is virtually absent from American and British literature of its era. Mary McCarthy, whose parents both died of the virus when she was six years old, briefly mentions the flu at the beginning of *Memories of a Catholic Girlhood*. In the novel *Look Homeward, Angel,* Thomas Wolfe devotes one chapter to the death of the main character's brother, clearly a double for his own brother Benjamin, who died of the flu when Wolfe was in college. Influenza appears in the background of Willa Cather's war novel *One of Ours* and Wallace Stegner's *The Big Rock Candy Mountain*. Only one canonical work of fiction written in English places the epidemic at the center of the plot: Katherine Anne Porter's "Pale Horse, Pale Rider," a novella narrated in a fever-ish, dreamlike manner by a young woman who falls ill, almost dies, and revives just in time to hear the discordant noise of Armistice celebrations.[2] How to bring the pandemic and the narrative form together? It is as if the project were unimaginable in the early twentieth century.

In stark contrast to the near silence that followed the 1918 pandemic, seventy years later a flood of texts appeared in response to the emergence of HIV/AIDS. In the United States, people with AIDS published a wide range of writing about their experiences of the disease, as did their doctors and caregivers. Journalists, playwrights, novelists, poets, memoirists, and diarists joined artists from other media in an effort to document the pandemic, create memorial art, and make meaning of suffering and loss on scales ranging from the individual to the global.[3] A good portion of the published texts, from articles to book-length autobiographies, fall into the category the medical humanities defines as "illness narratives"—autobiographical accounts of illness spoken or written by patients. For the purposes of this study, in which I am concerned with how contemporary writers compose illness and how readers receive the accounts, I expand the works covered by the term to include fiction and blogs, as well as academic and popular commentary, and I broaden the range of authors to include family members, physicians, caregivers—even novelists. This broadened category makes ever more apparent the thunderous cacophony of voices about HIV/AIDS, and the volume of their stories about loss, sorrow, struggle, rage, and redemption or its absence.

What can account for *all this writing?* Why, in the 1980s and 1990s, did the quantity of writing about HIV/AIDS exceed that of any previous disease—not just flu, but tuberculosis, polio, cancer, and more?[4] Much of the scholarship about these late-twentieth-century narratives tends to consider writing about HIV/AIDS in relative isolation, as if it were a product of a particular historical period when the virus threatened to decimate a generation of gay men.[5] No doubt, AIDS required and continues to require a powerful literary response because it forms such a complex knot of personal, scientific, cultural, social, and political issues and because in the United States it has so deeply scarred the artistic community.[6] But literature about HIV/AIDS did not develop in isolation, as I will explain in detail. It was preceded and accompanied by the emergence of a narrative form not available during the 1918 flu pandemic that has at its center personal accounts of illness and dying. As literary production about AIDS waned, however, the volume of autobiographical writing about illness and disability continued to grow, surpassing the rate of production of AIDS memoirs. Indeed, by the late twentieth century, illness and disability narratives were established as literary genres.

Since their ascendance, these narratives have shifted the boundaries of literary study. In the academy, for instance, accounts of illness have become central to the literary branch of medical humanism. Medical humanists who teach literature in medical schools and centers have drawn attention to how narratives about suffering sustain individuals and communities. They observe how autobiographical illness narratives reclaim patients' voices from the biomedical narratives imposed upon them by modern medicine.[7] They study, as well, how literary, popular, and medical narratives report and construct the experience of illness, from the personal level to the national.[8] And they encourage medical practitioners to respond to the stories of suffering people with attention, respect, and understanding.

Such an approach to personal narrative is, however, out of step with mainstream literary criticism, which has not, by and large, recognized the significance of the work performed by such texts. The gap between the pragmatic work done by medical humanists in professional schools and the theoretical projects of scholars in the academy has long been evident but has not been examined and explained. *Illness as Narrative* makes the argument that one cannot fully understand writing about illness without also recognizing the split in critical attitudes toward these works. I contend, in fact, that literature about illness poses a special challenge to those current critical practices that are based in what Paul Ricoeur called the *hermeneutics of suspicion*. In *Freud and Philosophy*, Ricoeur writes that dual motives underlie literary interpretation: "[the] willingness to suspect, [and the] willingness to listen" (27). He sees suspicion and phenomenology as ideally counterbalancing each other in critical practice. In more recent decades, however, critics such as Eve Kosofsky Sedgwick, Bruno Latour, and Rita Felski have noted that the hermeneutics of suspicion has displaced what Ricoeur called listening and become "nearly synonymous with criticism itself" (Sedgwick, *Touching Feeling*, 124). Distrust of texts' errors, lies, and manipulations has become prescriptive, and the project of much contemporary criticism has become to anticipate and contain textual and theoretical problems in advance (Sedgwick, *Touching Feeling*, 130). For scholars trained in such habits of reading, the idea of trusting a narrative to provide access to the experience of another person indicates a naïve understanding of how such texts function. Before a contemporary critic begins to read an autobiography about cancer or pain, she knows that it has been constructed by medical discourse and political, economic, and cultural forces. She also knows that common readers are likely to misread it because they will assume they can try on the experience of the author and that they will therefore succumb to the myriad powers of dominant discourse. She is also likely to assume that the narrative itself is not as sophisticated or knowing as the theory she uses to interpret it. Such a suspicious critical position is not necessarily wrong, but it is incomplete. Literary critics' disdain for or disinterest in illness memoirs suggests, above all, that contemporary critics have become alienated from ordinary motives for reading and writing.

How might literary critics in the academy reclaim the "willingness to listen" that would enable them to attend more fully to the cultural work of writing about illness (Ricoeur 27)? Providing an answer, or rather answers, to this question is the goal of *Illness as Narrative*. This book will explore how writers and readers use narratives of illness to make meaning of the experiences of living *at risk, in prognosis,* and *in pain.* It will also consider how narratives of illness invite reflection about the purpose and future of literature, the arts, and literary criticism. The academy has long rewarded readings that dismantle literature's illusions but, with regard to literary and amateur illness memoirs, it is also evident that critics need other options, interpretive approaches that enable them to assemble meaning in the face of life's fragility. This chapter begins the larger exploration of *Illness as Narrative* by charting the rise of illness narratives and considering how this history brings to the surface difficult questions about the evolution of contemporary criticism—what it has made possible, and what it has excluded.

The Emergence of Illness Narratives in the Twentieth Century

Having observed the remarkable cultural shift from the silence about the 1918 flu and the quantities of writing that appeared with the pandemic of HIV/AIDS, how do we account for the proliferation of illness memoirs in the late twentieth century? What changes occurred historically, culturally, politically, and medically to bring about this transformation in literacy and literature? A patchwork of answers is available in medical, scholarly, and popular writing on health and illness. In the early twentieth century, the flu evaded expression, in part because it spread so quickly and affected so many that it overwhelmed feeble governmental and medical, as well as narrative, responses. As terrifying as the plague was, it generally remained off the front pages of newspapers, where the war remained the primary concern. In an apparent effort to allay anxiety during the peak of the pandemic, journalists throughout the United States and much of Europe downplayed the severity of the virus (Kolata 51–54; Barry 335). In the *New York Times,* for instance, only four front-page articles appeared between August and December 1918, during the height of the outbreak. The strategy of journalistic understatement during the height of the pandemic may ultimately have triggered more alarm among the general public because "what officials and the press said bore no relationship to what people saw and touched and smelled and endured" (Barry 335; see also Kolata). At stake is more than the stories that journalists and editors consider appropriate to publish. The silence extended to other genres of writing.[9] Catherine Belling writes in a study of fiction about the epidemic, "in 1918 . . . , the story of the self was seldom told in public—or at all, especially if it involved private bodily suffering" (57).

In the aftermath of the outbreak, modernists such as Virginia Woolf, working against a different assumption—that illness is too ordinary to merit representation—began to make everyday life the subject of their art. Seven years after the end of the pandemic, Woolf argued in her essay *On Being Ill*, that the commonness of illness had prevented it from "tak[ing] its place with love and battle and jealousy among the prime themes of literature" (3–4). She titled one version of this essay "Illness: An Unexploited Mine"—a turn of phrase that in 1926 would have suggested *unexploded* mines—that is, land mines—from the recent war. With the war over, Woolf encouraged writers to turn their attention to the hidden drama of the sickroom, which she believed held more literary promise than the military detritus of war. "One would have thought," Woolf wrote, that "novels . . . would have been devoted to influenza; epic poems to typhoid; odes to pneumonia, lyrics to toothache. But no" (4). The story of the body, it seems, "lack[s] plot" (6). Such a claim ignores the presence of illness in the works of Chaucer, the Brontës, Dostoyevsky, and more.[10] It also disregards the ubiquitous Romantic association of tuberculosis and madness with creativity by suggesting that literature ignores the body, as if it were "a sheet of plain glass through which the soul looks straight and clear" (4). According to Woolf, "English, which can express the thoughts of Hamlet and the tragedy of Lear, has no words for the shiver and the headache" (6). In fact, however, she sees the problem as both the absence of words for embodied suffering and the inability of language more generally to communicate personal experience. Such failures render true comprehension of another's illness impossible. In the infirmary, naïve illusions about the possibility for sympathy, companionship, and the understanding of others dissipate, and one recognizes not only the profound indifference of the world, but also one's own insignificance.

There is no evidence that Woolf's argument about language, plot, and illness influenced the writers of her era. Certainly, no rush of novels, epics, or lyrics about influenza suddenly materialized. In the first half of the twentieth century, however, several types of narratives about illness began to appear regularly in professional medical journals and occasionally in the popular press, including biographical case studies by psychologists and psychiatrists, brief snippets of professional memoirs by nurses, and doctors' heroic narratives of discovery.[11] These were precursors to the patients' own illness narratives. By the 1920s and 1930s, tuberculosis patients composed and published what historian Sheila Rothman calls "sanatorium narratives" (226). Unlike nineteenth-century autobiographies that might integrate discussions of illness into a larger life story, sanatorium narratives more narrowly depicted "an encounter with disease, with staff, and with other patients" in large, impersonal medical facilities where routines were rigid and physicians aloof (Rothman 227). Anne

Hunsaker Hawkins observes in *Reconstructing Illness,* a study of book-length illness narratives (which she calls "pathographies"), that few such narratives, other than those set in the sanatorium, emerged until the 1950s (xiv). By the mid-twentieth century, however, patients with polio—many of whom were also isolated in institutions—began to publish their stories.[12] At the same time, medical journals printed dozens of articles about the "last illnesses" of famous people, from Katherine Mansfield to Charles, Duke of Albany, and from Mozart to Major Walter Reed.[13] In addition, the "paperback revolution"—which began in the United States with Pocket Books in 1939—made books more affordable to mass audiences and allowed different genres to become popular and profitable, including the therapeutic narratives of self-help and popular psychology, cousins of today's narratives of medical triumph (Illouz 162).

After 1950, profound changes in the patient-doctor relationship were brought about by the increasing professionalization and specialization of medicine. Modern medicine forced trade-offs for both patients and their physicians. Disease became isolated from everyday life because patients now traveled to physicians' offices and hospitals for diagnosis and care (A. H. Hawkins 11). The ill exchanged intimate relationships with local doctors for improved medical efficacy, even as both patients and physicians recognized that inattention to the patient's subjective experience was a detriment to treatment. Evidence that physicians were not blind to this loss can be found in *When Doctors Are Patients,* a collection of thirty-three case histories by physicians about their own illnesses, published in 1952. In the introduction, the physician-editors, Max Pinner and Benjamin F. Miller, state that their goal is to remind doctors that every disease "affects both body and soul" (xiv). "The patient-physician relation is complex and difficult at best," writes Pinner about his own experience seeking treatment for chronic heart disease. As a patient, he was able to find physicians who were "highly competent and able" and "showed genuine professional and human interest" and yet, he says: "with one or two exceptions, they did not understand the full extent of the help they could have given nor the type of help I had expected. The patient needs more than treatment and reassurance; he wants his physician to take the responsibility upon himself" (24). What Pinner needed most was not a list of rules and restrictions—not the mere exercise of technical knowledge—but rather to be shown "the possibilities for enjoyable and fertile living within new limitations" (25).

The loss of intimacy between patients and their physicians accelerated as medical research radically transformed the profession. The discovery of sulfa drugs in the mid-1930s enabled physicians to fight bacterial infections for the first time. Antibiotics, such as streptomycin and penicillin, were developed in the 1940s and did an even better job. Vaccines helped to control diphtheria, tetanus, and yellow fever, and later measles, mumps, rubella, and polio. By mid-century in the United States and much of Western Europe, the age of acute disease had come to an end (R. Porter 685). What followed, however, was not an age of health and medical triumph, as was expected. Instead, the industrialized world entered the "age of chronic disease" (R. Porter 685). With medicine's ability to cure infectious diseases, people lived long enough to develop ailments of age and prosperity such as heart disease, diabetes, cancer, and arthritis, and they also lived long enough to reflect on and write about their experiences. Although people were *doing* better after midcentury, they were *feeling* worse.[14] Scholars and other cultural critics therefore began publishing critiques of the medical profession that demonstrated that this matter of "feeling worse" did not represent isolated personal discontent, but rather a general cultural problem. In 1951, Talcott Parsons published *The Social System*, one of the first sociological studies of the modern medical institution, setting the stage for more analyses that focused on the experience of the patient and the weaknesses of the medical enterprise. In *The Social System*, Parsons defined the "sick role"— the theory that the treatment of illness within medical institutions transforms people into patients and inscribes them into a particular social script. The appeal of the sick role to the patient, according to Parsons, is that he or she is released from ordinary social roles and obligations; the danger is that he or she is thus compelled to behave according to the institutional norms of medicine. By the 1960s, patients began voicing Parsons's analysis on their own. Members of the antipsychiatry and women's health movements, as well as supporters of new community health centers and pain clinics, denounced their alienation from practitioners and expressed suspicion that medicine had overreached its authority and "medicalized" life by imposing its expertise and control on intimate experiences, from birth to death (R. Porter 691–93). It is also the case, however, that even as complaints about bureaucratic, institutionalized, and increasingly technological medicine grew more widespread, patients became ever more active medical consumers, eventually seeking out medical treatment for everything from attention deficits to weight loss, issues that were not seen as medical before the mid-twentieth century.

As frustrations with the medical system increased, critical commentaries about contemporary medicine began to reach wider, popular audiences. Among the most enduring and influential of these texts is Elizabeth Kübler-Ross's *On Death and Dying*, which appeared in 1969 and made the case for rehumanizing the processes of dying and grieving. This work, in which Kübler-Ross described what she saw as the five stages of grief—denial, anger, bargaining, depression, and acceptance—contributed to the growth of the hospice movement. *On Death and Dying* was quickly followed in 1970 by the first edition of *Our Bodies, Our-*

selves (under the original title *Women and Their Bodies*), which became the bible of the emerging women's health moment.[15] That same year, the founding document of the field of bioethics appeared, Paul Ramsay's *The Patient as Person: Explorations in Medical Ethics.* Three additional texts from the late 1970s would further prepare the ground for the proliferation of illness narratives. Intellectual gadfly Ivan Illich published *Medical Nemesis: The Expropriation of Health* in 1976, in which he attacked doctors, hospitals, and medical institutions for harming more than healing. Two years later, Susan Sontag's *Illness as Metaphor* came out, which documented the cultural and literary history of myths and metaphors for tuberculosis and cancer. She provides example after example of literature that mythologizes and misrepresents these diseases, assigning to them meanings that stigmatize the sick. In rejecting metaphor, Sontag implies that writing about illness should be a scientific and intellectual endeavor rather than a literary one.[16] Finally, Norman Cousins published *Anatomy of an Illness as Perceived by the Patient: Reflections on Healing and Regeneration* in 1979. This text combines Cousins's own illness narrative with an argument that the interconnection of mind and body is damaged by the dehumanizing experiences that are so common in medical institutions. To assist his own recovery from a debilitating rheumatic disease, Cousins took massive doses of vitamin C and checked himself out of the hospital and into a hotel. There, the story goes, he obtained a film projector, watched Marx Brothers movies and other comedies, and laughed himself back to health. Cousins thus concludes that a cold, mechanized, soulless hospital "is no place for a person who is seriously ill" (31).

Due to the popular success of books like these, by 1980 society was poised for the emergence of what critic Lisa Diedrich calls "the politicized patient" (26). Beginning with the women's health movement of the 1970s, Diedrich observes, patients and writers began to "challenge the structures and structuring of illness from the patient's side of the doctor patient binary" and to "present affective histories that are attentive to the rhetorics and practices of politics" (27). Women's health activists called for women to liberate themselves from the masculine medical establishment by becoming knowledgeable about their own bodies, particularly with regard to reproductive health. In the spirit of this movement, in her memoir *The Cancer Journals,* poet Audre Lorde refuses to accept breast cancer and mastectomy as a loss; instead she writes about her illness as an opportunity to redefine her body, her self, and her voice.

Then came AIDS.

When AIDS first appeared in the United States in the early 1980s, it was immediately defined as the "gay plague" or "gay cancer" and openly discussed as a divine punishment wrought on the culturally marginal communities it disproportionately infected—gay men, intravenous drug users, Haitian immigrants, and the urban poor. In this conservative morality tale, AIDS was retribution for the rejection of traditional social norms. To counter the prevailing explanations of the epidemic that were circulating in the mainstream media, early AIDS activists rallied around the slogan "Silence = Death," a call for people to speak up and educate others about the disease. As activist patients grew to know as much or more about their disease than their physicians, they fought for government funding of research and demanded changes in pharmaceutical clinical trials so that more people with AIDS could have faster access to potentially helpful drugs. Patients and their supporters protested, volunteered in health centers, and provided care. And they used writing as a weapon in a cultural battle against homophobia, the disdain of the medical establishment, and the indifference of the government. Activists and people with HIV/AIDS wrote letters, editorials, pamphlets, and manifestos, as well as plays and screenplays, poems, stories, essays, and memoirs. They got the word out.[17]

Following the exponential growth of illness narratives about HIV/AIDS in the 1980s and 1990s, the production of other kinds of illness narratives grew even more. This reflects the profound need people have to tell these stories in an era when religious and folk explanations no longer give a satisfying and complete meaning to their experiences, and when biomedicine largely excludes the personal story. In *The Illness Narratives: Suffering, Healing, and the Human Condition,* Arthur Kleinman observes that the sick person and the social group to which he or she belongs have always sought answers to the question, "Why?" and observes, "Whereas virtually all healing perspectives across cultures, like religious and moral perspectives, orient sick persons and their circle to the problem of bafflement, the narrow biomedical model eschews this aspect of suffering much as it turns its back on [the experience of disease]" (29). Historian Anne Harrington similarly notes that conceptual, therapeutic, and existential deficiencies in "physicalist medicine" open a space for the creation of explanatory stories about illness and healing, in particular mind-body medicine (17). Like Kleinman, Harrington maintains, "The physicalist approach to illness falls short, especially for patients, because it denies the relevance of the kinds of questions people so often ask when they become ill: Why me? Why now? What next?" Instead, patients are told, "Your illness has no meaning" (17). In Harrington's view, familiar contemporary narratives of mind-body medicine thus function "as amplifiers of a range of very distinctive moral and social concerns about the costs of modernity" (246). People are drawn to narratives about health and healing—including autobiographical narratives, I would add—in order to work through what she calls "cultural and spiritual dislocations" (230).

The arguments offered by both Harrington and Kleinman add another layer to the complex story about the multiple forces that accelerated the growth of illness memoirs throughout the twentieth century. Their work suggests that these narratives developed both as acts of resistance to the medical establishment and as necessary complements to modern medicine. If one of the consequences of modernity is that we no longer depend upon traditional explanations for suffering, loss, and mortality, and if doctors' offices and hospitals cannot function as spaces where personal meaning can be developed, then the existential questions about human fragility and significance have to be asked and answered elsewhere.

As this overview of the evolving genre of illness memoirs has shown, throughout the past century Americans have increasingly turned to *writing* to explore the meaning of illness and suffering, and they are more often choosing to make these narratives public in books, magazines, and now online. While critics and reviewers may grumble about the steady accumulation of "misery memoirs," the fact that illness narratives have proliferated is not a sign of a collapse in literary standards. Instead, it is the consequence of a variety of changes in culture, medicine, media, and literacy over the past century, which include medical professionalization; the rise of modern health care; the emergence of the women's movement and the gay rights movement; the etiology of the AIDS virus; the inability of master narratives to give meaning to suffering in the modern era; and technological advances that promote self-publication and the global distribution of information.

Misery Memoirs and Victim Art

As compositions about illness have proliferated in multiple genres, from memoir to journalism, essays, and fiction, and beyond the literary realm to art, film, and dance, no critical consensus has emerged about how to evaluate them. A subset of reviewers and readers sees illness memoirs as acts of testimony about trauma, or at least about the dislocations and transformations caused by disease or disorder. The term "testimony," however, sets a high standard, implying that such accounts should be verifiable and authentic. Few illness memoirs—constructed representations of the interior experience of illness— can fulfill such a standard, however. Those who write about illness, an experience that can break a life in two, face the nearly impossible task that confronts all who write about trauma: how to speak the unspeakable. If illness is beyond expression in language, translation of the experience into words misrepresents, even contaminates, the real event. In addition, because illness narratives provoke affective and intimate engagement, responses that have little currency in academic discussions of the arts and literature, they disrupt critical expectations and typical standards of judgment. Even when such works are written by respected writers such as Harold Brodkey, Anatole Broyard, Maxine Kumin,

Audre Lorde, or William Styron, they may seem to be self-indulgent manipulations of sentiment and goodwill. Other critics emphasize that life writing is a product of ideology and an extension of Enlightenment rationality that places the individual at the center of thought. In this framework, the project of personal writing about illness is doomed before it begins. One could say, in fact, that when such memoirs enter the literary world, these critics expect them to fail both as acts of testimony and as works of literature.

Whatever the critics say about the limits of the genre, however, writers continue to produce these memoirs. At what critic Leigh Gilmore calls "the limits of autobiography," they continue to test the possibility that a narrative will do meaningful work in the world.[18] This persistence leaves us with a fundamental question unanswered: What alternatives to suspicion are available as readers, especially critics, seek to understand narratives of illness that are overtly cathartic, therapeutic, or personal?

An array of pragmatic models for responding to narratives about illness exists beyond the mainstream in the medical humanities. In anthropology, for instance, Kleinman's *The Illness Narratives* draws attention to how patients' spoken explanations of disease can differ cross-culturally and offers guidelines for how physicians can do a better job of eliciting and understanding patients' explanations. In psychology, James E. Pennebaker conducts empirical research on the therapeutic benefits of expressing emotions, in particular the benefits of writing about trauma and other unsettling experiences. Although he does not promise that writing is a cure-all, his research demonstrates that the practice of composing provides a means for organizing an understanding of one's life and self, and for gaining insight into uncertainty and the unknown. Both *Reconstructing Illness* by medical humanist Anne Hunsaker Hawkins and *The Wounded Storyteller* by sociologist Arthur Frank catalog the common narrative patterns found in illness narratives. Rita Charon's book *Narrative Medicine* and her Program in Narrative Medicine at Columbia University seek to teach clinical practitioners—doctors, nurses, social workers, and therapists—to develop an active textual and cultural knowledge of narrative in order to "improve the effectiveness of care by developing the capacity for attention, reflection, representation, and affiliation with patients and colleagues" ("Mission Statement").

Much of this foundational work in the medical humanities has not, however, gained a foothold in mainstream criticism. In *The Invading Body*, Einat Avrahami observes that the encounter with illness narratives "creates ethical and emotional engagement in a way that affords something beyond a sense of the indeterminacy of meaning" (4). In the academy, however, critics tend to prefer indeterminacy to emotional engagement and imposed ethical obligations. Although an influential core group of scholars, including G. Thomas Couser,

David B. Morris, and Priscilla Wald, write about disability, pain, and narratives of contagion, much of the scholarship in the medical humanities attends primarily to the pedagogical or therapeutic value of writing about illness. Such approaches, in which personal expression is understood to provide an opening to the experience of another, can appear reductive to literary scholars who value complexity over utility. By contrast, medical humanists are more accepting of the emotional and ethical claims writers make on their readers. In other words, they attend to the *uses* of narrative, written, spoken, and received. They focus on writing about illness as a matter of literacy as well as literature.

For some critics, such pragmatic concerns threaten the status of their work, evoking unmistakable outrage and anxiety about the demands of personal testimony and other works that tug on the emotions. Perhaps the most dramatic example of this response is dance critic Arlene Croce's article, "Discussing the Undiscussable." She dismisses the dance "Still/Here" by Bill T. Jones, without having viewed it, as the most egregious example to date of "victim art"—that is, art that demands a personal, emotional response from each member of the audience (17). Jones, an HIV-positive African American choreographer created "Still/Here" as a dance and mixed-media piece that integrated videotaped interviews of people with terminal illnesses into the performance. Although Croce begins her article by stating that she has no plans to review Jones's dance, this does not stop her from condemning the project. "By working dying people into his act," she writes, "Jones is putting himself beyond the reach of criticism. I think of him as literally undiscussable—the most extreme case among the distressingly many now representing themselves to the public not as artists but as victims and martyrs" (16). Croce chooses not to watch performers she "feel[s] sorry for or hopeless about," either because of their "physical deformities" or because they use their race, gender, or sexuality to "make out of victimhood victim art" (17). Decrying Jones for "tak[ing] sanctuary among the unwell" (28), Croce defends the critic and criticism from the threat of the illness narrative, which "forces" sympathy and thus displaces and devalues dispassionate analytical judgment and appreciation (17). "Disease and death . . . are taking over and running the show," she warns, and "the wistful desire to commemorate is converted into a pathetic lumping together, the individual absorbed by the group, the group by the disease" (25). In her view, real, flawed, everyday bodies and the passions they inspire transform artistic expression into a "messianic traveling medicine show" (15).

Croce's argument generated a storm of responses and announcements of a "crisis in criticism."[19] In the world of literary studies where "the death of the author" is a familiar abstraction, it brought to the surface the question of what to make of an author or artist who is literally dying. Croce's nonreview placed in full view the empathy gap between creators of art about suffering and illness and disinterested critics. She had numerous supporters, among them Susan Sontag, who chided her "choice of occasion," but applauded her criticism of "the scourge of populism wielded by both left and right." She also faced an array of critics, the most forceful of whom was Homi Bhabha, who unveiled the hypocrisy underlying Croce's ideological attack on ideological art: without actually seeing Jones's dance, she assumed that it represented victimhood instead of survival (Berger 48).

In the years since its publication, "Discussing the Undiscussable" has become a common reference point for scholars who work with illness narratives. For them, Croce's article serves as an extreme example of the familiar complaint that contemporary memoir is "self-indulgent and unworthy of attention" (Conway 10).[20] Croce's piece and the critical reactions it inspired allow such critics to trace the battle lines and define the critical stakes in discussions of narratives about illness: on one side stands the dispassionate critic who is suspicious of art that elicits sympathy or empathy; on the other is the empathic critic who seeks to acknowledge the suffering bodies at the center of art.[21]

In recent years, with the rise of affect theory, Croce's diatribe against representing physical vulnerability is now recognizable as a radical articulation of the more general distrust of affect in the critical community, which sees emotion as more prone to political manipulation than reason. The concern is that, when public figures such as writers, entertainers, and politicians, evoke positive or negative emotions—from empathy and love to fear, agony, and shame—these feelings serve existing structures of power. Compassion, for instance, has been claimed by politicians across the political spectrum. In his 2000 presidential campaign, George W. Bush advocated a politics of "compassionate conservatism." He used the term to suggest that dependence on free-market economics demonstrated compassion for society as a whole and justified reduction of the social safety net for the disadvantaged. To Bush's opposition, the phrase came to signify a cynical politics that favored the wealthy while obscuring the deepening political and economic divide between the "haves" and "have nots." While Barack Obama does not evoke the stereotype of the bleeding heart liberal, he has repeatedly evoked compassion in speeches leading up to the 2012 election, positioning himself as more compassionate than conservative legislators who demanded cuts to federally supported health care. In contrast to the Republicans, whom Obama depicts as saying the country "can no longer afford . . . to be compassionate," he declares confidence that Americans can be both "competitive and compassionate" (Obama).

One might expect affect theorists to redefine and reclaim words such as "compassion" from blatant political posturing, but they have generally focused their attention on describing how feelings aroused by emotional rhetoric or sentimental literature reinforce political, economic, and social suffering.[22] In the essay "Trauma and Ineloquence," for example, Lauren Berlant questions the contemporary idea that testimonial accounts can stand as evidence for suffering or trauma by drawing attention to the sameness of testimonials written to solicit funds for global charities: "we see that they sing the same song; they are stuck in a social repetition; they produce beauty in contrast to understanding, or they produce beauty as a sign that their desires have defeated them, their intimacies betrayed them, their institutional faith mocked them, their optimism humiliated them" (55). When the smoke clears from the proclamation that testimonies are produced by agentless puppets of power, no one is left standing but the critic who sees what the rest of us, caught up in sentiment, do not. Berlant's implied argument here is that we need critics in order to understand how ideological constraints transform sympathetic readings of others' suffering into acts of complicity with the systems that produce that suffering. We need critics, in other words, to reveal how sentimentalism and ideology constrain common readers and writers.[23]

Berlant's argument should not be the last word on sympathy and testimony. While critical warnings to pay attention to how affect and ideology function in relation to texts have value, arguments that all testimony about suffering is mere repetition, and that our only hope as readers is to understand our failure to understand, express what I see as the academy's version of "compassion fatigue." Critics, like everyone else in this media-saturated age, are exhausted by the ceaseless supply of representations of pain, violence, and atrocity that come to us via ever more pervasive media, and that are intensified by our postmodern distrust of our own feelings.[24] Perhaps *some* emotional responses are distractions from a legitimate understanding of the structural origins of suffering. But a blanket dismissal of testimony and emotional engagement can only be made from a position of distance and privilege. Such a critical stance imposes a falsely absolute divide between everyday experience and critical engagement. It does not serve literary and cultural criticism well as a tool for understanding life's precariousness.

But what options are there other than the didactic humanism of those who see narrative as redemptive or the radical doubt promoted by contemporary cultural and literary criticism? How can literary criticism productively engage with the new genre of the illness memoir? For those whose training and careers have steeped them in the hermeneutics of suspicion, there seem to be few visible and viable alternatives.

Responding to Stories of Illness

As discussed earlier, models of such productive work exist in the study of literature and medicine: in Rita Charon's *Narrative Medicine,* Arthur Frank's *The Wounded Storyteller,* Anne Hunsaker Hawkins's *Reconstructing Illness,* David B. Morris's *The Culture of Pain,* and Priscilla Wald's *Contagious.* Each of these books discusses how embodied experience raises questions that are not central to current critical practices. The theories of narrative set forth in the work of Charon, Frank, and Hawkins respect the irreducibility of the writer's body. The experience of illness, their work demonstrates, finds expression in recognizable forms, yet the familiarity of the narrative patterns does not detract from the urgent work these narratives perform for the writers. These critics argue that we must attend to this meaning and practice in order to understand memoirs of illness. I find in these writers an admirable and refreshing willingness to be accused of unfashionable earnestness. Morris and Wald take a slightly different path. They shift their critical projects toward broader analyses of cultural discourse about pain and epidemics and thereby affirm the argument of the "Biocultures Manifesto" written by Lennard J. Davis and Morris: "Biology—serving at times as a metaphor for science—is as intrinsic to the embodied state of readers and of writers as history and culture are intrinsic to the professional bodies of knowledge known as science and biology" (411). Collectively, this group of writers demonstrates the limits of social constructionist practices that sharply separate the social and the biological. They recognize that culture and biology intersect in ways that can be mutually beneficial.

How and when will such insights influence those critics still committed to a disembodied criticism? There are indications that such change has begun. Bruno Latour, who built his reputation in science studies as a social constructionist, has lately called for a reconsideration of the goals of criticism, particularly criticism's focus on emancipating the general public from false beliefs (227). In "Why Has Critique Run Out of Steam? Matters of Fact to Matters of Concern," Latour maintains that critique has too often been reduced to the act of "ceaselessly transforming the whole rest of the world into naive believers, into fetishists, into hapless victims of domination," while simultaneously portraying that behavior as caused by powerful structures whose composition has not been thoroughly examined (243). Critics working in this vein decry trust in religion, fashion, and other conventions, explaining that human behavior is properly understood to be the effect of factors such as economics, discourse, systems of social power, or genetics (238). Latour now finds himself deeply concerned about the relevance of existing models of critique to matters "close to our hearts" (243). He seeks solidarity with his readers, asking if they, too, are exhausted by how explanations are churned out by the machine of critique, and then declares, "I am, I have always been, when I know, for instance, that the God to whom I pray, the works of art I cherish, the colon cancer I have been fighting, the piece of law I am studying, the desire I feel, indeed, the very book I am writing could in no way be accounted for by fetish or fact, nor by any combination of those two absurd positions" (243). The phrase "the colon cancer I have been fighting" leaps from Latour's list. By including the vulnerability of his own body as a matter as significant as faith, art, desire, and creative work, Latour repeats, with a difference, Virginia Woolf's argument from *On Being Ill*. While Woolf called for writers to acknowledge the importance of illness and embodied experience in epics, odes, and lyrics, Latour calls instead for scholars to approach matters of concern with new conceptual tools whose purpose is not to "debunk," but to "assemble" (246). Contemporary critique, he asserts, risks becoming irrelevant because it has overlooked experiences, beliefs, and passions that are engaged with but not reducible to the facts of material life (or the material facts of life). Thus, he presents his argument: "the critical mind, if it is to renew itself and be relevant again, is to be found in the cultivation of a *stubbornly realist attitude* . . . a realism dealing with what I will call *matters of concern*, not *matters of fact*. The mistake we made, the mistake I made, was to believe that there was no efficient way to criticize matters of fact except by moving *away* from them and directing one's attention *toward* the conditions that made them possible" (231).

As Woolf did in her essay some eighty years earlier, Latour encourages his readers to participate in a thought experiment. He invites us to reimagine the critic, not as "the one who lifts the rugs from under the feet of the naïve believers, but the one who offers the participants arenas in which to gather" (246). He continues, "The critic is not the one who alternates haphazardly between antifetishism and positivism . . . but the one for whom, if something is constructed, then it means it is fragile and thus in great need of care and caution" (246). He also asks us to imagine the circumstances in which we might *want* critics to address matters of concern we cherish—that is, to conceive of a critical practice that adds to our lived experience rather than stands apart from it (232). The challenge Latour poses is twofold: he wants critics to identify complex matters of concern that cannot be accounted for by existing critical approaches and for critics to allow these matters to enlarge the goals and the scope of criticism.

This critique of critique provides a framework for reconsidering why we write and read narratives about illness and what work these literary and folk narratives do in the contemporary world. In turn, such reconsiderations will bring new questions into view—questions to be addressed in the remaining chapters of *Illness as Narrative*. Does prioritizing concerns about risk, pain, human vulnerability, and the uncertainty of the future alter the critical project? What might the study of narratives about illness look like if the critic's task were to create intellectual arenas for the gathering of ideas, and to address matters of concern with care and compassion? If narratives of illness challenge critics to "combine a willingness to suspect with an eagerness to listen," how can we best respond to this challenge? (Felski 22). How can we define critical practices that are grounded in everyday life, practices that are rigorous, compelling and, at the same time, socially engaged and thoughtfully empathic? The project of *Illness as Narrative* is to explore and model alternative ways of engaging with matters that are, as Latour says, "fragile and thus in great need of care and caution" (246). I will examine a range of practices that are not central to current critical customs but that emerge in writing about illness and in critical work informed by embodied suffering. Practices such as acknowledgment, care of the self, attention, recognition, and repair point to the possibility of redefining the relationship of writers and readers to the books in their hands and the worlds they inhabit.

Two

Life Narratives in the
Risk Society

As we have seen, there are many explanations for why and how illness memoirs evolved into a thriving genre in the late twentieth and early twenty-first centuries. When science developed better explanations for disease and more effective treatments, personal stories of illness were displaced from clinical settings in the United States and surfaced elsewhere. With the growth of the publishing industry, changed attitudes toward personal disclosure, patient activism about women's health and AIDS, and the rise of the Internet, more people turned to the *written* word to give illness meaning. At least one more factor that motivated the emergence and popularity of this subgenre of life writing has been hidden in plain sight: our increasing awareness of statistically calculated *risk*.[1] During the twentieth century, with the rise of the field of statistics, a vast quantity of information about health risks became available. In the United States, increasing numbers of people have some knowledge of the health risks indicated by their blood pressure and cholesterol, smoking, drinking, and eating habits, as well as, in recent years, their genetics. As health statistics have proliferated, so have illness memoirs. Although we do not fully understand the function of these narratives, one of them appears to be to make personal meaning of the impersonal statistics that represent one's life "at risk."

The concept of the "risk society" emerged in the 1980s when Ulrich Beck coined the term in his treatise, *Risk Society: Towards a New Modernity,* about the central role of risk in the social transformations that took place in the shift from the modern to the late-modern era. Beck's *Risk Society* is one of the most influential academic books of the late twentieth century, having been translated into twenty languages and selling more than eighty thousand copies.[2] Before industrialization, Beck points out, natural hazards and disease constituted the greatest threats to survival. Later, during the industrial and modern eras, people grew confident that scientific and technical progress would enable humans to control the natural world. In the late-modern era, however, although natural threats remain, human-generated risks—global threats that are a hybrid of nature and culture—now occupy center stage, especially "ecological and high-tech risks" (22). Think, say, of planetary risks such as the oil spill in the Gulf of Mexico, the Japanese nuclear crisis, climate change, the global economic recession, and terrorism. These hazards are examples of what Beck calls "reflexive modernization," in which such risks are, in fact, the effects of modernization (12).[3]

Among the changes late modernism has brought to the common citizen is that probabilistic assessments of the nature and degree of particular risks compete with or supplant master narratives based on beliefs in fate or a divine plan.[4] If we accept that the prevalence of statistical assessments of risk has altered contemporary experience in much of the world, then for literary and cultural critics a key question should be, "What kinds of stories emerge and flourish in such conditions?" A small body of work in literary studies addresses the question of how statistics and risk have affected literature, and in these texts critics generally take the position that statistical science is a tool of the state and the medical establishment. Although none of this work directly addresses illness memoirs, some of it can inform a study of what I call "risk narratives," autobiographical and literary explorations of the meanings of risk.

In *Enforcing Normalcy,* for instance, Lennard J. Davis argues that statistical understanding of health and disease in the nineteenth century brought into being the idea of *normalcy,* a concept that was "promot[ed] and symbolically produc[ed]" by the novel (41). Statisticians studying facts and figures about the body saw that graphs of data generally looked like bell-shaped curves with most of the data points clustered in the middle. This central group of data came to be understood as representing what was *normal.* Consequently, in science and government—anywhere that data about populations was collected—the norm was redefined as desirable. The novel then evolved into a literary form suited to portraying normal, rather than ideal, lives. Davis maintains that "the very structures on which the novel rests tend to be normative, ideologically emphasizing the universal quality of the central character whose normativity encourages us to identify with him or her" (41). The genre's representation of the norm also, Davis maintains, brings into being "the abnormal, the Other, the disabled, the native, the colonized subject, and so on" (42). Thus, Davis's work suggests that the novel emphasizes norms over the risks that threaten norms. In his view, the genre works to contain fear and uncertainty rather than explore the complexities of risk and normalcy, and their relationship to each other.[5]

In a similar vein, critic Kathleen Woodward argues in "Statistical Panic" that statistics are an increasingly influential manifestation of biopower, which controls bodies and populations. Statistics, she maintains, are used to generate fear and compliance: "fatally, we feel that a certain statistic, which is in fact based on an aggregate and is only a measure of probability, actually represents our very future" (185).[6] Because a number or percentage implies a narrative, Woodward claims, people make the mistake of living their lives by the numbers instead of attending to the dissonance between those numbers and their experiences (189).[7]

Davis and Woodward, heavily influenced by Foucault, focus on distrust and panic. Among risk society theorists, however, less distrustful attitudes toward statistics suggest very different answers to the question of what kinds of texts emerge in a risk society. In the book *Individualization,* Ulrich Beck and his coauthor Elizabeth Beck-Gernscheim identify the central genre of the risk society as *biography.* They argue that late-modern individuals define themselves through life narratives that are shaped by uncertainties and choices rather than through tradition (3). (They use the term "biography," it appears, to refer to internal life narratives that are rehearsed and revised, but probably not recorded.) In the contemporary risk society, they explain, people feel less bound to the norms and institutions of the past, including those of "gender, corporeality, identity, religion, marriage, parenthood, [and] social ties" (Beck and Beck-Gernscheim 5). Biographies, in other words, are a means of contemplating and addressing life risks. In contrast to Davis's study of normalcy and the novel, Beck and Beck-Gernscheim claim that, in the current period, one must "create . . . [and] stage manage, not only one's own biography but the bonds and networks surrounding it and to do this amid changing preferences and at successive stages of life, while constantly adapting to the conditions of the labour market, the education system, the welfare state and so on" (4).

Anthony Giddens similarly maintains in *Modernity and Self-Identity* that, in late modernity, "A person's identity is not to be found in behaviour, nor . . . in the reactions of others, but in the capacity to keep a particular narrative going" (54). The pervasive awareness of risk in the contemporary world has, according to these theorists, altered the cultural work of life narratives. We use them to make sense of or contain the sense of being at risk of disease, accident, or death. For Beck, Beck-Gernscheim, as well as Giddens, the core questions for the individual in late modernity are: "What to do? How to act? Who to be?" (Giddens, *Modernity and Self-Identity* 70).[8]

These theorists offer literary and writing studies nothing less than a sociological theory of autobiography. It is also the case, however, that, while they argue that biography is a fundamental element of late-modern individual life, their work never addresses *actual* biographies or autobiographies. Thus, there are plenty of reasons for literary critics to dismiss their claims. Specialists in autobiography can take issue with their erasure of the history of the genre. After all, life writing emerged long before the late-modern era. In addition, memoirists and critics are likely to be rankled by the social scientists' sweeping claims about the cultural work of a complex and varied form of narrative. No doubt, the value of the sociologists' explanation of the role of biography in the risk society is limited because their methodology does away with the necessity of actually reading individual narratives once their function has been defined. Nevertheless, the field of literary studies owes a debt to risk society theorists for pointing to the evolving function of life writing and the centrality of risk to contemporary autobiography, especially illness memoirs. Their work suggests that memoir has become, in part, a means of responding to the uncertainties of the contemporary era.

There is important work left to be done in literary criticism concerning contemporary narratives about risk. In what follows, I want to explore the varied ways that these texts function for writers and readers. In particular, I am interested in how writers and readers negotiate with existing cultural narratives to generate alternative meanings for statistical risk. Thus, this chapter will review a range of contemporary texts—life narratives, memoir, journalism, and the novel—all of which address unique personal experiences of living "at risk." The writers whose texts I have selected have different backgrounds; among them are a scientist, journalist, poet, and novelist. This diversity quickly makes apparent that there is no single model of the risk narrative. Collectively, however, these narratives suggest it is no accident that the age of memoir emerged along with the age of statistics.

In Prognosis

Narratives about risk have displaced many traditional explanations for events such as illness, but risk itself is rarely the explicit subject of published autobiographies. There is a fundamental incompatibility between personal memoir and statistics: while general populations can be described with probabilities, the life of an individual cannot. To live "in prognosis" is to be in limbo between health and illness without a clear life narrative.[9] What story should one construct about the future if one has a 50 percent chance of inheriting

Huntington's disease from one's mother, or if one has been diagnosed with advanced prostate cancer for which there is a 31 percent five-year survival rate? How does the individual compose a personal story in the midst of uncertainty?

One might hope to depend on medical practitioners for guidance. According to medical historian Charles Rosenberg in "Banishing Risk," however, diagnosis creates a tension in the clinical relationship between patient and physician because it calls into question the patient's sense of self and autobiographical history. He explains: "Likelihoods and multifactorial complexes of causation do not easily fit into most people's way of thinking about themselves and family members. Nor [do they] fit nicely into the emotional necessities of the doctor-patient relationship; men and women want to know what is to happen next in their own lives or that of family members, not in that of a statistical aggregate" (46). Composing a story about "what's next" requires conceptual, linguistic, and narrative resources, as well as a grasp of statistics. Few patients have the confidence and knowledge necessary to quickly recast a sense of self in relation to a new and threatening prognosis.

Stephen Jay Gould, however, was one such patient, and his essay "The Median Isn't the Message," which he called his "personal story of statistics," may be among the most widely read risk narratives of the twentieth century. Gould is best known as a paleontologist and science writer, author of three hundred essays that were published monthly in *Natural History* in an unbroken stream from 1974 until 2001, and that were later collected in popular books. Among people with cancer, however, Gould's most important work may be "The Median Isn't the Message." He was diagnosed in 1982 with abdominal mesothelioma, "a rare and serious cancer usually associated with exposure to asbestos." As a scientist and a believer in the power of information and reason, he immediately asked his physician for "the best technical literature about mesothelioma," and she responded diplomatically, in his view, telling him that there was nothing worth reading. When Gould explored the holdings in Harvard's medical library, however, he found that "the literature couldn't have been more brutally clear: mesothelioma is incurable, with a median mortality of only eight months after discovery." Beyond that, little was known. On his own, he set out to determine his chances for surviving longer. Gould uses his experience of diagnosis to give readers a lesson in probability and to make an argument for the value of statistical understanding. He acknowledges common distrust, fear, and even contempt for statistics, but sees these reactions as a product of "an unfortunate and invalid separation between heart and mind, or feeling and intellect." Gould's revelation that the information he was given about his prognosis caused him unnecessary despair certainly speaks to physicians' difficulties communicating with patients, but his goal is to change the attitudes of patients. To counter frequent dread of statistics about health risks, he frames his essay as a "story of statistics, properly interpreted, as profoundly nurturant and life-giving." He seeks to humanize statistics and also to convince readers that knowledge, in particular "dry, academic knowledge about science," constitutes power.

Gould's passion for the skillful interpretation of data is evident as he lays out his assessment of risk. He explains, for instance, that when he discovered the median mortality for mesothelioma was only eight months, his training as a biologist made it possible for him to be optimistic. Gould imagines a graph of the survival rates of mesothelioma and recognizes that the distribution of points beyond the median would be "right-skewed," stretching off like a long, thin tail to the right side of the graph that measures the progression of time. That is, half of the points on the graph would "be scrunched up [on the left] between zero and eight months [representing those who die within eight months]. But the upper (or right) half can extend out for years and years." The right side of the curve opens up the possibility for hope, and Gould has good reasons to deduce that he would fall on that side of the curve. After all, he was diagnosed relatively young, at forty-two, his disease was identified at an early stage, and he was getting excellent medical care. In fact, by the time he published "The Median Isn't the Message" in 1985, he was three years past his original diagnosis and somewhere along the long, low arc to the right of the median. While neither he nor his doctors could ever know with certainty where his data point would appear on that curve, Gould lived for seventeen years after the publication of his essay on the meaning of median.[10] His essay demonstrates the limits of general risk assessments with regard to individual cases. But it also draws attention to the very thing that does not interest the risk society theorists: how one man's narrative makes personal meaning of impersonal statistics.

Gould's comfort and expertise with statistics makes immediately apparent that he is not representative of most inhabitants of the risk society. In fact, he is better at explaining the relationship of the median to prognosis than his own doctor, who is at a loss to know how to talk about numbers and percentages with her patient, even one who shares her conceptual framework and vocabulary. Despite the achievements of biomedicine, there can be no doubt it has encouraged physicians to set aside, ignore, or devalue the patient's experience of illness in all its dimensions, including anxiety about probabilities. Physicians are generally trained to think within a biomedical framework in which the body is an object and the focus of medicine is disease. As a consequence, according to psychiatrist and medical anthropologist Arthur Kleinman, contemporary physicians have no easily available language for suffering, no way of measuring it, and no "routine way of recording this most thickly human dimension of patients' and families' stories of experiencing illness" (28). In seeking a solution to this failure of education and empathy, Kleinman turns to biography and other forms of narrative. He argues that medical practitioners, educators, and researchers must study "ethnography, biography, history, psychotherapy" so they learn how to attend to the human dimension of disease (28). Gould's essay stands as a narrative bridge across the divide created by biomedicine. In teaching readers about the limits of what the median explains, he models for doctors how to explain risk, including how to embed it in narrative.

For all that Gould's essay accomplishes, it is also widely misread. It appears on many cancer-support Web sites not just because of how Gould explains the relationship of the median mortality rates to the "long tail" in mesothelioma prognoses. The piece has also been adopted by cancer survivors because it is uplifting. For some, the story of triumph over adversity obscures the narrative about statistics. Although the point of Gould's essay is that he recognized that the particularities of his case meant his individual outcome was unlikely to fall within the median range, readers generalize from his experience to their own. The essay's message becomes: if Stephen Jay Gould can beat the odds, so can I.

Such hopeful yet somewhat unfounded readings are predictable. In "Stories as a Tool for Thinking," narrative theorist David Herman explores the distortions created when narrative, "a basic pattern-forming cognitive system," is used to organize events (170).[11] He does not directly address the intersection of autobiography and risk, but he does write about the challenge of narrating indeterminacy. When one event follows another, he explains, the temptation is to tell a story of cause and effect, but such post hoc logic may not identify a valid relationship. Herman's discussion of narrative patterns and cognition explains the paradox that Gould's readers find a simple, familiar story in "The Median Isn't the Message," despite the complex understanding of probability that he tries to communicate. If Gould had died a month after he published his essay, it is fair to say that it would not be as popular as it is today because it would not resonate with hope. Readers' preference for triumph points to the problem at the heart of personal accounts of risk: because these chronicles follow narrative conventions, including closure, they contain the very essence of that which they engage—uncertainty.

If Gould's narrative allows readers to avoid the full complexities of living with risk and in prognosis, David Rieff's *Swimming in a Sea of Death,* his memoir about his mother, Susan Sontag, and her death, refuses all such consolations. For Rieff, trying to make sense of the risks his mother faced in her final illness ensnares him in ethical quandaries that he never resolves. Sontag's death from a lethal form of leukemia, myelodysplastic syndrome (MDS), is physically agonizing, but its traumas are also emotional and intellectual. She is certain that she can fight the odds, which are entirely against her, as long as she is willing to suffer. Like some of Gould's readers, she rejects the statistical prognosis, resists uncertainty, and refuses a narrative that does not end in survival. Rieff's struggle, however, is over what narrative he should support—the lie she wants to hear or the truth that she will die. Ultimately, he tells his mother the story she wants, but he remains haunted after her death about the ethics of his choice. His risk narrative thus becomes a meditation about the cruelty and confusion of living in and with prognosis.

Rieff's suffering is complicated because Sontag's writing about cancer in *Illness as Metaphor* does not align neatly with her final battle against the disease. When Sontag was first diagnosed with advanced, stage 4 breast cancer in 1975 at the age of forty-two, her prognosis was similar to Gould's and, like Gould, she approached the disease as a rationalist. Initially, doctors told her she had little chance of surviving, but she decided to have a radical mastectomy, choosing disfiguring removal of the entire affected breast, along with all the lymph nodes and the chest muscles underneath, in hopes of ridding her body of every last cancer cell (Rieff, "Why I Had to Lie").[12] She survived. In some ways, this episode presages her fight against leukemia: Rieff observes that "fighting cancer became for [her] a question of the right information, the right doctors, and the right follow-through" (*Swimming*, 38–39). Beginning with her first cancer, her belief in the value of science and reason informed a personal mythology. The myth that the best doctors, the most aggressive medicine, and her own courage saved her was reinforced by her survival of a second cancer, uterine sarcoma, in 1998. As the years passed, Rieff says, she "began more and more to think of her survival not as a species of miracle, since the miraculous had no place in the way she thought, nor as an accident of fate or genetics, let alone as a statistical anomaly, but rather as the result of medical progress and also of her willingness to have the most radical, mutilating treatment" (*Swimming*, 84). After her diagnosis with leukemia in 2004, the strength of her conviction that she would be cured through force of will transformed into magical thinking rather than trust in medical science. Even as the statistics indicated that, given the disease, her age, and her medical history, she had virtually no chance of surviving, she sought out a physician who could give her hope and a hospital willing to perform a bone marrow transplant. She, who had argued against battle metaphors in *AIDS and Its Metaphors*, fought; she fought like crazy. Although Rieff never states so explicitly, her fear of death and denial of risk—both understandable but also extreme—were defining elements of her final illness.

Rieff's meditation on mortality in *Swimming in a Sea of Death* serves as his own account of life in the risk society. After facing his mother's final fight against the odds and witnessing her death, he offers the perspective of a grieving son on the problems she had engaged in *Illness as Metaphor*. He makes plain that he loves and admires his mother, but he recognizes that the personal narrative that formed the foundation for her book was simply wrong. No matter how much trust a patient holds in biomedicine, no matter how willing the patient may be to seek aggressive therapy, no matter how fervently the patient refuses to accept stigmatizing metaphors, none of these acts are certain to heal the diseased body or vanquish death. For much of his memoir, he discusses how he is haunted by the question of whether he should have stripped away the myths of heroic recovery, forcing his mother to accept her dire prognosis, or if he should have told more lies to help shore up her spirit. Throughout, he contemplates what anyone can say to a patient when statistical prognosis leaves little room for hope. Ultimately, writing *Swimming in a Sea of Death* allows Rieff to voice, if not come to terms with, his lingering guilt and his doubt about what would have been best for his mother. Just as significant for my purposes, his memoir enables him to shine a bright light into the chasm between medical information about health risks and the meaning of risk in individual lives. Like his mother, Rieff sought to learn as much as he could about MDS, but unlike her, he is left openly wondering, "Is information, or knowing, power or is it cruelty?" (53).

Swimming in a Sea of Death is compelling in part because Rieff never resolves his confusion about what place statistical information should have had in his mother's experience of her final illness. Although he praises the physicians who allowed her to fight the odds, he also questions the false belief—presumably perpetuated by consumer culture—that encourages us to feel we should be protected from "pain, illness, and even death itself" (145). Through his memoir, Rieff reveals that the essential challenge to narrative in the age of risk is that our survival cannot be completely explained or accounted for by statistics. Even when we know the chances in general, we cannot know what will happen in individual cases. Some will make it; some will not. Thus, personal narratives— not probabilities and not polemical arguments—provide a structure for meaning in the face of evidence of one's own insignificance.

Before Prognosis: Genetic Risk

In the twenty-first century, the risk society has intersected with the genomic age, transforming life narratives and personal engagement with risk. With rapid growth of knowledge about genetics and the greater availability of personal genetic and genomic DNA testing, individuals are ever more likely to find themselves facing a disease prognosis even before they are sick. Although Gould and Sontag wrote as cancer *survivors*, in the twenty-first century, members of the risk society may now think of themselves as cancer "previvors" (Harmon). Those who can afford to have their DNA tested may discover that they are susceptible to certain diseases, such as Parkinson's, Crohn's disease, and various cancers, or that they are carriers of genes for Tay-Sachs or cystic fibrosis.

Press coverage has been particularly intense with regard to BRCA1 and BRCA2, inherited gene mutations that significantly increase the risk of breast and ovarian cancer. On average, 12 percent of women will develop breast cancer sometime in their lives ("Probability of Breast Cancer"), but if a woman has inherited one of these mutations, her risk of breast cancer leaps to between 50 and 85 percent before age seventy ("Breast/Ovarian Cancer"). These inherited forms of cancer are also particularly virulent; if they occur, they are more likely to recur ("Breast/Ovarian Cancer"). Some women with BRCA1 or BRCA2 have the resources to make choices that reduce their risk.

Amy Harmon's *New York Times* article, "Cancer Free at Thirty-Three, but Weighing a Mastectomy," is emblematic of new narratives of genetic risk.[13] Harmon's article focuses on Deborah Lindner, a thirty-three-year-old medical resident who tested positive for the gene mutation BRCA1. Women with BRCA1-related breast cancer—like Lindner's mother, from whom she inherited the mutation—often develop the disease before they are fifty. The cancer can be lethal: it is likely to recur and raises the risk of life-threatening ovarian cancer by 50 percent.[14] Lindner, whose family tree reveals alarmingly high death rates from breast and ovarian cancer among her female relatives, chooses to have a bilateral mastectomy after she learns the operation will decrease her chance of getting of breast cancer by 90 percent. Although she hopes to have children, she plans to have her ovaries removed by the time she is forty to eliminate the risk of ovarian cancer.

The story Harmon presents is journalistic rather than literary—a report more than a meditation. Lindner, who has medical training, gathered all the information available, spoke frankly with family and friends, made her decision about preventive treatment, and found excellent doctors to perform the mastectomy and breast reconstruction surgeries. Harmon makes clear, however, that no matter how sensible Lindner's decisions might appear, they are incomprehensible to some of her relatives. An aunt says the decision to "dismember her body" is "a course of action akin to 'leechings of the Dark Ages.'" Her mother tries to be understanding, but cannot help seeing her daughter's choice as risking that she might never marry or have children. Even if Lindner does have children, her mother is dismayed that she will miss out on the special bond created by breast-feeding. When the mother expresses this regret, her daughter responds sharply, "Wouldn't it be more special if I was around to have children in the first place?" Lindner's choice to shape her life narrative by weighing in-herited risk against personal priorities inevitably puts her in conflict with fam-ily members whose priorities and belief systems are different from her own.

Although Lindner's story is new, it is no longer rare.[15] According to Har-mon, although "only 30,000 of more than 250,000 American women esti-mated to carry a mutation in BRCA1 or . . . BRCA2, have so far been tested. . . . About a third opt for preventive mastectomies that remove the tissue where the breast cancer develops." More than half choose to have their ovaries re-moved (oophorectomy), cutting the risk of breast cancer in half and reducing the chance of ovarian cancer by 90 percent or more. Some readers may see these women as pawns of statistical rhetoric, consumer culture, and biomedi-cine because they choose preemptive mastectomy over vigilance and hope.[16] Given the exponential growth in information about genetic risk, however, such stories will only proliferate.

Harmon's story about Deborah Lindner represents a relatively straight-forward and uncontroversial account of prophylactic surgery to combat genetic risk, but as more people have their personal genomes scanned and learn about their risks for everything from Alzheimer's to vascular disease, different nar-ratives will emerge, especially when risks are known, but no treatments are available. Inevitably, gene discovery will outpace therapeutic research, plunging patients into psychological quagmires and physicians into ethical ones. Popular narratives of genetic determinism are likely to oversimplify and overwrite the complexity of individual experience. This is the origin of the "statistical panic" that Woodward warns about: we see our genome as a script rather than under-standing that the numbers refer not to facts, but to general probabilities that must be interpreted. This does not mean, however, that all statistical prognoses are mere conjecture. While one can never know to what degree one's own situ-ation will align with a statistical prognosis, it is reasonable to believe that the results of studies that have been replicated are grounded in reality. In sum, among other challenges, narratives about presymptomatic genetic risks must avoid the temptations of genetic determinism on the one hand, and fear of sci-ence and statistics on the other.

Among the very first genetic risk narratives is Alice Wexler's memoir, *Map-ping Fate: A Memoir of Family, Risk, and Genetic Research*. Wexler, a historian, offers an unusually nuanced discussion of how testing can affect lives and fam-ilies. Her mother died of Huntington's disease, one of the few heritable diseases that is carried on a single gene. Wexler thus entered her adult life knowing that she had a 50 percent chance of having inherited the gene from her mother, in which case she would be virtually certain to develop the disease herself. Hun-tington's causes progressive degeneration of nerve cells in the brain, which affects voluntary and involuntary movement, impairs cognition, and can cause psychiatric disorders. There are no treatments to cure or change the course of the disease. Few diseases inspire the sort of dread that Huntington's does. After witnessing the suffering of a parent, a child lives with understandable fear of sharing that genetic destiny.

Wexler's narrative complicates any received narratives about Huntington's by interweaving her own autobiography with a narrative about her family.[17] She describes her mother's diagnosis and death, as well as the uncertainty about whether she and her sister would inherit the disease and, if they had children, what it would mean to pass the gene to them. Because Wexler's father and sister were involved in research on Huntington's, she can also offer a personal account of the scientific search for its genetic origins. The genetic marker for the disease was discovered in 1983, when presymptomatic testing first became available, and the gene itself was found in 1993, making such testing much more precise. This was the occasion for scientific and family celebration, but also personal uncertainty. Ultimately, Wexler decided not to get tested. She preferred to live with risk rather than endure knowing that she would develop the disease. To live at risk for Huntington's, she explains, represents "an extreme example of what it means to be at risk for a wide range of other conditions. . . . [It] poses stark questions about the meanings of certainty and uncertainty and what it means to occupy a 'third space' outside the categories of either-or that we conventionally use to organize experience" (xiv–xv). Thus, she identifies one of the motives for life writing in the risk society. Being "at risk" constitutes a newly recognized social, cultural, and psychological position that must be made meaningful in order to be endured.

Literary Risk

We move from the conventional to the literary autobiography with the memoir *Body Toxic* by poet Susanne Antonetta.[18] Antonetta experiments with the poetic and formal challenges posed by narrating risk while writing about growing up at the New Jersey shore in the 1960s and 1970s amid a swamp of Superfund sites and coping with a worrisome genetic inheritance and a troubled family. The diseases and disorders she develops exceed any reasonable sense of bad luck. Antonetta and other members of her family are "wracked by infertility, tumors, organs malformed at birth and manic-depression" (27), and she reports that she had "one spectacular multiple pregnancy, a miscarriage, a radiation-induced tumor, a double uterus, asthma, endometriosis, growths on the liver, other medical conditions like allergies" (27–28). Throughout her memoir, Antonetta searches to understand how or whether the toxic stew of genetics, physical and psychological environment, and drug use caused or contributed to her maladies, all the while wondering if a final explanation can ever be found.

Antonetta pushes the risk narrative to its limit by composing a memoir in which risk is everywhere. She takes formal chances with her prose, exploring self-reflexive postmodern forms to express the confusion and indeterminacy of a life at risk. She recognizes that the story of the self that is composed of body, mind, culture, place, and DNA can only be approximated by narrative and suggested by metaphor. Thus, she employs an associative strategy, interweaving pieces of stories about genetics with others about illicit drug use and groundwater contamination. The narrative is discontinuous, but meaning accrues as one trope overlaps another—poisonous water, toxic clouds, monstrous secrets, and the intertwined strands of the double helix. As Antonetta circles back through tales of her summers at the Jersey shore, each return reveals a little more about the silences and secrets that have shaped her.

The spiraling, associative logic of her chapters serves as an example of the postmodern narratives of chance described by H. Porter Abbott in his article "Unnarratable Knowledge: The Difficulty of Understanding Evolution by Natural Selection." Abbott traces the complications involved in composing narratives about chance back to Darwin's *Origin of Species* and, in particular, to the theory of natural selection, which hypothesizes that heritable traits, which come into being by chance, become more common over generations, while unfavorable heritable traits become less common.[19] According to Abbott, acceptance of this theory by a popular audience was hindered by the narrative challenge it posed to readers, and to Darwin himself (144). Even the term "natural selection" suggests the problem inherent in giving an account of evolution. "Selection" implies an agent, a cause that creates an effect, and yet Darwin's project is to show that life evolves by chance—without a plan, without intentional selection. "Put briefly," Abbott writes, "the difficulty with evolution by natural selection arises because neither *natural selection* nor *species,* as they were conceptualized by Darwin, are entities with agency. Worse, they do not seem to be narrative entities at all" (144).[20] In fact, he maintains that, because evolution involves neither agent nor intention, it should be understood as "a cascade of algorithmic processes feeding on chance" (Dennett 59, quoted in Abbott 145).[21]

Although chance is, as Abbott points out, a fundamental element of narrative, when you "spread chance everywhere . . . you have something that transcends the limits of tolerable narrative" (148).[22] Telling the story of natural selection therefore "requires an active resistance to the narrative frames of common experience" (148). When chance is everywhere, he writes, the resistant and intolerable story that remains is "something strangely postmodern" (148). In the end, Abbott argues that in order to represent chance, familiar narrative scripts "must give way to a vision that includes a vast subsidiary field made up of *swarms of interacting micronarratives*" (157; emphasis mine). Although Abbott's fellow narratologist David Herman expressed concerns that conventional narratives simplify and contain indeterminacy (175–77), Abbott suggests that postmodernism addresses these challenges.

Abbott's work has further implications for the risk society, in which, its theorists argue, everyone composes an ongoing biography. It suggests that telling an appropriately complex risk narrative requires a *literary* approach. Experienced writers such as Antonetta, skilled at recognizing and manipulating narrative conventions, may produce the richest representations of risk. And, indeed, she composes a remarkably complex account of her interwoven genetic, cultural, and psychological inheritances. She sees her origins in her eccentric grandfather from Barbados and grandmother from England. Her odd, brooding Bajan grandfather was the thirteenth child of a mentally ill mother, and he married a self-mythologizing Christian Scientist nurse—a woman of passions and contradictions—whom he met when he was wounded in World War I. Antonetta appears to have inherited her grandfather's depression and distance and her grandmother's mania and flair for the dramatic. She is, in fact, bipolar.

In the midst of stories about her family, Antonetta also writes about the environment that shaped her. Growing up, she spent summers on the edge of the Pine Barrens of coastal New Jersey, two thousand square miles of bogs and forests of dwarf pitch pines, and the damage done to her by the invisible poisons in that landscape. Her family, including her grandparents, lived in handmade bungalows, with a lagoon on one side and a bay on the other. It was not a beautiful place. The bay, she writes, "tends to stagnate and grow what look like floating molds and mildews. Rather than sand beaches we have marshes and weeds spreading up to the water. Swimming's lackluster as is fishing; crabbing's good. We always had the things that needed cover and barrier to grow: crabs, cranberries, blackberries, the secret pleasures" (12).

While this place is naturally overripe with metaphoric potential, human and industrial greed and error have rendered it even more so. For decades, DDT trucks sprayed the roadsides to control the mosquitoes that bred in the marshes, and the children followed behind, breathing in the clouds. Ciba-Geigy Chemical Corporation bought 1,400 acres by the nearby Toms River and used it for disposing toxic waste. This waste contaminated the aquifer that provided drinking water to the area: "a poison plume a mile square and dozens of feet deep, containing ninety-five different chemicals" (18). A mile north of the bungalows was Denzer & Shafer X-Ray, which used its septic system to dispose of chemical solutions it used to strip silver from old negatives. A few miles away, an enterprising man named Nicholas Agricola disposed of five thousand drums of hazardous waste from Union Carbide on rented land, unbeknownst to his landlord or the residents who drew well water that was contaminated by the leaking drums. Five miles upwind was Ocean County's nuclear power plant, the Oyster Creek reactor, which Antonetta claims is either the worst or second worst nuclear plant in the country based on the quantity of toxic nuclear fission material it has released. The plant also ejected water used to cool the reactor into Oyster Creek, warming the water so much that local fish stopped migrating, an apparent boon to fishermen in this poor, rural "sacrifice" community (26). Antonetta drank in the landscape's secrets with the water, ingested them in local plants and fish, and soaked them in through her skin. Now that she is an adult, the place remains linked to her not only through memory, but also through illnesses that she believes were ultimately caused by the hazards to which she was exposed. Everything connects in her body.

Although she and her body were already compromised by genetics, family psychology, and environmental poisons, as a teenager Antonetta added the extra burden of massive quantities of drugs, especially heroin and LSD. Her old diaries reveal that she used heroin and other drugs daily for more than a year. Was she self-medicating? Perhaps. But she was also taking chances, hanging out with reckless boys, working for dealers, brushing as close as she could to death without being taken. Reflecting on a particularly terrifying diary entry written while tripping on LSD, her fifteenth trip in three weeks, Antonetta considers the intersection of the body, brain, and biography:

> In the twenty-six years since I wrote this my ten trillion cells have replaced themselves three times, except the doled-out brain cells, which don't replenish. In this period my thyroid cells, many of them, became something other than thyroid cells; their DNA altered, they lost their purpose and began filling up my neck [with tumors]. The ovaries I had then are gone. I've grown lesions on my liver. My uterine lining has moved out and now resides in the pelvis. I take pills that stream into the brain the GABA and serotonin that isn't naturally there. . . . There's no way to end the generations of poisoning: the years my landscape poisoned me, the years that, to compensate, maybe, I poisoned myself. (186–87)

For Antonetta, the challenge of writing an illness memoir in the risk society is that the multiplicity of possible causes and effects mean that she cannot compose a neat story of illness, cure, and redemption. It may well be that all writers of illness narratives struggle to find a narrative explanation for illness but, in this case, the author's experiments with a layered and spiraling narrative are a gesture toward an ideal form that reflects the intricacy of her subject.

While there are flashes of beauty and insight in her prose, Antonetta's experiments with narrating unnarratable knowledge do not always succeed. Although she generally avoids simple stories of cause, effect, and blame, she gets caught in the narrative drive toward certainty and closure when she discusses industries and government that gave little thought to the residents of this rural region. She is so certain that local industries caused disease clusters and the cluster of diseases in her own body, that she does not provide a complex picture of the evidence. The same year Antonetta's book appeared in print, the New Jersey Department of Health made public the results of a six-year-long, ten-million-dollar investigation of air and water contamination in the nearby town of Toms River that did not identify any single factor to explain elevated cancer rates, although it did affirm an "association" between leukemia in female infants and mothers who had lived near the Ciba-Geigy plant and consumed water from polluted wells (I. Peterson). Antonetta's narrative falters at this point, when she overlooks ambiguity and insists that her health has, without a doubt, been destroyed by industrial pollution. Narratives demand closure, and this demand is always at odds with the vast quantities of information that could be taken into account and the indeterminacy at the core of individual accounts of risk.

Despite the unevenness of *Body Toxic,* the narrative breaks new ground. As much as Antonetta wants an explanation for her ailments, at moments she admits that she cannot be sure when, where, or even if she encountered the toxin or toxins responsible for her sicknesses. Her infertility, she observes, could have happened "in my mother's body, the DDT, the swimming in Toms River, by the chemical pipeline into the woods." "These are facts," she continues, "that float without anything beneath them and even if you could tie them to the rock of a real event, no one would know what that might mean. It would only leave pretty ripples, circles to follow" (115). Echoing Herman, she concludes, "the mirror art holds up to nature isn't reflection but containment. A means of edging" (116). With her memoir, Antonetta shows that the act of composing a life narrative, especially a risk narrative, only momentarily contains the uncontainable. This is not a failure, but simply indicative of the relationship of narrative to risk. Throughout *Body Toxic,* Antonetta's narrative draws attention to its artfulness, and thus to the place of the literary in a world of risk. Her work thereby invites inquiry into questions about why and how art and literature matter in the twenty-first century.

These questions have been taken up with ever more urgency after the terrorist attacks of 9/11. Although risks of political violence have always been present, this day kindled a new awareness of vulnerability in societies where such dangers had previously felt distant. In response to 9/11, numerous novels have addressed concerns that have long been central to biographical narratives about risk, in particular how to make personal meaning of the impersonal dangers that threaten one's future.[23] Of the many such novels to appear, Ian McEwan's *Saturday* most directly examines the experience of both extraordinary and everyday risk as he describes a day in the life of his central character, neurosurgeon Henry Perowne.

As an exceptionally controlled writer, McEwan exists at the opposite end of the spectrum from Antonetta, and his manner of representing risk bears little resemblance to *Body Toxic*. McEwan's plots generally leave little to chance. Thus, in *Saturday*, his story may at first seem utterly paradoxical: he creates a tightly woven world, but it is a world in which risk is present and evident in every minute of every day. To a degree, McEwan normalizes risk in *Saturday*. Ultimately, however, in demonstrating how realist fiction can represent the risks embedded in the events of a single Saturday, McEwan makes an argument for the relevance of fiction in the risk society. He demonstrates how the novel can focus sharp attention on the meanings of risk in one man's life. In doing so, he does not seek to arouse additional anxiety, but rather to show that risk is a constant, if unpredictable, presence, and one's relationship to it must be managed if one is to find the will to get out of bed every morning.

The universality of risk is evident from the opening scene of *Saturday*. Perowne rises from bed in his London home, preternaturally awake before dawn. Standing at his bedroom window, he notices a strange light in the sky that he first thinks is a meteor and then a comet. After finding the correct local scale of reference, he realizes what he sees is a plane on fire, descending over the city as it makes its way to Heathrow. He expects it will crash. He wonders whether terrorists are involved. What this event means—whether it imperils the city, the nation, the world, or whether it is of no significance—remains unclear for much of the novel. The novel takes place over the twenty-four hours that begin at dawn on Saturday, 15 February 2003, a day of global protests against the impending attack by the United States, Britain, and a coalition of multinational forces on Iraq. On this day, eighteen months after 9/11, the world was on the brink of war. In London, more than 750,000 marched, while the BBC estimated that between six and ten million people took part in demonstrations around the globe.[24] With the stage set, McEwan proceeds to engage risk on every level, from the planet, to the city, neighborhood, family, and individual, all the way down to the subcellular level of the gene.

As Perowne's day unfolds, a sequence of random chances—some bad luck in an otherwise very fortunate life—leads to a minor car accident after which Perowne is nearly assaulted by the other driver, Baxter, the moody leader of a trio of street thugs. Although Perowne is outnumbered and physically outmatched, he is lucky. He escapes a beating because he recognizes that his assailant shows signs of a progressive genetic disorder and exploits his authority as a physician to manipulate him. Upon observing Baxter's unusual behavior—a persistent tremor, little nods and shakes of his head as he tries to follow movement across his line of sight, and a false sense of superiority—Perowne gambles that his assailant has inherited a mutation on a single gene that is now triggering the early symptoms of Huntington's disease. If his hypothesis is correct, then Baxter's future is determined at the genetic level. Assuming Baxter must be desperate for any hint of hope, Perowne distracts him from the assault with a lie. He tells him that there are new drugs to lessen symptoms of Huntington's (98), and in the confusion that follows this subterfuge, Perowne is able to escape, largely unscathed. Later, after he has exhausted his pent-up adrenaline by playing a viciously competitive squash match, he assumes the unpleasant episode is now behind him. After all, in a city as large as London, what are the chances he will ever encounter Baxter again? This gamble will catch up with him as the plot unfolds. The wholly rational man cannot escape chance events and bad luck. They will intrude with a vengeance.

McEwan makes an interesting choice when he creates a central character who favors science over literature, control over risk, and stability over change. By telling a story about risk through the experiences of a man of reason, McEwan considers the limits and possibilities of both scientific and literary worldviews. Perowne is so confident in natural law that Darwin's theory of evolution provides him with an explanatory framework for nearly all that happens during his day off. Everywhere he sees random chance, genetic determinism, and the struggle for survival. When he considers his grown children, for instance— Daisy, a poet, and Theo, a blues guitarist—he sees their successes as fortunate accidents of genetics and circumstance: "It's a commonplace of parenting and modern genetics," Perowne observes, "that parents have little or no influence on the characters of their children. . . . What really determines the sort of person who's coming to live with you is which sperm finds which egg, how the cards in two packs are chosen, then how they are shuffled, halved and spliced at the moment of recombination" (25). For Perowne, even a game of squash with a colleague becomes a competition in which his desire to defeat his opponent is "as biological as thirst" (115).

Perowne's character raises the question of whether the successes of science and the emergence of the risk society have diminished the value of literature. The neurosurgeon is fond of music but never turns to poetry or fiction for solace or understanding of life's indeterminacy, even as literature is richly present in his family and home. He is the son-in-law of one poet and the father of another, but insists he has no interest in the world reimagined. He's a rationalist; he wants scientific explanations. He sees imagined worlds as "a childish evasion of the difficulties and wonders of the real" (66). Instead, Perowne finds comfort in the aesthetics of repetition with variation, so he seeks out such patterns: in the *Goldberg Variations,* which he listens to while performing surgery; in the regular rearrangement of the same six chords as his son plays the blues; in the act of making love with his wife, to whom he has been married for more than two decades; and in the rhythm and syncopation of yet another Saturday. Only one text reliably engenders in Perowne a sense of aesthetic rapture: Darwin's *Origin of Species.* He is particularly drawn to the final paragraph in which Darwin sums up his theory of natural selection regarding the role of chance as well as natural law in the development of life. Darwin's final authorial gesture at the end of this revolutionary treatise is to affirm that his theory does not reduce nature to a set of dry rules; rather, he asserts, it should inspire wonder. "There is grandeur in this view of life," he declares (Darwin 490). Perowne's affection for this passage, which is alluded to several times throughout *Saturday,* implies that the transcendence offered by literature—the desire for grandeur—still matters in the risk society.

Although McEwan emphasizes Perowne's rationalist worldview throughout the book, he places Perowne in encounters with art and artists that compel him to acknowledge that something is lacking in his orderly, privileged existence. The sound of his son playing the blues "pierces him because it . . . carries a reprimand, a reminder of buried dissatisfaction in his own life, of the missing element" (28). The missing element is the "strange and worldly joy" at the heart of the blues; it is an "inventiveness, [a] style of being free" (28). Perowne longs for such experiences, especially to *create* as his son Theo does: to give "a glimpse of what we might be, of our best selves, and of an impossible world in which you give everything you have to others, but lose nothing of yourself" (176).

With such a character at the center of his novel, McEwan seems eager—perhaps overeager—to defend literature as redemptive and necessary in the face of broad cultural suspicion about its relevance in the risk society, and in an era of ever expanding scientific, technical, and medical knowledge. His efforts to rescue literature and the arts lead him, however, to concoct exactly the sort of literary contrivances that would annoy the character he has created. On Saturday evening, the Perowne family plans to reunite in their grand London townhouse—the doctor and his wife Rosalind, their children Daisy and Theo, and his father-in-law Grammaticus. As they assemble, their home is invaded by Baxter and his friend Nigel, who force their way in, holding Rosalind at knifepoint. With nothing to lose, Baxter has come to get revenge for having been disgraced by Perowne earlier in the day. When he learns Daisy is a poet, he seeks to humiliate her father by forcing her to stand nude before him to read one of her poems. When Daisy instead recites Matthew Arnold's "Dover Beach," Baxter is instantly transformed from a domestic terrorist into a sentimental lover (231–32). He is so moved by the poem's beauty and elated because he thinks the woman standing before him is its creator that his anger dissipates, his desire for revenge suddenly displaced by a desire to possess Daisy's book: "Baxter fell for the magic, he was transfixed by it, and he was reminded how much he wanted to live" (288).

Lest McEwan's readers conclude that the author has at last provided evidence for the redemptive powers of literature, he juxtaposes this account with Perowne's very different interpretation of the scene. To the neurosurgeon, Baxter's poetry-induced euphoria is less a mark of the power of language than a symptom of neurological deterioration. "It's of the essence of a degenerating mind," he observes, "periodically to lose all sense of a continuous self, and therefore any regard for what others think of your lack of continuity" (232). Quickly, Perowne and Theo distract Baxter and shove him down a flight of stairs, causing a near-fatal head injury. Improbably, Perowne then agrees to perform the surgery necessary to save Baxter's life.

What then are McEwan's readers to make of the value of literature in the risk society? Are the arts reminders of life's meaning or frivolous distractions? McEwan has carefully guided his plot to this point and placed Perowne in the operating room so that he can reveal that the work of the neurosurgeon is fundamentally like that of the novelist. Science and art are not as far apart as Perowne and generations of artists have made us believe. In the operating theater and the novel, Perowne and McEwan control the uncontrollable. Consider, for instance, how McEwan describes the first moments of Baxter's surgery: "At the very first stroke of sunflower yellow [Betadine solution] on pale skin, a familiar contentedness settles on Henry; it's the pleasure of knowing precisely what he's doing, of seeing the instruments arrayed on the trolley, of being with his firm in the muffled quiet of the theater, the murmur of the air filtration, the sharper hiss of oxygen passing into the mask taped to Baxter's face out of sight under the drapes, the clarity of the overhead lights. It's a reminder from childhood of the closed fascination of a board game" (258). That first stroke of the sponge on skin evokes the artist's brush or the writer's pen. Later, as he operates, Perowne experiences transcendence: "He feels calm, and spacious, fully qualified to exist. It's a feeling of clarified emptiness, of deep, muted joy" (266). Performing surgery transports him "into a pure present, free of the weight of the past or any anxieties about the future" (266). In Perowne's world, the essential element of aesthetic experience is this wondrous sense of completeness.

As the operation concludes, there is no escaping the parallel to McEwan who, having gotten inside the head of his character, is also busy at this point securing all the threads of the plot and tying off loose ends. Human creativity, ingenuity, or grace take place, McEwan implies, in what could be called, borrowing a phrase from risk theorist Deborah Lupton, "cocoons of invulnerability" (Lupton 78).[25] These are spaces, like the operating room, the dark concert hall in which Perowne watches Theo perform, or the bedroom where he and Rosalind make love, that allow temporary respite from the risks and uncertainties of everyday life, moments of self-transcendence that feel beyond the particular and individual, and thus beyond vulnerability. McEwan strives to achieve in *Saturday* the "self-enclosed perfection" Perowne finds in Darwin's *Origin*—"a coherent world, everything fitting at last" (177). He closes *Saturday* with a scene that parallels the novel's opening, bringing the day and the narrative full circle. Perowne stands at the window where he started his morning, but he is now badly shaken. He looks over the city: "London, his small part of it, lies wide open, impossible to defend, waiting for its bomb, like a hundred other cities" (286). He recognizes the ease with which we can all be wounded. Nevertheless, when Perowne turns from this view of London to his bed and his wife Rosalind, whom he has seen just hours earlier with a knife to her throat, he finds contentment: "He fits himself around her, her silk pyjamas, her scent, her warmth, her beloved form, and draws closer to her. Blindly, he kisses her nape" (289). And then he tells himself a necessary fiction that transports him, as surgery did: "There's always this. . . . And then: there's only this" (289). In this intimate moment, McEwan upholds his own art as an example of how anxiety and joy can be held in the same frame. Thus, he offers an explanation of the value of literature in the risk society: his text, like so many risk narratives, is an argument against cynicism and despair, a reminder that we want to live, not in spite of the world as it is, but because of it.

The Problem of Closure

Although McEwan's implicit demonstration of the function of narrative in the risk society is certainly compelling, the overtly manufactured quality of the novel's ending draws attention to the problem that any narrative conclusion—whether in fiction or nonfiction—will misrepresent the fundamental indeterminacy of life in the risk society. Indeed, in the narratives considered in this chapter, each of the writers struggles in one way or another with the friction between the demands of closure and the nature of risk. For example, Stephen Jay Gould's "The Median Isn't the Message" was not written primarily to tell the author's story of survival or to offer a message of hope, but to explain in simple terms how statistics about disease should be interpreted in individual cases. Gould may exhort his readers to develop a more sophisticated knowledge of risk and thereby to learn to accept variation and uncertainty, but his good luck undercuts this argument. He may argue that statistics, "properly interpreted, is profoundly nurturant and life-giving," but, in truth, statistics can only feel personally sustaining if one is lucky enough to match the profile of those for whom the odds are favorable. Readers who learn from Gould how to think statistically may not discover, as he did, that their prognosis is better than they expected. The ending of Gould's essay and his good fortune of surviving for twenty years after diagnosis allows readers to generalize about their own experience from his happy ending.

In *Swimming in a Sea of Death,* Rieff refuses to offer readers or himself closure with regard to the meaning of risk or the experience of grief. To let go of his grief, after all, would be to let go of the emotion that most strongly connects him to his mother. Knowing that it is too late to be the son he wishes he had been, he writes, "What does that leave? Closure? Again, I do not believe for an instant that there is any such thing" (178). Thus, he closes his book in equivocation. Looking at a diary Sontag kept when receiving chemotherapy for her first cancer, he sees that, in a rare moment of reflection on mortality, she wrote, "in the valley of sorrow spread your wings" (179). Did she believe these words? He does not know; he does not know if anyone can believe them. But he decides that this sentence expresses "the best that can be said of old mortality" (179). He ends his book by repeating the words that his mother probably did not believe and that he does not believe either, because it is the best he has to offer. Such ambivalence perfectly suits the risk narrative that precedes it.

The other authors considered here do not, like Rieff, explicitly reject resolution; rather, they seek to complicate the reader's experience of certainty and finality. Amy Harmon, Alice Wexler, and Susanne Antonetta bring their accounts of risk to a close with the proliferation of new narratives. They seek to open up new possibilities rather than shut them down. Harmon's article about Deborah Lindner's decision to have a double mastectomy ends as Lindner returns to consciousness after a seven-and-a-half hour operation. Because Harmon is writing a narrowly focused news feature about Lindner's choice, the larger story of risk does not come to a close at the end of the article. Questions about Lindner's life are left unanswered—whether she will be satisfied with her decision, whether she will have children, whether she will get cancer. The online version of Harmon's article offers more details about Lindner's decision, including a four-part video feature about Lindner's journey, the "Story of a Previvor," which gives a more intimate view of her experience. The Web page also opens itself to the many ways in which decisions about preventive mastectomies will be made in other lives. There is a detailed chart that analyzes the advantages and disadvantages of various diagnostic and treatment choices available to women with BRCA1 or BRCA2. There are also links to a range of additional resources for readers: links to support groups for BRCA carriers, information on genetic risk factors for breast and ovarian cancer, answers to questions about mastectomies, and links to both an article in *Nature* about genetic predisposition tests for other major diseases and to the *New York Times'* online "Health Guide to Breast Cancer." It remains up to readers to recognize where their own circumstances and choices differ from Lindner's and how they might compose their own risk narratives.

Wexler similarly ends her book without knowing her fate and by drawing attention to the variety of possible stories by people at risk for Huntington's. In an afterword, she reviews the literature about the psychology of people at risk for the disease. Rather than draw any sweeping conclusion, she emphasizes how little is known about the impact of knowing whether one carries the lethal gene mutation. She underscores that her story is not the only one and that, while psychological effects of having been tested for Huntington's or being symptomatic have been studied, the results are hampered by narrow definitions of "psychological." Too often researchers fail to contextualize individual responses with information about culture, class, and gender differences, as well as more specific differences regarding levels of support from counselors and family. Refusals to be tested are too often represented in the media as "a flight from truth and knowledge, a failure of courage, an avoidance of responsibility or a preference for 'ignorance'" (275). Wexler insists that people may forgo testing for a range of perfectly justifiable reasons, including pragmatic concerns about losing employment or health insurance. She concludes, therefore, that we need to respond to the stories of those who have or are at risk for Huntington's not as objects for judgment, but as resources worthy of thoughtful and generous readings.

The requirement of closure imposes awkward constraints on Antonetta's biography, which otherwise evokes the experience of risk as a complex movement between indeterminacy and control, anxiety and knowledge, and confusion and coherent narrative. The memoir ends with Antonetta having moved to the coast of Washington state, as far away from the Jersey shore as she can be in the continental United States. She acknowledges, however, that her escape is not a true escape. Even in this apparently pristine landscape, invisible risks threaten her adopted child, Jin, just as they threatened her childhood. Alongside this knowledge of risk, however, Antonetta places a different kind of knowing. She ends her text with anecdotes about Jin's playful mythmaking— his stories about monsters and witches that function to explore and contain his

fears. Thus, she reminds us that in a risk society imaginative narratives, including her own memoir, simply (or not so simply) provide a way to live creatively
with uncertainty.

Each of these conclusions offers a degree of closure, but none fully evokes
the complexity of the risk-centered world described by Darwin in *Origin of Species,* a world in which individual stories are particles in "swarms of interacting
micronarratives" (Abbott 157). In *Saturday,* McEwan draws readers' attention
numerous times to the final paragraph of Darwin's *Origin.* On Saturday morning, waking for the second time, Perowne recalls having encountered the
phrase, "there is grandeur in this view of life" in Darwin's book, and he finds
the words consoling (53–54, 263): "Those five hundred pages deserved only one
conclusion: endless and beautiful forms of life, such as you see in a common
hedgerow, including exalted beings like ourselves, arose from physical laws,
from war of nature, famine and death. This is the grandeur. And a bracing kind
of consolation in the brief privilege of consciousness" (54). If asked to construct
a religion, Perowne thinks, he would ground it in evolution: "What better creation myth? An unimaginable sweep of time, numberless generations spawn-
ing by infinitesimal steps complex living beauty out of inert matter, driven on
by the blind furies of random mutation, natural selection and environmental
change, with the tragedy of forms continually dying, and lately the wonder of
minds emerging and with them morality, love, art, cities" (54).

Darwin's conclusion resonates for McEwan and other writers in the risk
society because it demonstrates both the difficulties of writing about risk and
the problem of how such writing is received. One of the narrative challenges
Darwin faced was to bring his work to a close by affirming the open-endedness
of the story of natural selection. He chose to do so by stepping back for the long
view. In the first British edition of 1859, he brought his book to a close with this
paragraph:

> It is interesting to contemplate an entangled bank, clothed with many
> plants of many kinds, with birds singing on the bushes, with various in-
> sects flitting about, and with worms crawling through the damp earth,
> and to reflect that these elaborately constructed forms, so different from
> each other, and dependent on each other in so complex a manner, have all
> been produced by laws acting around us. . . . From the war of nature, from
> famine and death, the most exalted object which we are capable of con-
> ceiving, namely, the production of higher animals, directly follows. There
> is grandeur in this view of life, with its several powers, having been origi-
> nally breathed into a few forms or into one; and that, whilst this planet
> has gone cycling on according to the fixed law of gravity, from so simple a

beginning endless forms most beautiful and most wonderful have been, and are being, evolved. (489–90)

Darwin leaves his readers, including Perowne, with a sense of awe at the workings of natural, not divine, laws. With so many variables, and so many natural laws at work in every aspect of life, however, no single or simple scientific narrative can suffice to tell the story of even one small segment of an "entangled bank." This, too, is wondrous.

It is worth pointing out, however, that Darwin's original conclusion did not stand for long. He revised it for the second edition, which appeared only a month and a half after the first. In that brief space of time, he came to recognize the threat posed by the theological controversy that *Origin* had aroused (Browne 96). Thus, in the second and all subsequent editions of the book, the final sentence contains three words that alter the ending significantly. He writes: "There is grandeur in this view of life, with its several powers, having been originally breathed *by the Creator* into a few forms or into one" (490; emphasis mine). With the addition of "by the Creator," Darwin invites readers to assume the presence of a controlling agent in the narrative of natural selection, thereby turning a complex narrative about chance and risk into a far simpler story about divine cause and earthly effect.[26]

While this revision defused some of the controversy over the argument's religious implications, it also rendered Darwin's narrative more palatable to readers because it allows for a degree of closure. By inserting the Creator into the story, Darwin makes it possible for readers to see their lives as having a purpose and fulfilling a larger plan. However flawed this solution is, post-Darwinian writers of risk narratives will always share the double bind the scientist finds himself in at the end of *Origin of Species*. They must balance the responsibility to remain true to a scientific view of the world with the desire to give meaning to lives lived in uncertainty. The narratives they create will be imperfect but necessary fictions.

Three

Responding to the Pain
of Others

WHILE THE EXPERIENCE of being "at risk" is newly recognized as presenting a problem for language and literature, pain has long been understood to resist expression in words. At its worst, pain is unchosen, extreme, and without purpose; it obscures memory, thought, language, everything but itself. How can one communicate such an experience? Chronic pain does not present the same challenge to expression as acute pain and even agony can find its way into a story as time passes, but the problem posed by pain remains. How people express pain is highly varied, inherently subjective, and thus difficult—perhaps even impossible—to share or comprehend with certainty.

For writers, pain presents a paradox. Although pain resists expression, many writers have composed volumes about pain in a wide range of genres, from poetry, to drama, memoir, and scholarly writing. Pain is everywhere in literature. For examples of life writing about pain from disease, one can turn to Fanny Burney's "Letter of 1812" where she describes having a mastectomy without anesthesia or Alice James's late-nineteenth-century *Diary*, which contains passages about the pain of breast cancer. More recent book-length pain memoirs include Lynne Greenberg's *The Body Broken*, Lous Heshusius's *Inside Chronic Pain*, and Melanie Thernstrom's *The Pain Chronicles*.[1] This chapter will consider what renders pain communicable for some writers, but not for others. Are these differences attributable to the extremity of the pain, the speaker's or writer's skill with language, the chosen genre, the audience? And why, if there is a significant body of writing about pain, have critics been so convinced that it is beyond language?

One reason for the persistent belief that pain exceeds the reach of language is that pain poses the philosophical problem of subjective reality—that we are unable to have certain knowledge about another person's inner life. Another reason this belief endures is that, within the critical community, the most influential work about pain advances the argument that pain is unspeakable. Elaine Scarry's *The Body in Pain* has shaped criticism about physical suffering since it was published in 1985. Scarry famously asserts that "physical pain does not simply resist language but actively destroys it, bringing about an immediate reversion to a state anterior to language, to the sounds and cries a human being makes before language is learned" (4). Pain, she also argues, has the unique capacity to disrupt intersubjective experience: "for the person in pain, so incontestably and unnegotiably present is [pain] that 'having pain' may come to be thought of as the most vibrant example of what it is to 'have certainty,' while for the other person it is so elusive that 'hearing about pain' may exist as the primary model of what it is 'to have doubt'" (4). Thus, the sentence "I am in pain" signifies a fact for the person in pain; yet for the person hearing this sentence, especially if there is no visible or identifiable cause, the truth of the statement cannot be verified. This argument, which Scarry develops in relation to the extreme pain of torture, is the focus of the first half of her book, and scholars have used it again and again to shore up their analyses of the silences, fissures, and aporias in literature about trauma and suffering.[2] More than twenty-five years after the book's publication, this part of Scarry's argument—the idea that pain is unspeakable—has become part of the critical canon.[3]

Her claims may be valid with regard to the extreme of torture. But her argument has foreclosed a discussion of less extreme forms of pain. The very fact that there is an abundance of literature about pain calls into question the validity of her argument in relation to milder or chronic pain. In fact, many writers who have produced memoirs about such manifestations of pain suggest that the primary problem they face is not how to find language for pain, but rather how to make readers receptive to stories of pain. Their question is not how to find words for pain, but rather, who will listen and what will they hear?

Literary Performances of Pain

Across centuries, cultures, and genres, writers such as Emily Dickinson, Alphonse Daudet, and Margaret Edson have sought to communicate particularities about pain, while also drawing attention to the challenges that the subject itself poses. Dickinson, America's poet laureate of pain, describes pain as existing outside narrative, unlocated in place or time. At the same time, however, she finds the words to say this:

> Pain—has an Element of Blank—
> It cannot recollect
> When it begun—or if there were
> A time when it was not—
>
> It has no Future—but itself—
> Its Infinite contain
> Its Past—enlightened to perceive
> New Periods—of Pain. (323–24)

Dickinson suggests pain's inexpressibility by omission; she does not even attempt to describe the feeling of being in pain. Instead, she defines pain as a force that reduces people to passive objects. Out of time, without a point of reference to anything other than itself, pain cannot be contained in a narrative of personal experience. Dickinson can reasonably assume, however, that readers will recognize her account of her experience and understand what she means by its "Element of Blank." Unnamed, pain is still recognizable.

French novelist Alphonse Daudet turns to private prose to describe his pain. Daudet kept a notebook in which he recorded vivid accounts of the agonizing pain he suffered from neurosyphilis during the last decade of his life in the 1890s. These fragments were collected and published first in 1930 as *La doulou*. Then, in a remarkable rescue of a forgotten work by a nearly forgotten writer, the text reemerged as *In the Land of Pain* in 2002, translated and edited by British writer Julian Barnes. While Daudet struggles to express what his body feels, there can be no doubt that he succeeds in elaborating the "varieties of pain":

> Sometimes, on the sole of the foot, an incision, a thin one, hair-thin. Or a penknife stabbing away beneath the big toenail. The torture of "the boot."[4] Rats gnawing at the toes with very sharp teeth.
> And amid all these woes, the sense of a rocket climbing, climbing up into your skull, and then exploding there as the climax to the show. (21)

Despite Daudet's skill with metaphor, he confesses that writing about pain is difficult: "Are words actually any use to describe what pain (or passion, for that matter) really feels like? Words only come when everything is over, when things have calmed down. They refer only to memory, and are either powerless or untruthful" (15). This observation is followed directly by another, however, that reconsiders the nature of the challenge posed by pain: "No general theory about pain. Each patient discovers his own, and the nature of pain varies, like a singer's voice, according to the acoustics of the hall" (15). In this statement, the difficulty of communicating pain is caused less by the absence of language for pain than by the patient's interiority—"the acoustics of the hall"—which also determines what others hear. In addition, Daudet observes, "Pain is always new to the sufferer, but loses its originality for those around him. Everyone will get used to it except me" (19). Thus, he suggests that personal stories of pain, even those as inventive as his own, become flattened, generalized, and reduced to banalities by listeners.[5]

While Daudet's catalog of obstacles to expression documents his struggle to express his suffering, the fragments from his notebooks demonstrate that agonizing pain does not destroy language in every instance. Adding to his misery is his anxiety about how or whether his words will be received with their full force by a future audience. Will he be understood? He is not confident that he will. In a particularly despairing stretch of Daudet's rough and broken notes, he writes,

> Pain blots out the horizon, fills everything.
> I've passed the stage where illness brings any advantage, or helps you understand things; also the stage where it sours your life, puts a harshness in your voice, makes every cog-wheel shriek.
> Now there's only a hard, stagnant, painful torpor, and an indifference to everything. *Nada!* . . . *Nada!* (65)

How should one read this passage? At first, Daudet's sentences may appear to confirm the idea that pain destroys everything but itself. And yet, when the pain withdraws just enough, writing emerges. Suffering does not grant Daudet a new eloquence, but it also does not strip him of his way with words. Indeed, even when he writes that there is only nothing and more nothing, *something* happens due to the stroke of his pen. More than a century later, his words remain touching and instructive.

Writing before the rise of biomedicine, Daudet and Dickinson reveal that the challenge of communicating pain is neither entirely modern nor insurmountable. It also is the case, however, that there is a broader audience for such work in the contemporary era, as Julian Barnes's successful translation and republication of *In the Land of Pain* demonstrates. Playwright Margaret Edson takes full advantage of a new openness to personal accounts of suffering in her Pulitzer Prize–winning drama *W;t*. Edson presents pain as a modern problem—created by medical treatment and aggravated by physicians' indifference. She suggests that many people, but especially doctors, have forgotten how to listen deeply to expressions of suffering, and that this failure is the product of a culture that values a particular model of "success"—professional authority and status—over the skillful expression of empathy, compassion, and care.

Edson's script dramatizes again and again how specialized language necessarily limits one's ability to communicate with and comprehend others. Throughout the play, the central character, Vivian Bearing, demonstrates her authority through a language and a worldview shaped by her profession. She is an English professor, a renowned interpreter of Donne's *Holy Sonnets,* and a woman who, like Donne, possesses a sharp wit. Yet, at a particularly difficult moment, when she awakes in the hospital, agitated, afraid, and in agonizing pain, she struggles to address the play's audience clearly and in personal terms: "I want to tell you how it feels. I want to explain it, to use *my* words. It's as if . . . I can't . . . There aren't . . . I'm like a student and this is the final exam and I don't know what to put down because I don't understand the question and I'm *running out of time*" (70). At first, Bearing's faltering speech seems out of character: she has never before been at a loss for words. Her pain, it appears, is inexpressible, or at least she is unable to find her own words to name her pain. Bearing's nurse, Susie, calms her, and when her physician, Dr. Kelekian, enters, Susie speaks for her, telling him "the pain is killing her" (71). Although Kelekian turns to his patient and asks, "Dr. Bearing, are you in pain?" he does not hear her response, which seems to be spoken only in her mind (71). Unnoticed by the hospital staff, heard only by the audience, Bearing sits up and shouts: "Am I in pain? I don't believe this. Yes, I'm in goddamn pain. (*Furious*) I have a fever of 101 spiking to 104. And I have bone metastases in my pelvis and both femurs. (*Screaming*) There is cancer eating away at my goddamn bones, and I did not know there could be such pain on this earth" (71). In this scene, Edson dramatizes that pain can be expressed, if not named: there is no doubt about the quality of Bearing's agony. Even as her words do not represent her pain as Daudet's detailed metaphors sometimes do, they get her point across. And yet, they only do so for the play's literal and literary audiences, not for the people who are in the hospital room with Bearing. Immediately after she screams that she "did not know there could be such pain on this earth," she falls back onto her bed and cries out, audible now to those in the room—"Oh, God" (71)—and she loses consciousness. All they hear is this exclamation, which may be a prayer or a curse, or perhaps both at once.

The play closes soon after with Bearing's death, after which she rises from her bed, takes off her cap, two hospital gowns, and an ID bracelet, and walks forward, naked, arms reaching toward a light. Although this final scene implies transcendence of her flawed character and her life, the problem pain poses—not just for language, but for speakers and listeners—is never transcended in the play. Bearing's predicament points to a chasm between how her doctors define and interpret pain and suffering and how it is experienced and made meaningful in her life. Edson suggests that, although medical treatments may be more effective and scientific understanding of pain's causes more precise than in the past, medical institutions and practices too often dehumanize the person in pain. Patients give their bodies over to doctors and hospitals only to encounter inattention and indifference, not because they cannot express their suffering, but because their language is unvalued and unrecognized in medical culture.

Modern Pain

One of the elements that distinguishes Edson's consideration of pain from that of Dickinson and Daudet, aside from genre, is that her work presents the argument that understanding and empathizing with the pain of others has become even more difficult in the contemporary era, in large part because of modern medical attitudes and practices. Is Edson correct in implying that there is something unique about contemporary pain? In 1991, just two years before Edson's play was first staged, David B. Morris published *The Culture of Pain,* in which he similarly argues that biomedicine is responsible for creating a crisis in how we understand and treat pain. In this book, which examines literature, art, history, and medical science to see how pain was experienced and understood in Western culture, Morris maintains that, as medical accounts of pain have grown more specialized, they have lost any correspondence to nonmedical ways of conceiving pain (5–7).[6]

It is worth examining Morris's argument in detail because his work provides a context for understanding the critique of medical culture found in *W;t.* In *The Culture of Pain,* Morris expresses concern that, as biomedical epistemology has become the dominant framework for understanding health and illness, accounts of pain are valued for their contribution to diagnosis, not for their personal significance to the patient, family, or community. Within this professional culture, physicians are no longer attuned to the narratives that express pain's meaning.[7] This creates a crisis for patients, families, and communities, according to Morris, because pain is more than a medical problem involving the transmission of nerve impulses; it is, first and foremost, an experience that "engages the deepest and most personal levels of the complex cultural and biological process we call living" (7). Medicine, he argues, will always come up against the challenge that that pain is not simply physiological or neurological, but "emerges only at the intersection of bodies, minds, and cultures" (3). It is "biocultural."[8] Even if pain is expressed only in fragments, these fragments are sufficient to reveal that "'living pain'—pain experienced outside the laboratory and not reduced to a universal code of neural impulses—always contains at its heart the human encounter with meaning" (3). Morris does not use these problems to argue for abandoning biomedical knowledge about pain. Rather, his project demonstrates how scientific knowledge can be enriched by attending to what he calls "the neglected voices—within the history of literature and within the newest laboratories and clinics—that we have trained ourselves, like mere apprentices, not to hear" (5).[9]

If one looks at any of the tens of thousands of new articles about pain that appear in medical journals each year, it is clear that medical researchers have been paying a good deal of attention to pain. While most lay readers would have difficulty with the dense, specialized language in these studies, they might be intrigued that some of the articles concern methods for assessing pain that ask patients to describe their pain in language.[10] In the last decades of the twentieth century, it became established practice for healthcare workers to ask suffering patients to rate their pain on a scale from one to ten, with ten signifying the worst pain the patient has ever felt. The use of such relative numerical scales is meant to enable individual patients to evaluate the intensity of a pain and give medical practitioners a means of tracking that experience over time. But it must also be noted that this practice reduces language to the numbers one through ten and merely creates an illusion of precision. A more elaborate language-based inventory of pain, the McGill Pain Questionnaire, was developed in 1975. It asks patients to select from among seventy-eight sensory, affective, or evaluative adjectives the words that best describe their pain. According to its creator, Ronald Melzack, the McGill Questionnaire helps physicians see "that the word 'pain' refers to an endless variety of qualities that are categorized under a single linguistic label, not to a specific, single sensation that varies only in intensity" (278). Ideally, the questionnaire also provides patients with a vocabulary to name an experience that may be entirely new to them, a vocabulary that is functional because it is shared with their physicians. In theory and practice, this common language puts physicians in a position to better diagnose and treat pain. (Scarry herself praises the McGill Questionnaire for addressing pain as a problem of language.)[11]

If medical practitioners routinely ask patients to assess their pain in language, why are Morris and Edson so concerned about the linguistic divide between patients and their physicians? While the McGill Questionnaire attempts to provide patients and physicians with a shared vocabulary, its terminology is not generative for all patients. Patients select from a limited range of words, some of which may not be familiar. They must be able, for instance, to evaluate the *punishing* nature of their pain by selecting from among the words "grueling," "cruel," "vicious," and "killing," or to identify the *sensory* nature of their pain from among the words "tender," "taut," "rasping," and "splitting."

Although the recorded answers might allow a physician to initiate a conversation with the patient, too often the questionnaire displaces the patient's own story, sidesteps the issue of pain's private meaning, and disrupts the potential for humane communication between patient and doctor. After all, patients are asked for *words,* not narratives. All of Melzack's good intentions cannot mitigate the problem that isolated terms merely evoke a subjective experience that cannot be objectively measured and that is therefore likely to continue to frustrate biomedicine's scientific mode of inquiry. The McGill Questionnaire thus highlights the tension between the medical community's desire for objectivity and the highly variable ways in which people experience and describe their pain.[12] It may encourage doctors to pay attention to language, but it does so in a mechanical way, focusing attention on analyzing patterns of discrete terms. The problem noted by Morris in *The Culture of Pain*—that physicians regularly fail to attend to pain's biocultural meaning—is mitigated, but not solved, by teaching them to adhere to yet another clinical protocol.

The limits of the McGill Questionnaire raise questions about what attentive listening to pain requires. Morris makes clear that attention to language necessarily involves interpretation—a practice central to reading literature that is ideally both informed and imaginative. At the root of the movement to standardize how clinicians gather information about pain, Morris notes, is a scientific distrust of interpretation and a discomfort with the doctor's role as "a professional reader of pain" ("How to Read," 139). In *The Body in Pain,* Scarry shares this unease with the imprecision of interpretation. When she writes about pain, she narrows her focus to the capacity of language to represent the material world—to name objects—eschewing a more complex view of language that includes its social and creative functions. Language about pain fails, in her view, because it cannot identify its object and thus it cannot confer a verifiable reality upon an internal experience. Like physicians, Scarry wants language to name and validate what is real and true. For both, this desire creates the conditions for doubt and indifference.

It is also the case, however, that in the second half of *The Body in Pain,* Scarry complicates her original assertions and describes the paths by which pain, "this most radically private of experiences," enters culture through the creation of artifacts (6). She implies that language can be used to rebuild a shattered world or a shattered self. She writes that, while pain destroys language, "to be present when the person in pain rediscovers speech and so regains his powers of self-objectification is almost to be present at the birth, or rebirth, of language" (172).[13] How to interpret these creative responses to pain is not, however, an issue Scarry considers in detail. She discusses the creation of artifacts, including those made of language, but not their reception.

Scarry's Critical Legacy

The critical world's response to *The Body in Pain* itself points to the necessity of considering reception. Although Scarry discusses the potential for creativity after pain, this part of her argument has been overshadowed by the cultural force of her claim that physical pain "actively destroys" language (4). Critics routinely use the analysis Scarry presents in the book's introduction to justify focusing on the gaps and paradoxes rather than personal stories and empathic responses.[14] This aspect of Scarry's argument has influenced scholarship well beyond the realm of literary criticism. Her proclamations about pain and language appear again and again in texts about narrative and illness, including in foundational texts such as anthropologist Arthur Kleinman's *The Illness Narratives* and sociologist Arthur Frank's *The Wounded Storyteller*.

Two prominent contemporary ethnographies of pain by anthropologists Jean E. Jackson and Byron J. Good demonstrate how difficult it can be to attend to how people narrate their pain in a critical climate that emphasizes the ways in which pain resists expression. Even as Jackson and Good critique medical institutions and the restrictive biomedical language for pain, and even as they report in detail what patients say about their chronic pain, they remain so convinced that pain resists expression that they overlook the full significance of what they hear. The anthropologists listen to the language of pain in a particular, professionally sanctioned way. Like the physicians portrayed in Edson's play and discussed in Morris's study, their theoretical framework prevents them from listening fully and attentively, and this limits their analysis.

In Jackson's study, *Camp Pain: Talking with Chronic Pain Patients,* she reflects on her year as a participant observer at the Commonwealth Pain Center (CPC), a multidisciplinary pain center that offers chronic pain patients medical, psychological, and behavioral therapies. One might expect that, after spending a year conducting interviews with patients and staff members and transcribing conversations about their experiences, Jackson would be able to complicate or qualify Scarry's argument that pain actively destroys language or attend to her argument about creative, world-making responses to pain. Although Jackson's book presents "snippets" of interviews that reveal how patients describe and interpret their pain (14), her argument only slightly modifies Scarry's. She maintains that "a pain-full body occupies a world different from the everyday world" (162) and that the world of pain is an aversive version of the worlds of dreams or "deep religious or musical experience" in that it "has its own system of meaning, [and] its inhabitants [have] their own forms for communication" (162). Pain, she concludes, "resists *everyday-world* language" (163; emphasis mine), which she, following Scarry, defines as language that names a verifiable, objective reality. Certain that pain obscures all but itself, Jackson concludes it can only be expressed in an "anti-language" or "embodied communication" that is "antithetical . . . to ordinary natural language" (163).

While Jackson coins the term "anti-language," her argument is really more "anti-metaphor." To explain anti-language she offers the example of "the experience of 'seeing stars,' stripped of this metaphor" (163). For her, metaphors do not express pain as much as they point to pain's inexpressibility. Yet, the most vibrant accounts of pain she records involve metaphors. She quotes migraine sufferers saying that a headache "feels like a pair of pliers on the optic nerve" or "like a football helmet seven sizes too small." Another patient describes postherpetic neuralgia through mixed metaphors: it feels "like a blowtorch" and it also feels "as though the devil pulls his pitchfork out only to heat it up to put it back." A patient with thalamic syndrome pain asks: "Have you ever been burned by dry ice? Have you ever received a very severe electric shock?" and then explains, "I feel a severe burning sensation while at the same time a freezing sensation" (163).

There are multiple tensions within Jackson's analysis of the language of pain. She maintains that figurative language fails because it "does not describe . . . actual experience," as if any language could fully represent reality. She defines the embodied experience of pain as a language of its own, and also an "anti-language" (163). She acknowledges that patients turn to metaphor to explain their pain, while she argues that it cannot be expressed in everyday language, as if metaphor were not, in fact, part of ordinary language. Given that Jackson begins with the assumption that language cannot convey the truth of embodied experience, it is no wonder she finds that patients' statements, even those that reveal linguistic creativity and flexibility, do not communicate the experience of pain. Like Scarry, like the creators of the McGill Questionnaire, and like many doctors, Jackson seeks to remove ambiguity and interpretation from the encounter with language.[15] In the end, Jackson's certainty that metaphor can never be the true language of pain reveals less about how patients think or speak about pain than about how she has learned to evaluate evidence and construct an academic argument.

Jackson's fellow social scientist Byron Good also works with Scarry's argument about pain's inexpressibility and gets caught in a similar conflict between orderly theory and the messiness and uncertainties of actual lives. In his article, "A Body in Pain: The Making of a World of Chronic Pain," Good begins by announcing that he will offer the exceptional narrative of a pain patient named Brian—"a remarkable story of a life of pain—a pain with an incredible origin myth, a pain that radically shaped the life world of a young man, a pain for which he struggled to find meaning and a language for expression" (29). Good presents substantial passages from the transcript of a four-hour interview with Brian, who is articulate, reflective, self-aware, and capable of richly describing the pain he feels in his jaw, which may be from temporo-mandibular joint disorder (TMJ). The pain begins in his jaw joint, leading to spasms inside his mouth, and the spasms cause a choking sensation and anxiety as the feeling of restriction moves downward. This leads to heartburn, rapid breathing, and fear of not being in control (38). In a passage from the transcription of an interview, Brian explains that he visualizes his pain as "a demon, a monster, something very . . . horrible lurking around banging the insides of my body, ripping it apart. And ah, I'm containing it, or I'm trying to contain it, so that no one else can see it, so that no one else can be disturbed by it" (36). Even as Good includes pages of Brian's transcribed description and analysis of his pain, however, Good frames the discussion by asserting that "[Brian's] pain was unspeakable. It shaped a world. And it has resisted symbolization, refused to answer to a name, though many names have been proposed. It thus remains both untamed and ultimately unshared, for as Scarry says, 'pain comes unsharably into our midst as at once that which cannot be denied and that which cannot be confirmed'" (31).

How can one reconcile Good's presentation of Brian's multiple and overlapping narratives about his pain's origin and history with his own insistence on the inadequacy of Brian's accounts of his pain? Good's analysis of the inexpressibility of pain depends on a distinction similar to Jackson's differentiation of pain's "anti-language" and "ordinary natural language" (163). For both anthropologists, the pain sufferer need not be reduced to pre-linguistic cries in order for language to have failed. For Good, language "is perhaps more typically inadequate as a sufferer seeks a name for his pain, an individual name that accurately represents that pain, describes it with such clarity that its origins and contours are expressed, a representation possessing enough power that the pain can be controlled" (30). Like Jackson, Good's expectations show what kind of listener or reader he is. They both want the impossible: for language to be so precise that it provides a form of cognitive control over pain, giving the person in pain authority over the embodied experience.

What might Good have seen in Brian's transcript if he had been a different kind of listener, or if he were writing in a genre other than the academic article? Consider the distinction between a language that *names* pain—which is what Scarry, Jackson, and Good look for—and Brian's *narrative* of a life in pain. Good describes the narrative as "a remarkable story of a life of pain—a pain with an incredible origin myth" (29), but he also says that Brian's representation of pain is "inadequate to express the sentient quality of his suffering" (29, 35). Brian's own sense of why he fails to communicate is markedly different. He sees language failing him because his words are consistently met with disbelief and incomprehension. He asserts that people who do not have the disorder cannot possibly understand what it is like to have temporo-mandibular joint disorder: "If they don't suffer with it, they don't understand it. And they're really skeptical. They don't believe in you" (40). Unlike Good, Brian locates the failure not in language, but in the listener. Thus, the dynamic plays out exactly as Scarry would predict: Brian is certain of his pain, but his listeners are not.

The importance of attending to both the speaker and audience when studying accounts of pain is nowhere more evident than in the final section of Good's article, when he writes about how Brian turns to painting as a means of expression. Brian claims, "There are times when I, when a lot of things that are ineffable about what goes on internally, I can find expression in the art. A lot of bizarre things I can't verbalize come out in the images I get down on canvas" (46). Although Good asserts that "painting provides a medium for objectification of that which cannot be expressed through language" (47), this analysis does not fully accord with Brian's own statements about his turn to the visual. Brian is generally unwilling, it seems, to sell or display his paintings. He is reticent to reveal his work unless he is certain that the viewer will accept what his art reveals: "if I reveal something about myself, something that can be, that is very vulnerable and . . . is likely to be met with skepticism, people aren't going to understand it, or they're going to have a totally different impression; or they'll mock it in some way, so that's the kind of fear I have" (47). He cannot, he insists, show his art to ordinary acquaintances. Good wants to read "the world of images" as a place where "the scream can be expressed without a sound, where the ineffable can find expression" (47), and it may well be that Brian can express unique aspects of his experience in different media. But Brian's insecurity about how his art will be received, and his consequent desire to withhold it, suggests that this mode of creative expression is no more reliable than language for communicating uncommon and unshared experience. Although Good identifies the problem as language, in Brian's account it is *reception*. What he wants from his stories and his paintings is not release from his pain, but recognition that he is in pain. He has not yet figured out how to make that happen. Nor has Good, or Jackson before him, found the key to a form of attentive listening that would enable a more generous response.

Memoirs of Pain

Experienced writers and autobiographers have significant advantages over Good, Jackson, or any of their interview subjects when it comes to narrating and explaining pain. To begin, they have talent with language and practice with narrative. Their chosen genre is inviting to a wider audience because it tells a story, even when that story also makes an argument. Martha Stoddard Holmes, a literary scholar and former cancer patient, encounters no difficulty discussing her experience of pain in the article "Thinking through Pain," coauthored with Tod Chambers. In fact, Holmes explicitly examines the academy's reliance on Scarry's claim that pain is unspeakable. She explains that she began to resist Scarry's argument in her first book, *Fictions of Affliction: Physical Disability in Victorian Culture,* when she discovered "the lushness of language and literariness" that pain inspired in Victorian doctors (129). Later, ovarian cancer and six rounds of chemotherapy refined her understanding of pain and language. In her autobiographical contribution to "Thinking through Pain," Holmes refuses the idea that language is always inadequate in relation to pain because, she says, her own body in pain has been "a site not of language erosion but language generation" (131).

With this claim, Holmes's cancer narrative becomes an argument about the relationship of pain to language. She speculates that theorists who have given themselves over to the idea that pain destroys language are like doctors who prefer subjects who are still and silent—the better to get their work done without interference, complication, or contradiction: "The quiet of the anesthetized patient, like the screams of the unanesthetized sufferer, produces a scene of wordlessness that permits the generation of theoretical language—and even, ironically, the discussion of pain, as Scarry puts it, as 'language-destroying' (19). Acute pain is open to narration by witnesses, advocates, torturers, or theorists—all of whom may separate that pain, through representation, from the suffering body itself (one of Scarry's arguments). If the nonparticipatory anesthetized patient is in many ways more convenient for the surgeon, the inarticulate sufferer is so for the theorist" (132). Although Holmes seems to be on the verge of rejecting much of what Scarry says in *The Body in Pain,* she is instead inspired to reread the book. She finds things there she had overlooked, such as an acknowledgment that chronic pain is distinct from the acute pain of torture. "Perhaps the fault is not in *The Body in Pain,*" Holmes suggests, "but in how we have tended to read it": "Drawn to the keen lines of acute pain and the attractions of the unmaking of the world, we have bypassed the places in the text where the world is never quite unmade, but remade all the same. We have certainly sidelined those kinds of pain in which language is a constant companion, and a person on the continuum between pain and pleasure may drift to sleep in a sea of loose words" (133). Echoing my own sense of what is at stake in scholarship about language and bodily suffering, Holmes concludes, "What we may need is not to dismantle *The Body in Pain,* but to look at a wider range of relationships between pain and language" (133). She calls for more open engagement with accounts of pain—for a form of attentive listening that has eluded critics whose reading of Scarry focuses on the world unmade to the exclusion of the world remade.

Holmes's perspective is affirmed in novelist Reynolds Price's *A Whole New Life,* a memoir about his recovery from spinal cancer. Price describes the pain from cancer in visually vivid metaphors, which he uses in ways that invite reconsideration of the relationships between pain and language. He tells readers, for instance, that his pain felt like "a white-hot branding iron in the shape of the capital letter 'I' held against [his] upper spine from the hairline downward some ten or twelve inches and unrelenting" (26). Later, he sees his cancer as "a dark gray eel embedded live in the midst of [his] spine" (29). With such metaphors, Price persistently challenges readers to *imagine* the full agony of his pain. "There were times each day, for hours at a stretch," he writes, "when my whole body felt caught in the threads of a giant hot screw and bolted inward to the point of screaming" (88). Later, the pain reconfigures itself: "the searing burn down the length of my spine and across my shoulders and the jolting static in both my legs . . . soared in intensity. Like most real agony, the pain afflicted more senses than one; it often shined and roared as it burned. More than once I panicked in the glare and noise" (108).

Price's work makes a case for pain understood through metaphor and narrative. His goal is not to name pain at the moment it occurs or to confirm its existence through language. He chooses to let literature evoke his pain rather than expect that his words constitute truth or testimony. Price depends on the literary to entice readers to recognize that pain can generate language. He also uses his memoir to form a relationship with his readers that is more sympathetic and trusting than the one he has with many of his physicians, who forfeited their responsibility to interpret his pain with care. Thus, Price's memoir reconsiders not only the relationships between pain and language, but also how the presence of readers and listeners contributes to the full meaning of pain.

If the central crisis of Price's memoir is the author's cancer and the disabilities it causes, the secondary crisis is that Price's doctors do not fully listen or respond to his account of his suffering. Although Price is an award-winning writer, in medical settings he cannot make language do what he needs it to. The problem is not what Scarry would predict—that his descriptions of pain are met with disbelief. Rather, he suffers because he is overmedicated and wrongly medicated—his mind dulled, yet his pain unrelieved. Although he is given methadone at a pain clinic, he reports, "the help of the Pain Clinic stopped there, where so many American physical problems are grounded by doctors who've blindly or willfully impoverished their humane intelligence—on prescription blanks" (109). The physicians respond to pain as they were trained to;

they put Price's complaints through their algorithm for pain and arrive at the solution that medicine makes most readily available—regular doses of powerful painkillers. Price's personal experience, however, does not fit the algorithm. Dissatisfied by a life "clouded" by drugs, he becomes depressed and passive, lost in a "psychic bog of helplessness" (112). Neither he nor his physicians can see beyond the methadone solution. Eventually, Price learns that alternate treatments—biofeedback and hypnosis—are available in the very same building as the pain clinic, and these ultimately enable him to control his pain.

Price wonders how it is possible that these therapies were never mentioned—"not by anyone," Price says—"no doctor, nurse, orderly or physical therapist—not for twenty-four months after I'd described, as clearly as my verbal skills permitted, the nature and extent of my pain" (112). These responses were not Price's fault or a flaw in language but rather failures of sympathy and listening in which the guiding assumption that language about pain must refer to an object means that its personal significance cannot be recognized. Price refuses to temper his moral outrage at physicians by accepting the affective limits of medical training, the burdens of institutional practice and long hours, and the psychic strain of dealing with sick people (144–45). His prose snaps with anger when he writes that doctors should be expected to exhibit "the skills of human sympathy, the skills for letting another creature know that his or her concern is honored and valued and that, whether a cure is likely or not, all possible efforts will be expended to achieve that aim or to ease incurable agony toward its welcome end" (145–46). The extended diatribe from which this comment comes defines the kind of "sympathy" Price expects from medical practitioners: an expression of humane respect and a demonstration of sincere effort to help patients remake their worlds. In Price's view, when the doctors do not respond with their full professional and personal resources, they commit an ethical failure that is intimately intertwined with their failure to listen. What he needed from them and did not get was their total presence and their willingness to care about and for his particular experience of suffering.

Ultimately, however, Price's memoir is less about making doctors listen to and acknowledge him than about how *readers* attend to his story of pain. Throughout his narrative, he creates the conditions for readers to hear him in ways that his doctors did not. He presents an inviting narrative that makes it possible for the reader to face his suffering, not turn away. He explains in matter-of-fact language the details of a life complicated by disability: the dependence on others, the constant challenges of gaining access to buildings, and daily catheterization to avoid the embarrassment of losing bladder control in public. Without flinching—and, in so doing, daring the reader to flinch—he offers straightforward details about a life transformed by disease.

Price wants readers to imagine his pain, but he also explicitly preserves a clear distance between himself and his audience to demonstrate the limits of understanding. Reading about pain can bring one to sympathy, but not to complete knowledge. Unlike Scarry, who concludes that language about pain fails because it cannot name pain in a way that leads to certain knowledge, Price's goal is not transmitting his experience into another mind, but teaching sympathy. At one point Price extends to his reader a challenge: "If . . . you're presently free of chronic pain, and I could instantly transfer mine to you in all its savagery from neck to toe, I think I'm realistic in saying that you'd lay yourself flat instantly and beg to be hauled to a hospital, fast" (157). Here, Price indicates how he wants his pain to be read. He focuses at this moment only on those readers who are not in pain—those who are most likely to doubt him. He uses his story to address that doubt and also to invite them to imagine the terrible agony they would be in if his language could actually transmit his experience. He asks for more from his readers than most—including critics—are used to giving. He requests that they honor and value his account of suffering and recognize their role as witnesses to the remaking of his world.

Is Price's desire to elicit readers' sympathy realistic? In the current era, can writers reasonably expect that reading literature will train readers' imaginations and promote ethical interaction? Price is certainly not alone in hoping that this might be the case. In *Cultivating Humanity: A Classical Defense of Reform in Liberal Education*, Martha Nussbaum maintains that "the habits of wonder promoted by storytelling" form the basis of empathy and compassion. Through reading, she explains, one learns to "define the other person as spacious and deep, with qualitative differences from oneself and hidden places worthy of respect" (90). Thus, she maintains, "Narrative imagination is an essential preparation for moral interaction" (90).[16]

While Scarry holds a position of dominance in critical theory, Nussbaum and fellow philosopher Richard Rorty articulate a more commonplace view. Rorty maintains in *Contingency, Irony, and Solidarity* that reading literature can train the imagination to understand others across lines of difference. He argues that, now that the humanities are no longer grounded in the belief that there is a universal idea of the "human" or "humanity," novelists, ethnographers, and other writers who use thick description sensitize readers to the pain of others (94). They have the responsibility of "help[ing] us attend to the springs of cruelty in ourselves, as well as to the fact of its occurrence in areas where we had not noticed it" (95). Literary works that are richly descriptive of people's lives thus generate social solidarity by fostering "the imaginative ability to see strange people as fellow sufferers" (xvi). This solidarity, he explains, "is not discovered by reflection but created. It is created by increasing our sensitivity to the particular details of the pain and humiliation of other, unfamiliar sorts of people" (xvi).

Nussbaum and Rorty present impassioned arguments about the value of literature, but the hope that literature could generate an ethical transformation among readers has not been realized. For these philosophers, literature teaches compassion for those who suffer. As a writer rather than a theorist, Price's ambitions are less grand, more grounded in his local world and embodied experience. Although sympathy is the outcome he hopes to engender in *A Whole New Life,* he does not claim that other writers want such a relationship with their readers, or even that he might want to generate the same reaction with his other literary works. If, as Holmes maintains, writing about pain invites reconsideration of the many potential relationships between pain and language, an array of new texts about pain will offer a range of unanticipated possibilities.

Poet Sarah Manguso's memoir, *Two Kinds of Decay,* is particularly interesting in this respect because she writes in a way that seems to refuse narrative sympathy or empathy for her suffering. Her stark prose contains none of Price's effusiveness and elaborate metaphor, and she willfully keeps the reader at a distance. In a *New York Times* review, Emily Mitchell recognizes that Manguso's memoir is "not only about illness but also about the ways we use language to describe it and cope with it." But how does her writing communicate pain, and what relationship does that create between writer, text, and reader?

Manguso's restrained style makes clear that she wants readers to *pay attention* to her experience in ways that are neither easy nor comfortable. She describes spending her twenties fighting a rare neurological disorder, chronic idiopathic demyelinating polyradiculoneuropathy, for which she underwent a range of painful treatments, including regular apheresis, the removal and replacement of her plasma. The book proceeds less as a linear memoir than a set of austere vignettes, in which Manguso describes incidents from her nine years of treatment in clear, unornamented prose—prose that is clinical in both senses of the word: she observes herself as a patient, and often expresses herself with near scientific detachment. Her writing offers few distractions from the events of her illness; she integrates the precise, functional vocabulary of medicine into her sentences and avoids metaphor.

In one vignette, entitled "Metaphors," for example, she explains her disease in choppy prose and simple terms that seem especially blunt when they are removed from the context of her text: "My blood plasma had filled with poison made by my immune system. My immune system was trying to destroy my nervous system. It was a misperception that caused me a lot of trouble" (14). The words "poison" and "misperception" at first seem to be metaphors, words lifted from experience to describe the inner workings of the body. But on second glance, she is just describing what happens. The immune system does release material that is toxic to her nervous system; and it misidentifies the nervous system as something to get rid of. Then she addresses metaphor more directly: "All autoimmune diseases invoke the metaphor of suicide" (14). Because her body is, in fact, killing itself, this does not seem much of a metaphorical stretch either. Arthur Frank offers a striking reading of this sentence about suicide and her use of figurative language throughout her memoir. "As I read this," writes Frank, "a metaphor is no longer a trope, in the sense of a twisting of language. Instead, reality is what is twisted, and language is a straightening out process" ("Metaphors of Pain," 193). If readers recognize or even sense this, they have learned something profound about how illness and pain overturn experience and expectations, as well as language. Language, in other words, orders the disordered experience of illness, which makes it possible for readers to attend to the details of an otherwise unimaginable experience.

Manguso's desire to unsettle expectations regarding metaphors is most striking when she uses what might be best labeled a "literal metaphor" to explain the pain and discomfort of the medical procedure apheresis, the process of trading old blood plasma for new that she endures dozens of times. In preparation for apheresis, two liters of fresh plasma, which have been stored frozen, are thawed to room temperature just before use. Because blood vessels are normally thirty degrees warmer than room temperature, infusion is a chilling experience. "For the first twenty or thirty apheresis sessions," Manguso writes, "I lay under several blankets, which didn't help the cold but helped me think at least I was trying" (39). Eventually, a surgeon installed a permanent line that allowed the infused plasma to enter her body very close to her heart. This experience turns out to be even more unsettling. "I need to describe that feeling," she insists: "make a reader stop reading for a moment and think, *Now I understand how cold it felt.* But I'm just going to say it felt like liquid, thirty degrees colder than my body, being infused slowly but directly into my heart, for four hours" (39). Manguso's simile—"it felt like liquid"—is not a metaphor, of course. This is what she felt *in fact.* When she transforms this literal description into a simile, she suggests she knows that few, if any, readers are likely to have had an experience remotely like hers. No matter what words she uses, readers can only read her description hypothetically, figuratively, imaginatively. Thus, she draws attention to how foreign her experience has made her.

Manguso's atypical approach to metaphor refuses the sympathy that familiar tropes can arouse in readers. Even as metaphors distort, they often serve understanding by representing the unfamiliar in terms of the more familiar. Recall, for instance, Daudet's affecting account of the pain in his feet as feeling like "rats gnawing at the toes with very sharp teeth" (21), or Price's description of his cancer as "a dark gray eel embedded live in the midst of [his] spine" (29). Recall, as well, Susan Sontag's argument against metaphor in *Illness as Metaphor*. Figures of speech are dangerous in her view because they distort, and the distortions found in metaphors for illness tend to further stigmatize the sick. Manguso does not share Daudet's and Price's fondness for metaphor, or Sontag's reason for rejecting them. She prefers to avoid metaphor and use language to provide a bare account of her pain and suffering, a report that rewards attention without evoking emotion.

Manguso wants similar relationships with her readers as she has with her doctors. She recounts an episode when an elderly family practitioner expresses grief over her suffering. She banishes him from her hospital room with "no antipathy" and finds a new doctor (84). The warning is clear: as she wants no pity from him, she wants none from her readers. She does not want emotion about her experience to distract readers from what matters, which is that they come to better understand, without sentiment, what it is like to be seriously ill. In her final chapter, Manguso lists in spare, direct sentences eleven insights from her illness. Among them is that her memoir is, in the end, a conventional story of cure, not redemption, not transformation: "Someone gets sick, someone gets well" (183). In the middle of the list is her most direct statement of purpose: "This is suffering's lesson: *pay attention*. The important part might come in a form you do not recognize" (183). Quite simply, the work of language for Manguso is to focus attention on suffering.

Acknowledging the Pain of Others

While Manguso, Price, Nussbaum, Rorty, and Holmes all share an interest in literature about pain, they do not share vocabulary for what is entailed in reading about and responding to pain. The terms "sympathy," "empathy," and "attention," for example, suggest different affective, social, and cognitive reactions to narratives about suffering—and only a small portion of the possible responses. In the essay "Language and Body: Transactions in the Construction of Pain," anthropologist Veena Das offers a new perspective and vocabulary for reconceiving how the world is remade after it has been is unmade by pain. Instead of addressing how language names or fails to name pain, Das shifts attention to how expressions of pain move from body to language, and then to intersubjective transactions fostered by words and stories. She approaches these issues through her research on the history of violence against women in Partition-era India and Pakistan and the ways women in mourning express grief in their bodies. During lamentation, she writes, they injure themselves to "objectify" their interior wound, after which the objectified grief can be "finally given a home in language" (68). Thus, says Das, "the transactions between body and language lead to an articulation of the world in which the strangeness of the world revealed by death, by its non-inhabitability, can be transformed into a world in which one can dwell again, in full awareness of a life that has to be lived in loss" (68–69).

In this passage, Das echoes Scarry's discussion of worlds unmade and remade, yet she implicitly rejects Scarry's premise that pain destroys language. She argues that transactions between body and language, and between self and other, allow for the construction of pain's meaning. In Scarry's framework, language fails because it cannot refer to a pain that is objectively knowable by another. Das, however, does not expect language to name pain as an objective reality. She maintains that expressions of pain perform in the *imaginative* register, by which she means that, because pain cannot be fully expressed or known, approximate understanding is always constructed imaginatively (69). Thus, Das accounts for and accepts the uncertainty that Scarry defends against. She emphasizes proximity and connection instead of distance and solitude. Das's discussion of pain's intersubjective meaning is worth quoting at length: "In this movement between bodies," she writes,

> the sentence "I am in pain" becomes the conduit through which I may move out of an inexpressible privacy and suffocation of my pain. This does not mean that I am understood. [And] this is not an indicative statement, although it may have the formal appearance of one. . . . Pain, in this rendering, is not that inexpressible something that destroys communication or marks an exit from one's existence in language. *Instead, it makes a claim asking for acknowledgment, which may be given or denied.* In either case, it is not a referential statement that is simply pointing to an inner object. (70; emphasis mine)

With this account of pain's relationship to language—not only words or metaphors, but also claims and stories—Das moves her argument out of the dialectic of certainty and doubt. She allows us to see expressions of pain as social, contingent, and meaningful in specific, local situations. Through language, a person in pain can speak and receive an acknowledgment of suffering that reconnects him or her to others and the world outside pain.

In "Language and Body," Das does not explicitly define "acknowledgment"—or its relationship to empathy or compassion. Elsewhere, however, her work regularly engages that of philosopher Stanley Cavell, who argues that the skeptic's search for certainty is a problem in ordinary life because human insight into the world and others is inevitably uncertain and incomplete. The irresolvable conflict created by the quest for certainty in the context of social relations leads to what he calls "the scandal of skepticism" (132). That is, when skeptics frame the problem of other minds as a problem of knowledge, they justify avoidance, indifference, or insensitivity. Rejecting philosophical rationalism, Cavell points out that in ordinary social encounters one does not demand that all knowledge be confirmed or that one knows beforehand what the outcome of an encounter will be. Thus, he defines the philosophical problem of other minds not as a problem of *knowledge* (perhaps knowledge of another's pain), but rather as a problem of *acknowledgment*. Acknowledgment can take vastly different forms depending on the particular cultural, political, or ethical context, but it is always a social response that situates the listener in relationship to the speaker. One might engage, withdraw, ask questions, or admit confusion and, in return, accept a comparable range of replies. Practicing acknowledgment entails recognizing the complexity of living among others, where one is always performing acts of social reading and interpretation. In contrast to knowing or judging, acknowledging also entails recognizing one's own ignorance and vulnerability, as well as the unpredictability of social encounters and relationships.

Cavell's account of acknowledgment does not demonstrate how it might be exercised in ordinary life, so Das turns in her article to literary examples to ground her discussion of the particular and local. She justifies her focus on literature, which is quite unusual for an anthropologist, by explaining that "some realities need to be fictionalized before they can be apprehended" (69). Pain, she argues, offers a fundamental example of a reality that can be acknowledged and apprehended in literature. It might seem at this point that Das's interests naturally ally her with critics working at the intersection of trauma studies and literary studies, but acknowledgment is distinct from witnessing testimony. In trauma studies, testimony is understood to be the expression of a silenced *truth,* but Das chooses to work with fiction. The literary encounter serves as a model for social experience: one participates even though knowledge of others cannot be confirmed and one does not know ahead of time how things will end.

To show what fiction can reveal about the transaction between language and body and the complexities of responding to the pain of others, Das focuses on a short story by Pakistani writer Sa'adat Hasan Manto entitled "Khol Do."[17] Manto's story is set during the Partition riots of India and Pakistan in the late 1940s. After the countries were released from colonial subjugation, nationalist fervor was expressed in the abduction and rape of women, with Muslim women taken to India, and Hindu and Sikh women carried off to Pakistan. In "Khol Do," an aged father, Sirajuddin, becomes separated from his daughter Sakina as they travel across the border between the newly divided nations. At the father's urging, a group of eight young men find and rescue Sakina. The narrator observes that they are kind to her in the immediate aftermath of her rescue. They feed her and give her milk to drink and when she is embarrassed because she has lost the long scarf that usually covers her head and breasts, one of them gives her his jacket so that she can preserve her modesty. But Sakina is not returned until many days after the rescue, when four men carry her, near death, into the clinic where her father waits. It appears—though it is never made certain—that the men who rescued her also raped and nearly killed her. The narrator does not reveal what has happened to her in the days she was apart from her father until the doctor orders her father to open the window in the stiflingly hot room by saying "khol do," translated by Das as "open it" (76).[18] When the doctor says "open it," the daughter's body automatically responds by reaching to remove her pants and open her legs, gestures which reveal that she now hears the sentence as a sexual imperative, that she has been raped repeatedly, and that her relation to the world and language has been obscenely altered. The wordless gesture implies a terrible story. Nevertheless, when the father sees his daughter's movement, he does not address the evidence of her disappearance into sexual violation, but shouts with joy: "my daughter is alive—my daughter is alive" (qtd. in Das 76).

Using Scarry's theory that pain destroys language to interpret this story, one might conclude that the daughter has been rendered unreachable because her experience is unspeakable. In addition, one might decide, as Das did in a previous interpretation of the story, that the father's declaration that his daughter is alive constitutes another violation because he does not recognize—or perhaps even see—her suffering. Instead, he appears to talk over her silent body to console himself.[19] In "Language and Body," however, Das situates this story in its historical moment—a time and place in which many fathers sacrificed their daughters' lives rather than have their sexual violation bring shame upon their families. In Manto's story, Das maintains, although the sentence "'my daughter is alive' . . . has the formal appearance of an indicative statement, it is to beseech the daughter to find a way to live in the speech of the father. And it happens not at the moment when her dishonor is hidden from the eyes of the world but at the moment when her body proclaims it. This sentence is the beginning of a relationship, not its end" (77–78). The father could, as many others did during the Partition, reject his daughter for having been raped, but instead, his words demonstrate that, at a moment of crisis when the daughter cannot sustain herself, he will sustain her for the moment with his words. By acknowledging her pain, even as he may never know what happened to her, he can begin to bring her back into the family (76–78).

With Das's reading of Manto's story, she suggests productive ways for reconceiving the work of narratives—both fiction and nonfiction—about pain. The work of some texts about pain is less to create verifiable accounts or to pro-

vide knowledge than to seek, perform, describe, or offer examples of acknowledgment. Thus, one might say that Manto takes acknowledgment as his subject
in "Khol Do," holding it up for readers to contemplate.

Does acknowledgment, however, wholly displace empathy and compassion
as the ideal social connection? Is it the best possible outcome of the expression
of pain? Although Das uses the father's exclamation that his daughter is alive as
an example of acknowledgment, the term "acknowledgment" does not account
for his joy that she is alive or his repression of evidence of her victimization.
When he shouts, "my daughter is alive," the affective quality of his response suggests something more than acknowledgment as Cavell defines it. One could not
call his cry an expression of empathy because he does not seem to comprehend
or share her feelings. In fact, the ethics of empathy are ambiguous in Manto's
story. The most overtly empathic gesture in "Khol Do" is that of the anonymous
man who offers Sakina his jacket so that she can cover herself; this man's gen-
erosity, however, may precede his participation in her rape. She was last seen
with him before she disappeared. This reminder that empathy can be used for
reprehensible purposes does not preclude positive expressions of human connection in the rest of the story, however. The father's declaration that his daughter is alive is, at the very least, a declaration of love. Das's discussion of "Khol
Do" thus implies that love and compassion can be rescued from the ways they
are oversimplified and decontextualized in idealistic arguments about how literature serves civil society. If one believes social emotions must be grounded in
certainty or that particular emotions, such as love or empathy, necessarily lead
to ethical action, one will often be disappointed. But Das's discussion of Manto's
story suggests that acknowledgment, compassion, and love, like all acts of interpretation, are vulnerable to error, ignorance, and indeterminacy. And yet, she
shows they are also fundamentally necessary in embodied and social life.

While Das appears to have traveled far from Scarry's *The Body in Pain*, her
analysis of the limits and possibilities of language about pain ultimately builds
in productive ways on Scarry's critical legacy. Like Scarry, Das acknowledges
that pain can reduce the human voice to a wordless cry. Like Scarry, she also
sees that pain motivates creativity. Unlike Scarry, however, Das emphasizes that
the construction of pain in language—the remaking of the world—involves attending to the pain of others in ways that take into account its full historical and
social complexity. Her work also suggests an explanation for why pain narratives proliferate in this skeptical age, a phenomenon Scarry's argument cannot
account for. Writers and readers recognize that language and stories accomplish meaningful work in everyday lives, even amid all that remains uncertain,
unknown, and unknowable. While physicians and critics too often conceive of
physical suffering in ways that render them incapable of recognizing, acknowl-

edging, and empathizing with the pain of others, Das's work draws attention to the social transaction that takes place when bodily experience finds its way into language.

The challenge that pain poses to language and narrative is not one that literature can solve, but it is one that writers can and do address. Many of the literary writers considered in this chapter, from Daudet to Manto, invite readers to be attentive to the complexity of pain in lives that are embodied and social. They encourage them to be rigorous and responsive, to exercise reason and emotion, to be willing to suspect and to listen, to acknowledge what is not known, and also what is. And, as we will see in the forthcoming chapters, the question of *how* to communicate pain and suffering to others is as much a topic for literature as pain itself. Das and the writers of pain memoirs accept the difficulty of expressing pain in language and narrative, but they make abundantly clear that it is possible to respond to such expressions if one has an informed understanding of social and historical context, as well as a commitment to imaginative and generous interpretation.

Four

Sontag, Suffering, and
the Work of Writing

S USAN SONTAG HAS DONE more than any other single writer to bring attention to how literature documents and shapes the cultural meaning and experience of illness, pain, and suffering.[1] While Sontag's work on illness assumes center stage in *Illness as Metaphor* and *AIDS and Its Metaphors,* she wrote about suffering throughout her career, from *On Photography,* to novels such as *The Volcano Lover,* and to her final book, *Regarding the Pain of Others.* Sontag's body of work reveals a deep and sustained exploration—with many turns, conflicts, and contradictions—of the ethics of reception, how audiences regard and respond to representations of other people's pain. Over the course of many years, she returns to questions about what writing and photography can do to communicate and alleviate the pain of others. What good, she wants to know, is art that arouses sympathy for the suffering of distant others?

In studies of literature and medicine, no critic has yet fully examined how Sontag's ideas on these issues evolved through her four decades as a writer. Work in the field tends to focus more narrowly on her texts about illness and, even then, few critics take into account the full complexity of her arguments. Many articles, for instance, quote the famous metaphor that opens *Illness as Metaphor:*[2] "Illness is the night-side of life, a more onerous citizenship. Everyone who is born holds dual citizenship, in the kingdom of the well and in the kingdom of the sick. Although we all prefer to use only the good passport, sooner or later each of us is obliged, at least for a spell, to identify ourselves as citizens of that other place" (3). These famous sentences are the twentieth century's most cited metaphor for illness and have made *Illness as Metaphor* central to discussions in the medical humanities. Although this analogy is influential, it is also one of the century's most misread or misinterpreted metaphors.[3] Immediately after Sontag's introductory paragraph, she knocks readers from their sense of firm footing by launching a polemic against metaphor. She insists that we must speak, write, and think about disease without using figurative language or mythical narratives. "My point," she declares, "is that illness is *not* a metaphor, and that the most truthful way of regarding illness—and the healthiest way of being ill—is one most purified of, most resistant to, metaphoric thinking" (3).

Indeed, Sontag's project in *Illness as Metaphor* is to counter popular and literary accounts of illness that perpetuate stigmatizing myths that diseases such as cancer are caused by moral failure and signify social disorder. The purpose of her argument was, she explains later in *AIDS and Its Metaphors*, "not to confer meaning, which is the traditional purpose of literary endeavor, but to deprive something of meaning: to apply that quixotic, highly polemical strategy 'against interpretation,' to the *real* world. . . . To the *body*" (102; emphasis mine).[4] Metaphors, she maintains, distance us from knowledge if we mistake them for reality. They shield us from the shock of the real and thus dull the pain and knowledge of our vulnerability.

Since the point of Sontag's argument is that metaphors arouse our imaginations in ways that overwhelm reason, she must have known that her concise, memorable parable about the kingdoms of the sick and well would compete with her argument. She took a risk in order to grab the reader's attention with a metaphor that emphasizes human commonalities—we *all* have two passports—over differences. She later called this gambit "a brief, hectic flourish of metaphor, in mock exorcism of the seductiveness of metaphorical thinking" (*AIDS and Its Metaphors,* 93). Whatever her intentions, the split between her powerful metaphor and her argument that disease is "without 'meaning'" (*AIDS and Its Metaphors,* 102) is indicative of tensions in the argument of *Illness as Metaphor* and tensions that are present throughout her long career as a writer.

This chapter will examine the contributions Sontag made over a lifetime to conversations about the representation of illness and suffering, paying particular attention to evidence of the uncertainties that underlie her performance of certainty. From her first works to her last, she struggles with the ambiguities and conflicts that, to this day, preoccupy literature and criticism about the representation of illness, risk, and pain. Her work even anticipates the split between theoretical literary criticism and the pragmatic medical humanities. She is allied with skeptical critics who distrust affect and are committed to revealing the indeterminacy of meaning, but at times, like humanist critics, she explores the personal and cultural work narratives about illness perform for writers and readers. In considering the competing forces in Sontag's work, the goal of this chapter is not to explain them away, but to recognize them as central to the struggle of all who read and write about illness and all who seek to understand the ethics of regarding the pain of others.

Sontag approaches the challenge of defending the truth of suffering as, in part, a problem of genre. She adopts and rejects modes of address and representation—the essay, photograph, and novel—on the basis of whether she thinks they advance understanding of the "real." The critical essay, with its origins in philosophical meditation, was her genre of choice as she developed her reputation and fame in the 1970s, and she continued to produce them at an astonishing pace into the 1980s. In these essays from her early and middle career, Sontag denounces photographic representations, metaphors, and even personal narratives for concealing true human misery and rousing too-easy compassion. Although she knows the world cannot be rid of images and stories about misery, she calls for them to be somehow purified so that they communicate the reality of suffering. Sontag also questions the critic's role in relation to representations of suffering. As a critic, she is often didactic and polemical—forcefully defending standards against sentimentalism. For her, educating readers about simplistic or false sympathy is the work of criticism.

In the 1990s, however, she turns away from the abstractions of the essay, exploring other literary means to deeper, truer understanding of human distress. In what appears to be a radical reinvention of herself as a writer, she begins to write historical fiction, extolling the capacity of narrative to educate sympathies and inspire ethical engagement with the world. For Sontag, the novel, unlike the essay, provides readers with an education in sympathy by enticing them to consider the lives of others. While Sontag continues to see herself as a novelist, in 2003 she returns to the critical essay and the topic of photography, still searching for a firm sense of how to respond to the representations of human misery that the world and media continue to supply. Whatever the genre, her writing seeks to express the urgency of attending to the real. For Sontag, this means shaping the reception of literature and art in ways that assure that the feelings aroused by representations of misery are bound to an understanding of historical, cultural, political, and aesthetic context. Representation and emotion, in her view, generally fail to live up to reality. The continual challenge she poses to herself as a writer is to find ways to get closer to the real. She never finds a resting place.

Genre, Representation, and the Reality of Suffering

From her earliest essays, Sontag provokes readers to think about art, literature, and the world differently. In *On Photography*, for instance, she argues against any number of forces that she sees as barriers to understanding, but she focuses in particular on photographs of human suffering. Sontag begins with a rare autobiographical anecdote about seeing images as a child that awakened her to distant horrors. This brief narrative helps her to make a point about the emotional distancing from reality that she believes takes place through photographic representations of anguish. When she was twelve, she saw photographs of Nazi concentration camps that aroused a storm of feeling, and the experience made her realize the ethical complexity of looking at such images. "One's first encounter with the photographic inventory of ultimate horror is a kind of revelation, the prototypically modern revelation: a negative epiphany," she begins (19).

> For me, it was photographs of Bergen-Belsen and Dachau which I came across by chance in a bookstore in Santa Monica in July 1945. Nothing I have seen—in photographs or in real life—ever cut me as sharply, deeply, instantaneously. Indeed, it seems plausible to me to divide my life into two parts, before I saw those photographs (I was twelve) and after, though it was several years before I understood fully what they were about. What good was served by seeing them? They were only photographs—of an event I had scarcely heard of and could do nothing to affect, of suffering I could hardly imagine and could do nothing to relieve. When I looked at those photographs, something broke. Some limit had been reached, and not only that of horror; I felt irrevocably grieved, wounded, but a part of my feelings started to tighten; something went dead; something is still crying. (19–20)

This traumatic confrontation with evidence of the human capacity for cruelty marks the end of her childhood, and the impact of those images did not fade with the passage of time. When Sontag was interviewed by Bill Moyers upon the publication of *Regarding the Pain of Others* in 2003, he asked her to discuss the most vivid pictures she had ever seen. Fifty-eight years later, her memory of those photographs from Dachau and Bergen-Belsen was still vivid: "I thought when I saw those pictures . . . 'Oh, my God. This is what human beings can do to other human beings. . . . This is reality.'"

The shock of these photographs and the complexity of her own and others' emotional responses to such images provides a foundational narrative for Sontag's lifelong intellectual apprehensions and powerful feelings about representing suffering. The images of horror shook her out of a comfortable complacency, "a childhood in which [she had] never seen any violence at all," and pushed her to confront issues and questions that people generally do not want to think about (Interview with Bill Moyers). In *On Photography*, she describes her own reaction as genuine and appropriate, but she distrusts others' responses. Either one is shattered by such photographs, she writes, or one has not recognized the reality they represent. Her concern about others' responses may have been aroused by the wide distribution of these images. She was by no means unusual in casually and unexpectedly encountering photographs of the liberation of the camps in 1945. These images appeared in a number of mainstream magazines. Photographers from *Life*, which employed Margaret Bourke-White, *Time*, and even *Vogue* accompanied the liberating troops.[5]

Sontag's rare personal revelation opens up questions about representation and ethics—what *good* was served by seeing these images. She can envision only two positive consequences: that facing them might contribute to alleviating the pain they represented, and that she and others might learn from them. Because she was not able to mitigate, imagine, or understand the suffering she saw in the photographs that she stumbled upon in the Santa Monica bookshop, they caused disquieting ruptures between knowing and feeling. The experience thereby raised questions that she would struggle with for decades: Is it moral to look at or create representations of human misery? How can one respond ethically to images of suffering? If a representation inspires compassion that is felt privately and not translated into thought and public action, is it ethical?

"In Plato's Cave," the first essay in *On Photography*, is one of Sontag's earliest efforts to distinguish her own writing from problematic representations that create a false and dangerous sense of unmediated connection to the real.[6] Implicitly, her critique of photography upholds the essay as a form that better advances an understanding of reality and enacts an ethical response. Sontag's critical distance allows her to enumerate the many ways these images are not what they seem. "Photographs are often invoked as an aid to understanding and tolerance," she observes: "But photographs do not explain; they acknowledge" (111).[7] In fact, she argues, when people falsely assume that they represent the real, photographs actually obscure reality. She is concerned that "what seeing through photographs really invites is an acquisitive relation to the world that nourishes aesthetic awareness and promotes emotional detachment" (111). Photography, she maintains, has inaugurated a new era of inauthenticity in human experience. She is particularly disturbed that photographs can overwhelm viewers emotionally. There is a great danger, she warns, that when compassion is exhausted or unmoored from the real, ethical action will be thwarted, if not rendered impossible. Sontag thus declares that little can be learned from images, and that "the knowledge gained through still photographs will always be some kind of sentimentalism, whether cynical or humanist. It will be a knowledge at bargain prices—a semblance of knowledge, a semblance of wisdom" (24).[8]

Sontag thus argues that repeated exposure to images of horror threatens both "conscience and the ability to be compassionate" (*On Photography,* 20). Even those who are attuned to suffering cannot allow themselves to be repeatedly devastated when faced with more and more representations of horror. "The ethical content of photographs is fragile," she explains: "At the time of the first photographs of the Nazi camps, there was nothing banal about these images. After thirty years, a saturation point may have been reached. In these last decades, 'concerned' photography has done at least as much to deaden conscience as to arouse it" (21). Viewers would do better, she thinks, to attend to the form of the images and their context, not just their content.

In exposing what photography fails to do, Sontag suggests what she would like her writing to accomplish. Sontag clearly wants her writing to give access to what is real, transmit knowledge, and create the conditions for compassionate understanding and ethical action. Indeed, the project of many of Sontag's best known, early essays is to protect reality from the distorting influence of representation. She wants her ideas to affect and change minds and culture. So at the end of *On Photography,* she announces, "If there can be a better way for the real world to include the one of images, it will require an ecology not only of real things but of images as well" (180). She calls for a "conservationist" approach to the dissemination of photographs that would prevent the public from becoming inured to the suffering of others (180). Of course, the rationing of images is not a solution that could ever have been carried out. Indeed, she could not have imagined in 1978 the vast archive of images that would, in a few decades, be instantly available to anyone with a computer and access to the Internet.

In *Illness as Metaphor,* published only one year after *On Photography,* Sontag again explores the ethical and persuasive possibilities of the essay—this time to argue against cultural myths and metaphors about illness. If literature frightens patients away from seeking treatment, then her essay serves as a corrective. In arguing against metaphor, Sontag's essay also makes a case for the superiority of the critical essay over personal narrative. Although she has an autobiographical motive for writing *Illness as Metaphor*—one that is at least as powerful as her motive for writing *On Photography*—she refuses to tell that story. "I didn't think it would be useful," she writes in *AIDS and Its Metaphors,* "to tell yet one more story in the first person of how someone learned that she or he had cancer, wept, struggled, was comforted, took courage." And then she concludes, "A narrative, it seemed to me, would be less useful than an idea" (101). So, when Sontag wrote *Illness as Metaphor,* she deliberately did *not* write an illness memoir. Nowhere in this book, half of which is about literary metaphors for tuberculosis, does Sontag tell her readers that her father died of the disease in 1939 ("Finding Fact from Fiction"). At that time, the stigma of TB was so great that her mother at first concealed his death and later told her daughters he had died of pneumonia ("Finding Fact from Fiction"). She also does not reveal that she composed *Illness as Metaphor* in the two years after she was diagnosed with breast cancer, or that doctors informed her she had a 10 percent chance of surviving those two years after diagnosis (Rollyson and Paddock 171). Not until she writes *AIDS and Its Metaphors* a decade later does she acknowledge that when she became ill with breast cancer she was "enraged" and "distracted . . . from [her] own terror and despair" by seeing "how much the very reputation of this illness added to the suffering of those who have it" (100). There is a message in *Illness as Metaphor* that has not yet been noted by critics who work in the medical humanities: the book contains an implicit argument against the therapeutic ideal of the illness narrative and in favor of the illness essay.

Sontag's exclusion of the personal contributes to tensions, even subtle contradictions, in *Illness as Metaphor*. She argues that access to the real requires intellectual and critical distance from personal experience. Counterintuitively, she suggests that experience is not strongly linked to reality. She writes passionately that passion should have no place in our discussions of illness because disease is best known by rational science. An avowed literary formalist and antirealist, she seeks to protect the reality of disease. She loves literature, yet she argues against what literature has contributed to the cultural understanding of disease. In an interview with Jonathan Cott after the publication of *Illness as Metaphor,* she presents herself as rejecting traditional binarisms of "the heart and the head, thinking and feeling, fantasy and judgment" (118). But, after proclaiming that "one of my oldest crusades is against the distinction between thought and feeling," she upholds superiority of the mind over the body: "we think much more with the instruments provided by our culture than we do with our bodies, and hence the much greater diversity of thought in the world" (117–18).

An Education in Sympathy

This friction between thinking and feeling continues to surface throughout her career. Even as she asserts that thinking and feeling are interconnected, she creates an intellectual landscape that does not allow for their integration. To figure out how to sustain a long career in which she could connect her embodied, affective, and intellectual life, in the late 1970s and early 1980s she produces critical studies of a set of writers—men with long, illustrious careers —who could serve as models. In *Under the Sign of Saturn,* a collection of essays about the works of individual writers or filmmakers, her studies of Antonin

Artaud, Walter Benjamin, and Elias Canetti pay tribute to their work, their dedication to the life of the mind, and the ways in which their characters—whether
alienated, melancholic, or passionate—shape and sustain their work over time.
These essays, along with a 1982 essay on Barthes entitled "Writing Itself: On
Roland Barthes," provide her with a forum for contemplating her own character
and ambition.

When she writes about Canetti and Barthes, in particular, she focuses implicitly on their similarity to herself.[9] In exploring the role that affect can play
in the life of other writers, she again reflects on her own writing and character.
In "Mind as Passion," Sontag praises Canetti for his "passionate but also acquisitive relations to knowledge and truth" (187). She admires him for saying
that he needed a long life in order to feel everything inside himself. To him, "to
die prematurely means having not fully engorged himself and, therefore, having not used his mind as he could" (200). Canetti, she notes, "had to keep his
consciousness in a permanent state of avidity, to remain unreconciled to death"
(200). This passage predicts her own future.

Just two years after "Mind as Passion" appeared, Sontag wrote her tribute
to Roland Barthes in which she even more firmly searches for a way to integrate
thought and feeling. She lauds Barthes for being "the latest major participant
in the great national literary project, inaugurated by Montaigne: the self as voca-
tion, life as a reading of the self" ("Writing Itself," 139). She also compliments
his bold, at times contradictory, assertions, "his aphorist's ability to conjure up
a vivacious duality" (124), and his "bid to have the final word [that] is inherent in
all powerful phrasemaking" (124). "For Barthes, as for Nietzsche," she writes,
"the point is not to teach us something in particular. The point is to make us
bold, agile, subtle, intelligent, detached. And to give pleasure" (128). Notable in
her account of Barthes's career is her attention to the ideas of play and pleasure,
not terms associated at this point in her career with her often adversarial style.
Sontag closes the essay on Barthes, for instance, by praising his "commitment
to intellectual adventure," his "talent for contradiction and inversion—those
'late' ways of experiencing, evaluating, reading the world; and surviving in it,
drawing energy, finding consolation (but finally not), taking pleasure, expressing love" (141). Barthes's work thus offers an example of the integrated writing
that seemed missing in her earlier volumes of essays. In Barthes, she identifies
her ideal: in his work, "the thinker (writer, reader, teacher) and the lover—the
two main figures of the Barthesian self—are joined" (139).[10]

There is a moment in "Writing Itself" that would resonate a decade later
when Sontag published the novel *The Volcano Lover: A Romance*. She notes that,
before Barthes's untimely death, he said that he no longer wanted to write as a
critic and instead wanted to write a novel (140). He was finished, she says, "with

the aesthetics of absence, and now spoke of literature as the embrace of subject and object" (141). In an interview with Leslie Garis when *Volcano Lover* was published, Sontag stated that she began to lose interest in the essay as early as 1980 when she was writing "Mind as Passion" about Canetti.[11] "As I was writing," she explained to Garis, "I thought, 'Why am I doing this so indirectly? I have all this feeling—I'm in a storm of feeling all the time—and instead of expressing it I'm writing about people with feeling.'" In a later interview, Sontag recalled her increasing frustration with her "essay voice," and the persona who kept her at a distance from what she wrote. "I think very early on I developed a way of dealing with painful information, which was to say, that's interesting. Instead of allowing myself to be hurt by it" ("Finding Fact from Fiction"). She remained hesitant, however, about writing something other than essays, "because they have a powerful ethical impulse behind them, and I think they make a contribution" (Garis). When she expressed such concerns in therapy, she says, her psychiatrist replied, "What makes you think it isn't a contribution to give people pleasure?" "That sentence launched me," she said (Garis).

Although Sontag had turned away from fiction after writing several early, experimental novels, at this point she began to explore how narrative can communicate or alleviate the pain of others.[12] To free herself from critical guardedness and to integrate the thinker and lover, she reinvented herself as a writer of realist, historical fiction. This signifies a dramatic change from the early views she expressed in *Against Interpretation*. In an essay from that collection entitled "Nathalie Sarraute and the Novel," Sontag made a strong case against realism in the novel, raising doubts about the "cozy recognition" induced by "lifelike" fiction (105). "The genius of the age is suspicion" (105), she asserted, allying herself with what *New Yorker* reviewer Joan Acocella calls the "knowingness" of the essay instead of the "innocence" of the novel (Acocella 456). Sontag was convinced by Sarraute's objections to "old-fashioned" novels ("Nathalie Sarraute," 105)—a category that, for her, contains works ranging from Thackeray's *Vanity Fair* to Mann's *Buddenbrooks* (106). After rereading these texts, she complained, "I could not stand the omnipotent author showing me that's how life is, making me compassionate and tearful; with his obstreperous irony, his confidential air of perfectly knowing his characters and leading me, the reader, to feel I knew them too" (106).[13] Following Sarraute, Sontag dismissed the "traditional machinery" of realist description: "Who really cares," she asks, "about the furniture of so-and-so's room, or whether he lit a cigarette or wore a dark gray suit or uncovered the typewriter after sitting down and before inserting a sheet of paper in the typewriter?" (106).

With the publication of *The Volcano Lover* in 1992 and *In America* in 2000, Sontag completely revises her earlier position. When Acocella asks Sontag about her rediscovery of the novel, she responds, "I thought I was a ruminator. . . . I thought I was a student. I thought I was a teacher. And then I discovered that I liked to tell stories and make people cry" (443). The experience of writing also transformed for Sontag; in an interview with the *New York Times,* Sontag described being swept away by the pleasure of writing fiction and declared in her typically emphatic manner that the essay had become a "dead form for her" (Garis). Although Sontag's transformation may seem unfathomable, she had long recognized the importance of emotionally powerful experience. In the essay "Against Interpretation," she called for the rejection of strong theory in favor of "an erotics of art" because she wanted people to have a richer experience of art—to see, hear, and feel more (14). The turn to fiction, however, marks a shift in her understanding of how readers gain access to reality and meaningful experience. Early in her career, Sontag used her essays to defend Platonic truths that she believed were diminished by representation in literature or photographs. In "In Plato's Cave," she coaxed her audience out of the cave of shadows and into the light of the sun to see the real. By turning to fiction, she now seems to understand Plato's "Allegory of the Cave" differently: it is, after all, a *story.* Plato represents humans' alienation from the truth using the vehicle of narrative. Novels will now provide Sontag with a medium for exploring the human dramas and meanings that her critical essays kept at bay.

After reinventing herself as a novelist, Sontag argues that fiction is better suited than the essay for shaping moral understanding. In a 2004 speech, "The Truth of Fiction Evokes Our Common Humanity," she proclaims that the fiction writer is a "moral agent" who grapples with problems of evil and suffering, asking such questions as "what are we to do . . . when the pain that is endured is the pain of others?" Elsewhere she states that reading "should be an education in sympathies"; it "reminds you that there is more than you, better than you" ("Desperately Seeking Susan"). It is the work of serious fiction writers like herself to "evoke our common humanity in narratives with which we can identify, even though the lives may be remote from our own. They stimulate our imagination. The stories they tell enlarge and complicate—and, therefore, improve—our sympathies. They educate our capacity for moral judgment" ("Truth of Fiction").

Sontag thereby demonstrates an intellectual alliance with the philosopher Martha Nussbaum. Nussbaum uses the term "compassion" rather than "sympathy," but similarly maintains that compassion constitutes a "complex sentiment" that links emotion, imagination, cognition, and action, and that can be learned, or perhaps deepened by both tragic drama and realist novels ("Compassion," 38–40).[14] Although the philosopher recognizes that modern moral theories have treated compassion as nonrational, she argues, "the correct perception of a practical situation requires emotional as well as intellectual activity, [and] that the emotions have a valuable informational role to play within the ethical life as forms of recognition" (*Love's Knowledge,* 290). Thus, she makes a case for the "human importance of a fine-tuned responsiveness to complex particular cases and of a willingness to see them *as* particular and irreducible to general rules" (290). She also maintains that narratives with complex structures allow readers to learn this manner of responsiveness (290). Compassion, in other words, is a "narrative emotion" (286).[15]

Sontag's historical fiction puts Nussbaum's theory into practice, using realist narrative to create conditions for attunement with the pain of others. *The Volcano Lover,* which was both a critical success and a best seller, offers an education in Sontag's version of sympathy, which is not simply sentimental or simple, but emotional as well as thoughtful and intellectually engaged.[16] The novel considers many familiar Sontagian themes, among them passion, aesthetics, feminism, and power, but it also unfolds into a consideration of suffering and pain. Sontag invites sympathy for actual historical figures, not all of whom have been understood sympathetically over time, and reinterprets them. She takes figures who have been ridiculed or celebrated by history and, by creating conditions for a sympathy that is not ignorant of historical, political, and cultural contexts, complicates readers' responses to them. Unsympathetic characters become more sympathetic; heroes become more human and flawed. She concludes by holding up each character for judgment, showing that one can feel sympathy for someone whom one must nevertheless recognize as having made terrible choices and contributed to great suffering.

The Volcano Lover retells the well-known story of the scandalous love triangle of Sir William Hamilton, a British envoy to the court of Naples in the eighteenth century; Emma Hamilton, who was first his mistress and later his wife; and Lord Nelson, a British naval hero during the Napoleonic Wars.[17] When Nelson arrived in Naples to recover from injuries after winning the Battle of the Nile, he lived with the Hamiltons and soon began an affair with Emma. Aggravating the scandal, Sir William approved of the arrangement and the threesome lived together for the rest of the envoy's life, even after they returned to England. Although Sontag adapts a well-known historical narrative, she does not identify her characters by their historical names, but instead reclaims them for her operatic plot as generic figures: the Cavaliere (Sir William Hamilton), the Cavaliere's Wife (Emma Hamilton), and the Hero (Lord Nelson).[18] The backdrop for Sontag's "romance" is natural and political turmoil. Vesuvius, the roiling volcano, always threatens to erupt, and political unrest in the wake of the French Revolution imperils the monarchy.

At first, Sontag's portraits of Sir William and Emma demonstrate far more sympathy than has generally been granted them by history. She depicts them as passionate aesthetes, largely ignorant of politics. Instead of portraying the envoy as a foolish, willing cuckold, as history generally has, Sontag emphasizes his passion for collecting Greek vases and art of all kinds—paintings, sculpture, books, antiquities. He is also drawn to Vesuvius and its uncontrollable energy, which he seeks to tame through reason, transforming it into measurements, figures, and collected fragments of rock. He is like an obsessive and disengaged scholar who focuses on details, ignoring that the world around him is about to explode. For Sontag, Emma is more than one of history's fallen women. She renders her as an intelligent artist, the creator of a popular form of performance art that she called "attitudes." At parties, she poses to depict scenes from mythology and classical history, each capturing, in the words of the visiting poet Goethe, a "significant moment" that is "most humane, most typical, most affecting" (149). Even the great writer finds her performances "remarkable" (149). Sontag also renders Nelson a more complicated hero than his legend has allowed. While she admires his courage and willingness to endure suffering, she assails him for his brutal suppression of the short-lived Neapolitan Republic and for the torture and execution of the intellectuals who were the republic's leaders. When Nelson turns against the republicans, even after a treaty is signed that allows for their passage into exile, Sir William and Emma reveal the weakness of their political characters. They do nothing to oppose him. At this point, Sontag turns her attention to the political consequences of the egocentrism and self-indulgence that accompanies the trio's amorous and aesthetic passions. While she earlier rescued them from notoriety, she ultimately condemns them. Sontag's Cavaliere, his Wife, and the Hero are not noble or tragic in the end; they are doomed because of their particular choices, active and passive, in relation to the politics of their place and time. Sympathetic understanding, she shows her readers, does not preclude ethical judgment.

The Volcano Lover, like the Cavaliere's home, is crammed with evidence of a curator's interests and obsessions, among them Sontag's familiar concern with the relationship between the aesthetic and the political. Can art contribute to a just society? What does art have to say about suffering? Sontag suggests some answers in the final section of the novel, where the narrator (with whom Sontag explicitly identifies herself in the novel's prologue) meditates on the evolving ways suffering has been depicted in art and understood in culture. Contemplating the stoic ways in which many of the republicans faced their executions, Sontag states, "Even the most horrifying stories can be told in a way that does not make us despair" (295). She continues: "Because an image can show only a moment, the painter or sculptor must choose the moment that presents what the viewer most needs to know and feel about the subject. But what does the viewer need to know and feel?" (295). As she considers the famous sculpture of the death of Laocoön and his sons, and a painting of the flaying of Marsyas, she explains that, in the Cavaliere's era, "the significant moment for the depiction of an intolerable situation was before the full horror had reached its apex, when we can still find something edifying in the spectacle. Perhaps what lies behind this curious theory of the significant moment, and its prejudice in favor of moments that are not too upsetting, is a new anxiety about how to react to or represent deep pain. Or deep injustice. A fear of minding too much—of unappeasable feelings, feelings that would cause an irreparable rupture of protest with the established social order" (296).

Sontag contrasts this eighteenth-century taste for art that "showed people able to maintain decorum and composure, even in monumental suffering" to modern sensibilities (296). Writing about the contemporary moment, she asserts, "We admire, in the name of truthfulness, an art that exhibits the maximum amount of trauma, violence, physical indignity. (The question is: Do we feel it?) For us, the significant moment is the one that disturbs us most" (297). Thus, she ends her contemporary novel in a manner that is clearly intended to disturb. In narrating Nelson's suppression of a new Neapolitan Republic, she depicts torture, hangings, and beheadings. She details the slow decline of each of her central characters, and she closes the novel with four posthumous monologues about suffering. In the last of these, Eleonora de Fonseca Pimentel, a poet, revolutionary, and editor of the newspaper of the short-lived Neapolitan Republic, curses those who betrayed her and describes her own gruesome hanging. To be certain that her neck would break, the hangman's assistant held onto her ankles as the rope was raised and the hangman himself leapt onto her shoulders. "We became," she says, "a dangling, swaying chain of three" (413). In a review, A. S. Byatt comments that Sontag's conclusion makes readers feel the traumas experienced by others: "She sees all her people through their deaths, clinically and passionately, and makes us imagine what we would rather not imagine" ("Love and Death"). Sontag invites readers to sympathize with her characters, as well as to understand them for their gifts and their flaws.

Numerous critics have observed that even with Sontag's commitment to fiction, she never entirely leaves the essayist behind.[19] Regarding *In America*, Acocella writes, "some people will say, as they said of *The Volcano Lover*, that Sontag is not really a novelist, that she is still an essayist. But what is wonderful about the book is exactly this counterpoint of novelist and essayist, of innocence and knowingness" (456). Leslie Garis concurs that Sontag, and by extension her novels, are "a hybrid of reason and romance."[20] Part of what these critics imply with their statements is that Sontag has not made a seamless transition to her new genre. It would be a mistake, however, not to recognize that narrative does make a difference in how Sontag conceives of the role of affect in under-standing representations of suffering. In *The Volcano Lover,* Sontag works with, rather than against, the contemporary era's sense of "the significant moment for the depiction of an intolerable situation" (296). She uses narrative to com-municate what she believes her audience most needs to know and feel about the moment that depicts "trauma, violence, physical indignity" (297). Rather than precluding representations of pain or using argument to impose her way of in-terpreting the image or narrative at hand, she creates an elaborate context that she hopes will allow readers to *feel* in ways that inform what they know. Admit-tedly, the prose is not fluid. Sontag remains didactic. But *The Volcano Lover* is an achievement. Sontag writes from and for her own era, offering representations of pain and suffering that have accrued complex layers of meaning to deepen readers' understanding of their world and themselves.

"Narratives Can Make Us Understand"

If Sontag began to strongly identify as a novelist in the 1990s, why then did she to return to the extended essay when she wrote about photographs of war in her final book, *Regarding the Pain of Others?*[21] Perhaps something about the topic seemed best addressed with argument. After all, *Regarding the Pain of Others* returns her very directly to the subject of *On Photography.*[22] Her reex-amination of the ethics of representation indicates that after twenty-five years she has not yet succeeded in resolving her struggle with photography's power to foreclose access to the real, which in this case is the reality of war. At the same time, however, this essay is markedly different from her work from the 1970s and 1980s. She imbues it with a strong narrative element, which suggests she has discovered that no single genre communicates all that needs to be known about the suffering of others. While fiction can provide an education in sympa-thy, or at least an education *about* it, criticism directly warns readers about the dangers of easy sympathy.

As Sontag once more engages the issues that preoccupied her throughout her career—pain, representation, and reality—she specifically focuses on the problem of iconic war photography and the ethics of looking at representations of pain. The sense of moral outrage that she felt when she saw photographs of Bergen-Belsen and Dachau at the age of twelve was aroused again in the early 1990s when she, moved by the plight of Sarajevo under siege during the Bosnian War, made several extended visits to the once cosmopolitan city.[23] Al-though *Regarding the Pain of Others* seems in many ways to be a revision of *On Photography* produced by a more mature, experienced writer, to assess the book as a simple reworking of her earlier argument incorrectly assumes her stasis as a thinker and writer and dismisses important elements of its context and form.[24] From the vantage point of the early twenty-first century, Sontag now believes that our collective failure to comprehend the suffering of war is due to several factors: the scale of suffering that photographs now enable us to see; the skepticism in which we are inculcated; and the passivity that images of suffering and skepticism together promote. As an essayist, she builds here on what she learned from writing realist, historical novels, which required that she focus on the particular. She places blame for failures of understanding on how photography functions in specific situations, not on the medium itself. Images of suffering, she says, "cannot be more than an invitation to pay attention, to reflect, to learn, to examine the rationalizations for mass suffering offered by established powers" (117).

Certainly, one inspiration for returning to this topic must have been the terrorist attacks on the World Trade Center and the Pentagon on 11 September 2001, eighteen months before Sontag's book was published.[25] The photographs and videos of the events of 9/11—many taken by amateurs—appeared in every possible media outlet: in newspapers and magazines, of course, but also in extraordinary quantities on the Internet. Perhaps because so many photographs were available, the only image that now seems iconic is "The Falling Man" by Richard Drew, which shows a single man falling, head first, his body aligned with the vertical intersection of the north and south towers. This image has retained its power, in part, because it shows what the American news media refused to display: one of the hundreds of people who died by jumping or falling from the towers. Journalist Tom Junod points out in an article about "The Falling Man" that, "In the most photographed and videotaped day in the history of the world, the images of people jumping were the only images that became, by consensus, taboo—the only images from which Americans were proud to avert their eyes." And they still do not want to see them. A commemorative sculpture, "Tumbling Woman," was displayed at Rockefeller Center in 2002, but due to complaints was removed after only one week (Flynn and Dwyer). Viewers also complain that such images posted on the Internet are distasteful and disrespectful (Brottman 167–68).

The publication of *Regarding the Pain of Others* was also framed by the intensification of military actions in Iraq. In the months leading up to its appearance, the governments of the United States and Britain were known to be preparing a unified and aggressive attack. By coincidence, the book appeared on the shelves less than two weeks before these countries invaded Iraq, an invasion that began with the televised bombing of Baghdad on 20 March 2003. As Sontag reminded audiences on her book tour, her new work was profoundly relevant in a world that had recently been exposed to the live broadcast of Baghdad's destruction. These images were not taboo.

At first, much of Sontag's argument in *Regarding the Pain of Others* feels familiar, even as she focuses much more explicitly on the experience and ethics of sympathy and compassion than she did in *On Photography*. She maintains that sympathy for people affected by war is diminished by distance as well as by the relative inexperience of Westerners, particularly Americans, with life in war zones. Americans may feel sympathetic when they see images from Iraq, Afghanistan, or Darfur, but what seems like sympathy, according to Sontag, can actually be a defensive mask covering impotence and indifference. In her view, "the imaginary proximity to the suffering inflicted on others that is granted by images suggests a link between the faraway sufferers. . . . and the privileged viewer that is simply untrue, that is yet one more mystification of our real relations to power" (102). With this point, Sontag circles back to the dilemma posed many years ago by the photographs taken in the concentration camps. While photographs may engender an emotional response, they cannot teach us about the complex intersecting global and local structures that create the conditions for suffering, and they cannot be relied upon to generate ethical action in the world.[26]

In *Regarding the Pain of Others*, Sontag still seeks to produce moral understanding and action, but she no longer blames photography and the profusion of photographs for habituating us to the suffering of others. Instead, she now believes that "harrowing photographs do not inevitably lose their power to shock" (89). In fact, she mocks the excesses of her previous statement that there should be an ecology of images, asking, "What is really being asked for here? That images of carnage be cut back to, say, once a week?" (108). She recognizes now that "No Committee of Guardians is going to ration horror, to keep fresh its ability to shock. And the horrors themselves are not going to abate" (108). Having conceived of the problem differently, she must take a new approach to finding a solution. And she does.

As Sontag draws *Regarding the Pain of Others* to a close, the book becomes a defense of the work of narrative in the world. She maintains that narrative is an "antidote" to the allure of war (123): "Harrowing photographs . . . are not much help if the task is to understand. Narratives can make us understand" (89). Twenty-five years earlier she rejected narrative as a means of addressing the problem of illness; in *Illness as Metaphor* she chose to write an essay rather than a memoir because she believed "a narrative . . . would be less useful than an idea" (*Illness and AIDS*, 101). It is also the case, however, that even as her emphasis on narrative appears to be new, the idea that "narratives can make us understand"—indeed virtually the same words—appeared in *On Photography*. There she wrote that "functioning takes place in time, and must be explained in time," and she concludes, therefore, that "only that which narrates can make us understand" (23). What is new in 2003 is Sontag's emphasis on and use of narrative. Stories govern our thinking, she demonstrates in *Regarding the Pain of Others* because, more than photographs, they require us to sustain attention, stand back, slow down, reflect, and thus see a subject in a new way.

It is not entirely clear what Sontag's ideal antiwar narrative might be. She offers just a few examples of particular works of literature that can change readers' minds when she asks, "Could one be mobilized actively to oppose war by an image (or a group of images) as one might be enrolled among the opponents of capital punishment by reading, say, Dreiser's *An American Tragedy* or Turgenev's 'The Execution of Troppman,' an account by the expatriate writer, invited to be an observer in a Paris prison, of a famous criminal's last hours before being guillotined?" (*Regarding*, 122). Although Sontag implies that her answer is "yes," her choice of exemplars—a novel by Dreiser and a short story by Turgenev that is so obscure she must summarize it—reveals that the answer for most readers will be "I don't know." Few of Sontag's readers (even this elite group) are likely to have read these texts, let alone to have been moved to ethical decisions or actions by them.

More useful for understanding Sontag's project is her own performative use of narrative within *Regarding the Pain of Others*. She moves back and forth between the voice of the critic and that of the storyteller, using narrative with particular skill in the opening and closing sections of the book. Sontag the essayist presents information and argument; Sontag the novelist stages scenes that involve the reader in the ethical dilemmas that underlie her interest in representations of human suffering. She begins *Regarding the Pain of Others,* for instance, by retelling the story with which her fellow novelist and essayist Virginia Woolf began *Three Guineas.* She represents her own project as the same as Woolf's—to present "brave, unwelcome reflections on the roots of war" (Sontag, *Regarding,* 3). Woolf began her essay by recounting a fictional correspondence between herself and a London lawyer who has ostensibly written to her to ask, "How in your opinion are we to prevent war?" (Woolf, qtd. in Sontag, *Regarding,* 3). Woolf rebuffs the lawyer by arguing that women and men cannot communicate with ease about the topic of war because they have different ways of being and thinking and, as Sontag puts it, "war is a man's game" (6). Woolf then maintains that, through resistance to militarism, women can help prevent war. Sontag begins her argument at that point: "Who believes today," she asks, "that war can be abolished? No one, not even pacifists" (5). Her primary objection, however, is to Woolf's assumption that women hold a common position about war. "No 'we' should be taken for granted when the subject is looking at other people's pain," she asserts, and then launches into her own essay (7).

After the narrative introduction, Sontag returns to the essay. She discusses one familiar image of war after another, explaining its origin, construction, and reception, and exercises control over readers' reception of her argument by withholding reproductions of the photographs, drawings, and paintings she describes.[27] She recounts the history of manipulation in war photography, debunking the authenticity of many of the most famous photographs. She informs readers that, in the Crimea, Roger Fenton scattered cannonballs across the road to create his 1855 photograph, "The Valley of the Shadow of Death." Felice Beato's 1858 image of the ruined Sikandarbagh Palace after the British slaughter of two thousand Indians was reconstructed three or four months after the event. During the American Civil War, Mathew Brady's team moved and posed dead Confederate soldiers in their photographs of Gettysburg. Even the famous photograph of American soldiers raising the flag at Iwo Jima in 1945 actually records a restaging of the morning capture of Mount Surabachi (Sontag, *Regarding*, 55–56). Today's war photographs, those that are not censored by the government or the media, continue to fulfill the dual purposes of documenting and transforming events. The tension between these purposes contributes to the uneasy ethics of regarding the suffering they depict.[28]

Not until the final pages of *Regarding the Pain of Others* does Sontag fully explain her new position on how one should regard the pain of others, and she does so in prose that mixes argument and narrative. Sontag tells the antiwar story that she believes is conveyed by one of Jeff Wall's Cibachrome transparencies, "Dead Troops Talk (A Vision after an Ambush of a Red Army Patrol Near Moqor, Afghanistan, Winter 1986).[29] Wall's photograph is an imposing seven-and-a-half feet high and more than thirteen feet wide and depicts the staged scene of a ruined Afghan hillside in the aftermath of a battle.[30] The artist's task, Sontag says, is "the imagining of war's horror" (123), which Wall accomplishes by posing actors as Russian soldiers scattered across a desolate hillside—bloody, wounded, missing limbs. From their injuries, it appears these men must be dead, and perhaps they are, but they laugh and joke with each other. Unnoticed by or invisible to the Afghan scavenger and soldiers who appear on the scene's borders, these ghosts appear still to be alive to one another. Sontag concludes by offering her own interpretive narrative about Wall's image. She recounts what she thinks might be a typical experience of viewing "Dead Troops Talk." The viewer is, Sontag concludes, "engulfed" by his "accusatory" image, and thus imagines "that the soldiers might turn and talk to us. But no, no one is looking out of the picture" (125). She continues, drawing her text to a close:

> These dead are supremely uninterested in the living: in those who took their lives; in witnesses—and in us. Why should they seek our gaze? What

would they have to say to us? "We"—this "we" is everyone who has never experienced anything like what they went through—don't understand. We don't get it. We truly can't imagine what it was like. We can't imagine how dreadful, how terrifying war is; and how normal it becomes. Can't understand, can't imagine. That's what every soldier, and every journalist and aid worker and independent observer who has put in time under fire, and had the luck to elude the death that struck down others nearby, stubbornly feels. And they are right. (125–26)

This ending echoes so much of what Sontag has written previously about representation, reality, pain, and compassion, but with differences both personal and formal. When she disclosed in the early pages of "In Plato's Cave" that her life was split in two by photographs that revealed the human capacity for cruelty, she recognized that she was an outsider who felt too much but could do too little. Now, however, a lifetime later, experience has brought her closer to an embodied, intellectual, affective, and physical understanding of what she saw. In Sarajevo, she became an insider, at last. She is the independent observer named in her penultimate sentence who, like the soldiers, knows how it feels to tremble at the sound of bombs, witness the deaths of others, and face death herself. Whereas, at the age of twelve she looked at photographs of World War II prisoners and was overwhelmed by grief and confusion, she is now confident that her understanding and response to the reality of war and pain is not facile. She does not know precisely the experience depicted by Wall—which is, after all, a fiction—but she knows enough. She is one of those who has "put in time under fire and had the luck to elude the death that struck down others nearby," and she believes, therefore, that she, too, is "right" (126).

Given Sontag's new commitment to narrative, her conclusion that audiences "can't understand, can't imagine" the experience of war is paradoxical. She has stated that "narratives can make us understand" (89), but now she maintains that neither images nor narratives about war can reach audiences who have not experienced the pain of war directly. Sontag's closing sentence, "And they are right," returns us to the opening of *Regarding the Pain of Others* and her critique of Woolf for separating viewers into "we" and "they" by gender and for assuming these categories define a particular way of comprehending war. Sontag redefines a "we" and "they" that are not rooted in gender, but in different kinds of embodied experience, and this shapes her work as a writer and her relationship to her audience. If experience defines the ground of difference and most of her readers have not experienced war, then her writing can only inspire a negative epiphany; she can only make readers grasp what they do *not* understand. The projects of Sontag-the-narrator and Sontag-the-essayist remain in tension: the narrator pulls at our sympathies, the essayist tells us our feelings are facile; the narrator uses fiction to educate our sympathies; the essayist insists that knowledge of the real only comes with experience.

If one interprets Sontag's work as performative, however, then it is possible to appreciate the conclusion as an effort to generate a particular kind of experience. For the reader who accepts her explanation of Wall's photograph, she re-creates something like her own foundational experience of standing in a bookstore and looking at images of human suffering that she did not want to see but that seared her mind so that she could never look away. At that moment she could not understand or imagine, and now she places her readers in this position. Although Sontag's conclusion might simply discourage readers from regarding the pain of others, her goal is to provoke thought and action. In an interview about *The Volcano Lover*, Sontag said that she wanted her writing—essays and fiction—to say to readers, "be serious, be passionate, wake up" (Garis). In this conclusion, her performance integrates her work as an essayist and a narrator. She provokes readers to pay attention to the pain of others by telling them a story, and that story helps them to understand how difficult it is to know that pain. This, too, is an education in sympathy.

Sontag's Narrative Legacy

Sontag's reevaluation of narrative explains a phenomenon that would otherwise appear to be a paradox to those who only know her early work: after the death of this writer who refused to pen her own illness memoir, her son David Rieff published a literary memoir about her final illness, and her partner of fifteen years Annie Leibovitz published a photographic memoir that documents Sontag's second cancer and her death. These accounts of their lives with Sontag during her illnesses and her death overtly help them come to terms with their grief and loss. While the younger Sontag would have been appalled by the sentiment that motivated these tributes, the older Sontag would more likely recognize the narratives as deeply felt efforts to make meaning of their pain.

Sontag died of leukemia on 28 December 2004, only nine months after her diagnosis. Her final decline was rapid, dramatic, and, as described by Rieff, tragic. On 28 March, she and Rieff were informed by a doctor that blood tests and a bone marrow biopsy were "completely unambiguous" (Rieff, *Swimming*, 7). The doctor's assessment of her chance of survival was equally unambiguous: no treatment could bring about cure or remission. Despite what she argued years earlier in *Illness as Metaphor* and *AIDS and Its Metaphors*, Sontag approached her illness as a battle. She was willing to endure any degree of pain to survive. Convinced that she had survived breast cancer because she had the most aggressive treatment, including surgery more radical than most doctors recommended, she was certain that "when it came to cancer treatments more was always better" (Rieff, *Swimming*, 39). She found a doctor who said he did not think her case was hopeless, and that was what she needed to pursue a cure (32). Rieff believes that "her experience of surviving confirmed for her that sense of specialness that had sustained her from childhood forward. Contemptuous of the false optimism of the age . . . my mother nonetheless shared it, if only unconsciously, where the question of illness was concerned" (88). To his dismay, she made it clear she wanted him to sustain the fiction that she might survive, which he did.

One year after Sontag's death, Rieff published an essay in the *New York Times,* "Illness Is More than Metaphor," in which he described her fight to survive against the odds. Ten months later, in October 2006, Leibovitz launched an autobiographical retrospective of her professional and personal photographs, and published a companion book, *A Photographer's Life: 1990–2005.* The exhibit and book consider the years Leibovitz spent with Sontag, her friend, mentor, travel companion, and lover. Sontag is not the sole focus of the work, but she is a constant, grounding presence. While the exhibit of *A Photographer's Life* was touring museums in 2008, Rieff published *Swimming in a Sea of Death: A Son's Memoir,* in which he explores his mother's vehement refusal to accept her grim prognosis and his own unrelenting guilt about participating in her self-deception.

Although Rieff and Leibovitz are motivated by love and grief for the same woman, their reflections on her life barely intersect at all; in fact, they nearly write each other out of Sontag's life. In Leibovitz's collection of photographs, Rieff appears only once—sitting in a hospital room, framed by the doorway, absorbed in his newspaper, which he holds in front of him, a barrier between him and his mother's sick bed (*A Photographer's Life*). Leibovitz appears twice in Rieff's text. He belittles her relationship with Sontag, calling her his mother's "on-again, off-again companion of many years" (*Swimming in a Sea of Death,* 66). Later, in the text's angriest sentence, he attacks Leibovitz for including in her book a number of grim photographs of Sontag when she was ill and dying, and also of her body after death. He writes that his mother was "humiliated posthumously by being 'memorialized' . . . in those carnival images of celebrity death taken by Annie Leibovitz" (150).

While this may be all that Rieff can see through his grief and rage, Leibovitz uses her photographs to compose the story of a life in which work and love are integrated, and in which illness, aging, and death are acknowledged as natural and inevitable. Leibovitz's visual memoir brings together photographs from different parts of her own public and private life, but nearly all define her in relationship to others: her meticulously composed celebrity portraits, informal shots of her large, extended family, and intimate images of her life and travels with Sontag. While Leibovitz is clearly close to her parents and family, she gives Sontag a position of prominence as she constructs her visual narrative. The dust jacket shows a contact sheet of foggy landscapes, with two images of Leibovitz, the one in the center roughly outlined with red grease pencil. This portrait was taken by Sontag. That Leibovitz chose it for the cover of her memoir suggests that Sontag was key in shaping how Leibovitz saw herself from 1990 until Sontag's death. Leibovitz also places a portrait of Sontag in Petra, Jordan, as the first image in the book, an image that both celebrates and memorializes her. Sontag stands in silhouette, dwarfed by the walls of a dark stone gorge. Just beyond her, illuminated by bright sunlight, are the pillars of the ancient Treasury that are carved from a sandstone cliff. Leibovitz also punctuates the book with photographs of Sontag's drafts and notes for *The Volcano Lover,* which was composed in the early years of their relationship. On the page preceding Leibovitz's introduction, she places an image of Sontag resting on a bed in Milan, with notes, books, and manuscript pages strewn around her. Later there is an image from 1990 of pads and piles of paper covered with handwritten notes. Among the images from 1992 is a shot of a page from Sontag's draft on the glowing screen of an old Macintosh SE; the just-legible words describe the Cavaliere climbing Mount Vesuvius. In the final pages of *A Photographer's Life,* more notes for *The Volcano Lover* appear, followed by a photograph of Sontag climbing Vesuvius in 1992 and then an image of the mouth of the volcano, empty of human figures.

While these images of Sontag's work suggest Leibovitz's regard for her companion's art, the photographs of Sontag in the hospital during her second cancer and her final illness offended not just Reiff, but also many other critics and viewers.[31] Leibovitz puts on display photos of Sontag lying limp and glassy-eyed in a hospital bed after surgery for uterine sarcoma. Later pages show her during her final illness—bloated and unrecognizable—and finally laid out on a funeral bier in her burial gown. Is the publication of these images from their life together a violation of Sontag's dignity, an expression of intimacy, a commentary on death and relationship, or all of the above? In my view, Sontag's illnesses and death are dreadful to see, but they are framed and made meaningful in the context of Leibovitz's well-populated autobiography. In the pages that precede the images of Sontag's final illness Leibovitz places photographs of three generations of her extended family—from her daughter at age three to her father at ninety-one. The pages that follow Sontag's death suggest both the fragility and wonder of embodied life. They display photographs taken only six weeks later of Leibovitz's father's very different death—at home and in his wife's arms. This second death is directly followed in the text (although three

months later in the calendar), by the surrogate birth of Leibovitz's twin daughters, one named Susan, after Sontag, the other named Samuelle, after her father. Death is followed by renewal. Life goes on, differently.

It might appear that Leibovitz has simply folded death and loss into a commonplace therapeutic story about life changing and continuing. She has, after
all, stated in interviews that putting the photographs into a narrative helped her
come to terms with her loss.[32] While that may be a benefit of composing, Leibovitz can also be seen as engaging with the very situation that concerned Sontag
in *Regarding the Pain of Others.* In that text, Sontag argues that "compassion can
only flounder" in the face of large-scale suffering (79). Leibovitz shifts the focus
to a more intimate scale and reveals that even in everyday life, knowledge of the
other is mediated and inadequate. Thus, the composition of the photographs
of Sontag in the hospital is rough, suggesting that these images of Sontag's
decline are only a shadow of the real agony they depict. The camera clearly
acts as a distancing device here—separating Leibovitz from full absorption in
Sontag's misery. In presenting these images within a larger memoir, Leibovitz
nevertheless makes the case to her audience that illness, pain, dying, and death
are matters worth attention and examination. She reveals herself figuring out
love and loss through the process of composing photographs and then arrang-
ing them to tell the story of her time with Sontag.

If Leibovitz's book engages the issues that concerned Sontag in *Regarding
the Pain of Others,* Rieff's *Swimming in a Sea of Death* engages his mother's earlier work, especially *Illness as Metaphor* and *AIDS and Its Metaphors.* He takes
on the role of the rational one for whom his mother's death represents a failure
of knowledge and a betrayal of truth. He is particularly disturbed by the limited
language and stories that were available to shape her experience. He critiques
how doctors talk to them, rails against euphemism and cliché, and offers an
extended critique of a brochure from the Leukemia and Lymphoma Society for
the "unconscionable . . . way in which the brochure is written in the language
of hope, but in fact offers none to anyone reading it with care" (55). He admits
he has no alternative to propose, but insists, "the gap . . . between language and
reality is simply too great, and is actually a disservice to most patients and their
loved ones, and, I suspect, even for physicians and nurses as well" (58). Rieff
emulates his mother's characteristic search for what is "right." He is haunted
because Sontag refused the medical certainty the leukemia would be fatal and
wanted to be told there was hope she would survive. He is both convinced it
would have been an act of extraordinary cruelty if he had refused to tell her she
would survive and unforgiving of himself for affirming the hopeful lies that
made it harder for her to die.

Rieff's essayistic memoir revises Sontag's early arguments against repre-

sentation. As Sontag argued against metaphors about illness even as she employed them, Rieff similarly doubts the value of memoir while he composes
his own. He openly distrusts his motives for writing and his ability to tell the
story: "Am I supposed to be ironic about what, in retrospect, was to be the last
of her Indian summers, perhaps quoting the P. G. Wodehouse line about how
'unseen, in the background, Fate was quietly slipping the lead into the boxing
glove' . . . ? Or am I to ascribe some special meaning to the intensity of her final
years . . . ? Or is all of this just that vain, irrational human wish to ascribe meaning when no meaning is really on offer?" (18–19). No meanings are adequate,
no narrative sufficient. He dismisses, as well, how palliative care specialists
often speak of "reframing hope" with their dying patients, a phrase that means,
he says, "helping mortally ill people find a way to shift from hoping to live to
connecting in some final, profound way with their loved ones" (152). Skeptical
about this invitation to choose a different narrative, he says, "'hope' is far too
strong and sentimental a word. I hear something of the same wishful thinking that overwhelms when I hear the word 'closure.' There is no 'closure' on
offer for the death of someone you love. Of that, at least, I'm certain. And I very
much doubt that 'hope,' framed or reframed, offers much to someone trying to
organize his or her thoughts and feelings in the shadow of extinction" (152). In
refusing closure, a fundamental element of narrative, he assures that he will
be unconsoled and inconsolable. Art's "solace," he maintains, is "also its men-
dacity" (170). Without reframing events, however, Rieff is trapped in his sense
of personal failure. His writing does not lead to forgiveness or understanding,
even though he desperately wants relief of some kind.

It is tempting to praise Leibovitz's visual memoir over Rieff's because she
appears to achieve a resolution that Rieff either does not want or cannot attain.
His mother's death forces him to confront what he does not know, and he cannot accept his inability to reason his way to certainty about the "right" course
of action. While Reiff's text seems to emerge from the closed fist of frustration,
Leibovitz sets forth her narrative on an open hand. It is also the case, however,
that their projects are very different. Working from their own particular experiences, with contrasting artistic and analytical viewpoints and in the different
media of photography and text, they present divergent interpretations of Sontag's death.

What can be learned from Leibovitz's and Rieff's discordant reflections on
suffering and death? Significantly, the two people closest to Sontag chose to
compose memoirs. This choice aligns their work more with her narratives, and
less, especially in Leibovitz's case, with her early arguments against the representation of illness. Thus, their memoirs suggest that scholars in the medical
humanities who have focused on her argument against metaphors have only

inherited half the story. These critics have missed that Sontag turned to narrative to address her sense of disconnection. Despite the radical differences of Leibovitz's and Rieff's memorial texts, together they confirm what Sontag asserted in *Regarding the Pain of Others* and enacted in her novels—that stories can be tools of understanding. In *Swimming in a Sea of Death,* Rieff creates a mantra of Joan Didion's statement: "we tell ourselves stories in order to live" (38, 43, 121).[33] If Sontag had recognized this earlier in her career, she might have tempered her stance against myths and metaphors of illness. This is not to say that she was entirely wrong in *Illness as Metaphor;* some stories do stigmatize. But others—such as her own account of the kingdoms of the sick and the well—make available new ways of thinking about the unthinkable. All those writers who quote "illness is the night-side of life" in their articles, Web pages, and blogs recognize the power of her metaphor, which is influential because it provides a *narrative* framework for engaging with the suffering of others (*Illness and AIDS* 3). In "misreading" the story of the kingdoms of the sick and well, they are actually true to Sontag's later belief that narratives can help us to understand.

Five

Theory's Aging Body

To ask about the function of criticism at the present time is to invite nearly as many answers as there are critics. The profession has traveled a long way from Matthew Arnold's confident declaration in 1865 that the only rule a critic must follow is "disinterestedness" in order "to know the best that is known and thought in the world, irrespectively of practice, politics, and everything of the kind" ("Function," 17). While a good number of today's critics might define their work as motivated by "interest," rather than disinterest, there is no consensus on what the focus of that interest should be. Even those who use criticism to draw attention to the ways that suffering, pain, and illness challenge representation, do not not agree on criticism's function. As we have seen, Susan Sontag, Veena Das, and Elaine Scarry define the relationship of language and pain in divergent ways and see literature as performing different roles in the systems of power that create and control embodied experiences of suffering. In addition, those who write about literature and medicine—such as Rita Charon, Arthur Frank, and David B. Morris—would have difficulty reconciling their approaches to narratives about illness with Lauren Berlant's arguments against empathic or compassionate reading practices.[1]

In "Poor Eliza," Berlant offers a particularly negative assessment of the kind of commonplace reading practices that might be called "reading to connect"—that is, reading with the hope or intention of experiencing an affective connection with the subject of a text or its author. Berlant unveils the hidden politics of such sentimental reading practices. Feeling an empathic connection allows one to appear to transcend structural problems such as racism and sexism, but, of course, this is a false transcendence. She warns that "witnessing and identifying with pain, consuming and deriving pleasure and moral self-satisfaction" from reading sentimental literature has no public consequence ("Poor Eliza" 645). Indeed, she argues that, when readers consume narratives of suffering privately, the experience prompts passivity rather than political action.[2] Working within Berlant's framework, the ethical function of criticism is clear: the critic must intervene to ensure that lay readers do not lose sight of the differences between themselves and those who suffer.[3] To be a serious, theoretically engaged critic requires attention to the systems that produce suffering, not local and particular examples of suffering. From this position, it appears that contemporary memoirs about pain, trauma, illness, and disability should be read, if they are to be read at all, with caution. Readers must guard against manipulation that renders them sympathetic to the trials and tribulations of individuals in pain and distracts from more significant issues, such as the degradation of reality for Sontag, the use of torture for Scarry and, for Berlant, the manipulation of affect to perpetuate the status quo.

What is lost when distrust and suspicion shape critical reading practices? In an effort to distance criticism from humanism's unexamined belief in the wholeness and autonomy of selves, suspicious criticism has swung to the other extreme and now disrupts and invalidates ordinary approaches to reading. In *Uses of Literature,* Rita Felski reframes the issues at stake for criticism. Because critics have disregarded ordinary motives for reading for too long, the field has lost an understanding of why literature matters to most readers—and, I would add, to many writers as well. Critics do not possess a deep, collective understanding of the everyday uses of literature as a form of "social knowledge" (Felski 14). Nor do they have a vocabulary for what interested, rather than disinterested, criticism might accomplish. This is a deficiency for many reasons, among them that literature about illness, pain, and suffering—which engages readers intellectually, affectively, and socially—can appear unserious and unworthy of critical attention.

Criticism is not stable or unified, however, and numerous literary theorists who built their reputations during the theory boom of the 1980s have begun to argue openly for connecting their work with everyday concerns, among them illness, vulnerability, and mortality. The body of theory has aged, as the theorists themselves have, and issues that once seemed only opportunities for suspicion and critique have risen to attention in new ways. For these critics, professionally honed modes of reading now seem inadequate to the task of providing insight into a mundane fact that has not changed over time: we are all mortal. Recall Bruno Latour's provocation in his essay "Why Has Critique Run Out of Steam?" cited in the opening chapter of this book. He warns that criticism risks becoming irrelevant because it overlooks experiences, feelings, and ideas that are not reducible to facts. Criticism can become relevant again, he argues, but only through "the cultivation of a *stubbornly realist attitude*" and a commitment to addressing "*matters of concern*, not *matters of fact*" (231). Latour's comments suggest that the profession's dedication to disinterest and ever more heightened skepticism has limited the scope of criticism too much. With the hermeneutics of suspicion so entrenched, however, what can reinvigorate critical practice? How can literary critics begin to address the problem that the culture of critique has rendered them inattentive, and perhaps insensitive, to foundational issues such as illness, pain, and suffering?

Mortality and Critical Self-Fashioning

Evidence of the divide between theoretically informed critical practice and narratives about illness appears not only in work by critics such as Sontag, Scarry, and Berlant. It surfaces throughout criticism of the past few decades, including in some surprising places, such as the epilogue to Stephen Greenblatt's *Renaissance Self-Fashioning*. This example is worth discussing at length because the epilogue and the critical conversation it generated reveal so much about a moment in critical theory that has shaped what is considered a worthy subject for criticism. At the close of Greenblatt's paradigm-shifting study of cultural forces on the Renaissance self, he turns from discussing self-fashioning in the life and work of early modern writers to telling a story about a plane flight he took to Boston. The nation's preeminent Shakespeare scholar found himself sitting next to a distressed middle-aged man who asked for his help.

> [The man] was traveling to Boston, he said, to visit his grown son who was in the hospital. A disease had, among other consequences, impaired the son's speech, so that he could only mouth words soundlessly; still more seriously, as a result of the illness, he had lost his will to live. The father was going, he told me, to try to restore that will, but he was troubled by the thought that he would be incapable of understanding the son's attempts at speech. He had therefore a favor to ask me: would I mime a few sentences so that he could practice reading my lips? Would I say, soundlessly, "I want to die. I want to die"? (255)

Greenblatt begins to form the words, but he stops before he reaches the word "die" and says he cannot fulfill the request. Instead, he asks, "Couldn't I say, 'I want to live?'" Then he suggests to the father that "he might go into the bathroom . . . , and practice on himself in front of a mirror" (255). In a "shaky voice," the man replies, "It's not the same" (255). The critic apologizes, and the two spend the rest of the flight in silence.

Greenblatt recognizes that some of his reaction was caused by ungrounded fears: "I could not do what the man had asked in part because I was afraid that he was, quite simply, a maniac and that once I had expressed the will to die, he would draw a hidden knife and stab me to death or, alternatively, activate some device secreted on board the plane that would blow us all to pieces" (256). But then things take a turn from the paranoid to the theoretical. Greenblatt returns to preparing for a class by picking up, of all things, the chapter "Deep Play: Notes on the Balinese Cockfight," from anthropologist Clifford Geertz's *Interpretation of Cultures*. In this chapter, Geertz gives an ethnographic account of the cockfighters of Bali whose participation in the sport gives expression to their sense of manhood. This particular detail about Greenblatt's choice of reading matter echoes the topic of his own book—self-fashioning. He juxtaposes the scene of reading Geertz's text with the story of the ailing son in Boston who is contemplating whether his diminished life is worth living, and with the image of this man's distraught father, who is trying to embolden himself to save his speechless son. Each man appears to fashion or refashion himself, but only Greenblatt, it seems, is aware that he is the subject of larger cultural forces.

So why did he refuse to mouth the words "I want to die" to help his neighbor? What cultural forces were in play during the long, uncomfortable flight to Boston? He explains, "I was aware, in a manner more forceful than anything my academic research had brought home to me, of the extent to which my identity and the words I utter coincide, the extent to which I want to form my own sentences or to choose for myself those moments in which I will recite someone else's. To be asked, even by an isolated, needy individual to perform lines that were not my own, that violated my sense of my own desires, was intolerable" (256). True, in the preceding pages he has argued that the perception that one fashions of oneself is a powerful fiction, that we are never free from ideology, institutions, and relations of power, and that choice is an illusion. Nevertheless, he fears that to speak the words "I want to die" would be to relinquish his sense of autonomy and even to invite death.

It might seem odd that, having defended his thesis about self-fashioning, the critic cannot step back from the scene and disengage from the idea that the words he speaks could determine his identity. In the end, however, Greenblatt deftly subsumes any apparent inconsistency into his argument, explaining that his unshakable faith in his ability to alter his fate with words simply validates that the illusion of self-fashioning is a *necessary* fiction. Greenblatt's conviction that he *must* form his own sentences may constitute false consciousness, but he assures us he is aware of its falseness. Thus, he is able to explain, even justify, withholding assistance to a fellow traveler: he has no choice. In the pages preceding his conclusion, he asserts, "the Renaissance figures we have considered understand that in our culture to abandon self-fashioning is to abandon the craving for freedom, and to let go of one's stubborn hold upon selfhood, even selfhood conceived as a fiction, is to die" (257). With this dramatic claim, Greenblatt asks his reader to recognize that the idea of a free, autonomous subject is an illusion so powerful that maintaining it is a matter of life and death, shaping what can be said and what can be done, even for those who are aware of the illusion.

This is indeed a strange story, especially given that, in the situation Greenblatt describes, there can be no doubt that the life at stake is that of the ailing son, not the critic. Taking Greenblatt's lead, however, one can read his ruminations about Geertz and self-fashioning while remaining mute on the flight to Boston not only as an autobiographical story, but also—and primarily—as a story about self-fashioning, the function of criticism, and the profession of English. The anecdote provides a portrait of a profession that, in addition to respecting intelligence and dedication to work, values suspicion and abstraction over attention to actual expressions of human suffering. In Greenblatt's epilogue, theoretical analysis that gives primacy to the written word is a particular kind of self-fashioning that fends off the risks of embodied and social existence.

Although this interpretation of Greenblatt and the profession may seem harsh, my point is not at all that he is monstrous, or that critics more generally are, but that a reader with the privilege of hindsight can see how the critic in the anecdote is "the ideological product of the relations of power in a particular society" (*Renaissance* 256). In this case, the story reveals that Greenblatt's commitment to his theory of self-fashioning renders him insensitive to the pain of the man next to him and the dire situation of his son, and shows, as well, that this insensitivity is rewarded, if not actively promoted, by the profession. This portrait of the critic would be less significant if it were an anomaly, but it is not. A number of critics have written about Greenblatt's epilogue, yet none that I have read acknowledges being troubled by his refusal to help the distraught father whose son has lost the ability to speak. Instead, critics tend to focus on the epilogue's concise, forceful restatement of Greenblatt's argument that his study of Renaissance texts revealed "no moments of pure, unfettered subjectivity" (256). He explains that, as his research advanced, "the human subject itself began to seem remarkably unfree" (256). Fellow critics often push back against this radically constructionist conception of subjectivity.[4] They resist

Greenblatt's assertion that the human subject is so completely determined and generally concur that, when he denies agency and the possibility of resistance, he pushes Foucault's argument too far. At the same time, in nearly every critical discussion of the epilogue, Greenblatt's choice to withhold help from the man traveling next to him goes without mention. To his critics, who also operate within the dominant critical framework of the moment, the father's suffering is irrelevant and Greenblatt's withholding of help is not notable as an ethical mistake. The pressing issue for them is whether he makes a valid claim that people are entirely fashioned by cultural institutions.

What happens on the rare occasions that Greenblatt's anecdote *is* taken up by the critical community is even more revealing about critical attitudes toward suffering. In *Ariel and the Police,* Frank Lentricchia observes that Greenblatt uses the "theatrical fiction" of personal anecdote to support the "theatrical fiction" of selfhood (101).[5] Framing his reading of Greenblatt's story, Lentricchia writes, "the personal story that he tells in the epilogue of his book functions as a cautionary tale of the archetypal political awakening of liberal man to the realities of power" (97). Lentricchia argues that, by refusing to say "I want to die," Greenblatt clings to self-fashioning and thereby shields himself from his fears that he is not free. In Lentricchia's judgment, Greenblatt offers "the best if unwitting account of new historicism and its political quandary" that he has ever come across: "Hating a world that we never made, wanting to transform it, we settle for a holiday from reality" (101). Lentricchia can only interpret Greenblatt's anecdote as demonstrating *the* "political quandary" of new historicism, however, because he repeats Greenblatt's own erasure of the particular social occasion that prompted his argument. He omits discussion of the encounter between the critic and the grieving father and thus can interpret this scene as signifying the critic's fear of "the realities of power" (97) rather than his terror of illness, human fragility, loss of language, and death. Lentricchia, like Greenblatt, conforms to a critical worldview that separates its understanding of culture from the experience of everyday, embodied life.

At least one critic does attend to Greenblatt's account of the events that took place on the plane to Boston, but not because she perceives an ethical problem. In "Shakespeare as Fetish," Marjorie Garber draws attention to the first sentences of *Shakespearean Negotiations,* the book Greenblatt published immediately after *Renaissance Self-Fashioning.* He opens the book with a powerful statement about its origins: "I began with the desire to speak with the dead" (1). This is, he says, "a familiar, if unvoiced, motive in literary studies, a motive organized, professionalized, buried beneath thick layers of bureaucratic decorum" (1). Ultimately, through study of the "textual traces" of the dead, he hopes to

make the voice of Shakespeare heard in his own voice (1). In discussing Greenblatt's dream of speaking with the dead, Garber observes a continuity between
the opening to *Shakespearean Negotiations,* in which he writes about speaking
with the dead, and the conclusion to *Renaissance Self-Fashioning* in which he
could not say "I want to die" (255). Garber is intrigued by the connection:

> From the unvoiced, taboo pronouncement (who would say it when a plane
> was taking off?), "I want to die, I want to die," to the professed desire to
> speak with the dead (and to the acknowledgment that to do so he had to
> hear his own voice) is not, after all, so far to go. It is, if you like, to go from
> the Hamlet of Act 1, scene 2, to the Hamlet of Act 1, scene 5. . . . But the
> movement from the secular text (Geertz's *Interpretation of Cultures*) back
> to the fetishized universal Shakespeare is striking. (244)

In this passage, Garber appropriates the story of the awkward exchange to serve
her argument and to perform her own playful act of fetishizing Shakespeare,
comparing Greenblatt's transformation between books to Hamlet's transformation between scenes.

What does Garber have to say about the suffering father who seeks to restore his son's will to live? Regarding Greenblatt's inability to fulfill the father's
request, Garber focuses on the mise-en-scène and asks, "who would say ['I want
to die'] when a plane was taking off?" No one, she is certain. To me, a better
question is: why *wouldn't* someone say these words if asked to do so to help the
father of a son in suicidal despair? In asking such a different question, I want to
shift attention away from the discussion about the foundations of new historicism or the fear of flying and toward the individual who asks the critic for help
figuring out how to speak to someone whose life no longer seems worth living.
If criticism is largely motivated by a desire to give voice to the textual traces left
by the dead, which is a compelling formulation of one of the profession's goals,
what would it mean to emphasize how our work speaks to and with the living?
What critical practices might support a more empathic response to stories like
the father's and encourage attention to the cultural work of narratives about
personal suffering? Throughout *Illness as Narrative,* I have noted the evolution
and proliferation of narratives about illness, and I have observed the emergence
of a range of voices, such as those of Bruno Latour, Veena Das, and Susan Sontag (in her novelist mode), that express dissatisfaction with critical detachment.
While it may seem as if their calls for attention to "matters of concern," acknowledgment of pain, and education in sympathy are personal and unrelated
to one another, together they map the pervasiveness of the "hermeneutics of
suspicion" and chart out ways to revive what Ricoeur calls criticism's "willingness to listen" (27).

Intimations of Mortality

Latour, Das, and Sontag are not alone in searching for ways to *listen*. As the twentieth century came to a close, many of the literary theorists who gained renown with the rise of theory began to see that their professionally honed modes of reading were inadequate to providing insight into a universal fact: we are all mortal beings. The experience of illness and aging and the inevitable confrontation with the impermanence of bodies and ideas have dimmed the appeal of arguing exclusively about how selves, bodies, texts, communities, and cultures are objects of power. While it may be tempting to dismiss this shift in attention to the nostalgia of scholars reaching the ends of their careers, a temporary suspension of suspicion reveals that these critics identify elements of life and literature that many current approaches do not or cannot adequately account for.

One of the most biographically and theoretically rich examples of how mortal illness can affect critical interests is found in the late work of Michel Foucault. When Foucault was dying of AIDS, he reexamined the practices, or "technologies," by which individuals know themselves and make choices about their thoughts and actions. In the third volume of *The History of Sexuality, The Care of the Self,* he turned his attention to a set of Hellenistic and Greco-Roman texts, especially those from the first and second centuries, where he discerned evidence of a growing apprehension about sexual pleasures among elite men.[6] At that time, moralists did not call for legislation, punishment, or medical prohibitions to control the pursuit of sexual pleasures. There was no "tightening of the code that defined prohibited acts" (41). Instead, an ethic of sexuality arose via the "cultivation of the self," whereby one saw oneself as an ongoing work to be constructed and refined. Such cultivation, he explains, "took the form of an attitude, a mode of behavior; it became instilled in ways of living; it evolved into procedures, practices, and formulas that people reflected on, developed, perfected and taught" (45). Particular "technologies of the self" included regimens of exercise and diet, as well as practices to improve thought and behavior. "There are," Foucault writes, "the meditations, the readings, the notes that one takes on books or on the conversations one has heard, notes that one reads again later, the recollection of truths that one knows already but that need to be more fully adapted to one's own life" (51).[7]

In *The Care of the Self* and several additional works on ethics and subjectivity, "Self Writing," "Technologies of the Self," and the interview "On the Genealogy of Ethics," Foucault develops his understanding of *writing* in the form of the *hupomnemata* as a practice of self-care. In "Self Writing," he explains that the *hupomnemata* "could be account books, public registers, or individual notebooks used as memory aids"—a form of ancient personal writing in which

men recorded "extracts from books, examples, and actions that one had witnessed or read about, reflections or reasonings that one had heard or that had
come to mind" (209). The thoughts and quotations recorded in the notebooks,
however, were not simply stored there. Writing provided a way of adapting "the
traditional authority of the already-said" for one's particular character, circumstances, and actions (212). Thus, the *hupomnemata* are unlike contemporary
private journals in which one constructs a narrative of the self (209). The purpose of these notebooks was "not to pursue the unspeakable, nor to reveal the
hidden, nor to say the unsaid, but on the contrary to capture the already-said,
to collect what one has managed to hear or read, and for a purpose that is nothing less than the shaping of the self" (210–11). Foucault emphasizes that this
writing was a "true social practice" that often took place within institutional
structures, such as schools, as well as within "customary relations of kinship,
friendship, and obligation" (*Care* 51, 52–53). In addition, the notebooks provided
the raw material for another technology of the self: letter writing. Correspondence is social and self-cultivating, Foucault explains, because "to write is thus
to 'show oneself,' to project oneself into view, to make one's own face appear in
the other's presence" ("Self Writing" 216).

Foucault's enthusiasm for the *hupomnemata* may be unexpected, given
his earlier discussions about the relation of writing to the self. In the closing
paragraph of the introduction to *Archaeology of Knowledge,* for instance, he char-
acterizes his own writing as aiding the erasure of a coherent narrative of self:

> What, do you imagine that I would take so much trouble and so much
> pleasure in writing, do you think that I would keep so persistently to my
> task, if I were not preparing—with a rather shaky hand—a labyrinth into
> which I can venture, in which I can move my discourse, opening up un-
> derground passages, forcing it to go far from itself, finding overhangs that
> reduce and deform its itinerary, in which I can lose myself and appear at
> last to eyes that I will never have to meet again. I am no doubt not the only
> one who writes in order to have no face. (17)

This account of theoretical writing provides a Foucauldian reversal of expectations. Rather than dedicating himself to his writing in order to show his face or
reveal truths, he hopes to find ways lose himself in the maze of his words and to
reveal that he, like all selves, can never cohere. Elsewhere, Foucault unveils the
dangers of confessional narratives. In the first volume of *The History of Sexuality,* he argues that confession—religious or legal—is a technology of regula-
tory power to compel subjects to speak, not an expression of a true self. Much
later, in "About the Beginning of the Hermeneutics of the Self," he complicates
his conception of the relationship of confession to the subject. Confession, he

maintains, is a public presentation of the self that replaces the self's internal manifestation. Through these revelatory stories, he writes, one "destroy[s] [one] self as a real body or as a real existence" and gives oneself over to public performance (221).

The few available details about Foucault's final months of life suggest that his new interest in writing as self-cultivation was motivated in part by his illness. In the years just before his death in 1984, AIDS was widely rumored to be a "gay cancer" and conspiracy theories were building about how it had emerged and spread. In addition, public health dictums directed at gay communities about the dangers of bathhouses intersected with efforts to suppress gay sex and culture.[8] At that point in time, the cause of AIDS was still unknown, which inevitably fed a generalized paranoia. The situation seemed ready-made for Foucauldian analysis about the power of medical discourse to discipline gay bodies. Foucault's own sick body, however, called into question the idea that the story of how AIDS spread was only a myth. In "The Final Foucault and His Ethics," Foucault's friend the historian Paul Veyne tells a story about noticing Foucault's persistent cough and fever. Without thinking about the possibility that his friend could actually have AIDS, he commented that Foucault's doctors might think he had the disease and Foucault replied, "That is exactly what they think." Veyne artlessly pursued the line of questioning, asking, "Does AIDS really exist, or is it a moralizing medical myth?" He recalls that Foucault replied, "I've studied the question closely, I've read quite a bit on the subject. Yes, it exists, it's not a myth. The Americans have studied it very carefully" (8).[9]

Assuming Foucault was aware that he had AIDS, as biographers Didier Eribon, David Macey, and James Miller all believe is likely, he was in a bind regarding his public face. What could he say or write about his situation? He was known to be gay and had spoken about the pleasures of bathhouses. To go public with his disease might therefore strengthen the disciplinary discourse that had emerged around AIDS. And yet, to remain silent about the relationship between cultural and medical discourse and the bodily realities of AIDS risked suggesting that he felt shame or guilt. He chose silence. Problematic as this was, it allowed him time to take care of himself and the life that he lived through his work.[10] He devoted his final months to writing. This influential thinker, who theorized "the death of the subject" faced his actual death by thinking instead about how lives and selves can be made into works of art. His final work is *about* the care of the self and also *performs* care of the self. Paul Veyne confirms that in Foucault's last months the cultivation of the self took on personal meaning: "During the last eight months of his life, the writing of his two books played the role for him that philosophical writing and the personal journal played in ancient philosophy: that of a work of the self on the self, a self-stylization" (8). Veyne does not mean that Foucault's project was merely, or even mostly, personal. Rather, Foucault's ill health and his suspicion or expectation that he would die from AIDS prompted a reconsideration of the relationship between social, historical, and cultural coercions, on the one hand, and the possibility of composing the self through reflection and action on the other. In his writing, Foucault focused on the ancient idea that "the principal work of art which one must take care of, the main area to which one must apply aesthetic values, is oneself, one's life, one's existence" ("On the Genealogy of Ethics" 271). He sees this "practice of the self" as "diametrically opposed" to the contemporary cult of the "true self" (271). "It seems to me," he says in "On the Genealogy of Ethics," "that all the so-called literature of the self—private diaries, narratives of the self, and so on—cannot be understood unless it is put into the general and very rich framework of these practices of the self. People have been writing about themselves for two thousand years, but not in the same way" (277).

Foucault's late theory offers a position from which to imagine different ways in which illness can be engaged in writing and criticism. His discussion of the *hupomnemata* describes how one cultivates the self through meditations upon the ideas assembled from readings, lectures, or encounters with others ("Self Writing" 211). Such writing does not seek to create the appearance of completion; it is an ongoing practice in the service of a self who is never final or complete. Thus, Foucault's late work indicates that philosophical, essayistic, and meditative writing, even if it is not explicitly about illness or suffering, can perform a function similar to that served by illness narratives—the transformation of the self as it makes meaning of the body's fragility and life's finitude.

Critical shifts such as Foucault's are evident elsewhere in recent academic history, where questions about how to understand and respond to illness, mortality, and the suffering of others have moved closer to center stage.[11] When Edward Said died of leukemia in 2003, after fighting the disease for twelve years, he was in the midst of completing *On Late Style: Music and Literature against the Grain*, a study of ambitious works often composed late in artists' careers. Said was intrigued by "artistic lateness not as harmony and resolution but as intransigence, difficulty, and unresolved contradiction" (7). Drawing on his earlier work and experience, he also locates in "late style" a sense of exile, the expression of "anachronism and anomaly" (xiii). With regard to Beethoven's "late style," for instance, Said describes the composition of the Ninth Symphony as tantamount to exile—"a moment when the artist who is fully in command of his medium nevertheless abandons communication with the established social order of which he is a part and achieves a contradictory, alienated relationship with it" (8). It is not a coincidence that the late style Said finds in Beethoven—as well as in the work of Theodor Adorno (who first wrote about Beethoven's "late style"), Thomas Mann, Richard Strauss, and Jean Genet—aligns so neatly with his own theoretical preoccupations. Although Said may revel in the late style of works that "remain unreconciled, uncoopted by a higher synthesis" (12), music critic Edward Rothstein believes there is something more at stake in Said's own late work, something the critic conceals inside his own desire to remain intransigent. "The reason we care about these works," writes Rothstein, "is not that they express irreconcilable contradictions or exile. Rather, each constructs an alternative universe in which something is actually being understood about our world: some things are rejected, some are accepted, some are greeted with horror, some with resignation. Beethoven's late music, for example, embraces incongruities because—we are convinced—that is precisely what it means to see the world whole. There is accumulated knowledge here: recognition and reconciliation, not just 'intransigence' or 'unresolved contradiction.'" Rothstein suggests that "late style" is an acknowledgment and performance of a complex, mature view of the world, one that, in some cases, may be informed by a deep sense of the fragility of life.

For Judith Butler, the terrorist attacks of 11 September 2001 and the global context in which they occurred gave rise to *Precarious Life: The Powers of Mourning and Violence,* which asks what political good can be made from grief and loss.[12] Concerned by what she sees as a reluctance among scholars to voice political criticism after September 11, she maintains that it is possible, and indeed urgent, to be outraged by the attacks on the World Trade Center and the Pentagon, to participate in public mourning, and also to take part in critical debate. She argues that critique should be nothing less than a force to minimize violence. "That we can be injured," Butler writes, "that others can be injured, that we are subject to death at the whim of another, are all reasons for both fear and grief" (xii). Does such human vulnerability lead inevitably to violence? Her hope is that, "to be injured means that one has the chance to reflect upon injury, to find out the mechanisms of its distribution, to find out who else suffers from permeable borders, unexpected violence, dispossession, and fear, and in what ways" (xii).

At the conclusion of her book, Butler reveals that her defense of criticism is inspired by her concerns over the precarious life not only of humans, but also of the humanities. She closes her book with an affirmation of the relevance of the humanities to this moment in history: "If the humanities has a future as cultural criticism, and cultural criticism has a task at the present moment, it is no doubt to return us to the human where we do not expect to find it, in its frailty and at the limits of its capacity to make sense. We would have to interrogate the emergence and vanishing of the human at the limits of what we can know, what we can hear, what we can see, what we can sense" (151). This moving statement challenges critics to reach beyond the already-said and the already-done and invent new practices. But Butler, like Said, ultimately contains her desire for renewal. In the final sentences of the book, she calls for humanists to "reinvigorate," rather than to reimagine, "the intellectual projects of critique" (151). The justification for this call has been diminished, however, by the passage of time. Since September 2001, economic and political inequities and violent struggles continue, and it is clear that cultural criticism has not and will not rescue humanity from the horrors we inflict on one another. That criticism and cultural commentary cannot save the world does not mean, however, that they are useless.

Although Butler cannot imagine a function for criticism beyond critique at the end of *Precarious Life,* had she looked at the connections between her own work and that of Foucault, Latour, and Das, she might have seen that they search for ways to acknowledge the fragility of embodied experience that are not currently central to the profession's ways of reading: care of the self, return to the human, attention to matters of concern, and acknowledgment. Collectively, these terms indicate a turn toward reading and writing *practices* that define and redefine one's relation to the world, the self, and others. In the context of contemporary criticism, attention to repair, recognition, or acknowledgment also indicates a shift in emphasis toward local, social, and affective activity.

Sedgwick's Reparative Practices

In recent years, no critic has addressed the need for alternative critical reading and writing practices with as much intellectual and affective force as Eve Kosofsky Sedgwick, a queer theorist who came to prominence in the same era as Greenblatt, and who died in 2009, eighteen years after her original diagnosis with breast cancer. Sedgwick integrates an illness narrative into her final critical work, *Touching Feeling,* which introduces valuable new critical terms: paranoid and reparative practices. In the chapter "Paranoid Reading and Reparative Reading," Sedgwick offers a fresh explanation for how the "hermeneutics of suspicion" has become "synonymous with criticism itself" (124). Today's criticism is grounded, she asserts, in a *paranoid* perspective. Critics are driven to predict and contain textual and theoretical problems and risks so that "bad news" about oppressive forces of power is always known in advance (130). As critics tirelessly seek to unveil texts' errors, concealed meanings, and lies, she concludes, paranoia has become "less a diagnosis than a prescription" (125).[13]

Sedgwick's goal is not to undermine the legitimacy of such projects, but rather to question the *imperative* that we must always and only attend to that which is hidden beneath, behind, or beyond. Informed by her experience of illness, pain, and mortality, she seeks to recognize the limits and possibilities of current criticism and then to explore alternatives. She describes paranoid criticism as favoring "strong theory" that can account for a range of phenomena that otherwise appear remote from one another. Freudian theory, for example, which defines sexuality and desire as universal sources of human motivation, has been used to explain everything from family dynamics, to trauma, dreams, and narrative structures. If the strength of strong theory is its range, its weakness is its potential for reductiveness and circularity. Sedgwick points out, for instance, that D. A. Miller's theory of the carceral in *The Novel and the Police,* is ultimately tautological: "everything can be understood as an aspect of the carceral, therefore, the carceral is everywhere" (135). She might also have turned to Greenblatt's argument in his epilogue: self-fashioning is a fiction, but our unshakable faith in the illusion of our own agency is proof that we *need* such fictions.

The biggest problem with strong theory and the paranoid criticism that depends on it is its "faith in exposure" (139). Thus, scholars in literary and cultural studies regularly perform a set of familiar critical moves. They "expose residual forms of essentialism lurking behind apparently nonessentialist forms of analysis"; "unearth unconscious drives or compulsions underlying the apparent play of literary forms"; and "uncover violent or oppressive historical forces masquerading under liberal aesthetic guise" (8). Because revealing cultural secrets demonstrates the critic's specialized access to a more "real" reality, the profession has embraced this practice as the primary way of organizing knowledge. Sedgwick also observes that suspicion has effectively delegitimized any other stance, so that "to theorize out of anything *but* a paranoid critical stance has come to seem naïve, pious, or complaisant" (126). We have overlooked evidence that "paranoia knows some things well and others poorly" (130).[14]

What then is to be done about rediscovering those objects, relations, or elements of experience that paranoia cannot know well? Obscured from our vision, Sedgwick observes, are the connections that exist when elements stand *beside,* rather than beneath, behind, or above, one another (8). She is quick to point out that "beside" can be used to describe a wide range of relations, and they are not necessarily amicable, equitable, or harmonious (8). Next to—*beside*—paranoid reading and writing practices, Sedgwick wants to place practices that are "reparative" (150). Her concept of the "reparative" draws on Melanie Klein's "depressive position," a mature psychological stance from which one can acknowledge feelings of loss, ambivalence, and guilt.[15] Sedgwick's account of reparative practices is more evocative than prescriptive: "No less acute than a paranoid position, no less realistic, no less attached to a project of survival, and neither less nor more delusional or fantasmatic, the reparative reading position undertakes a different range of affects, ambitions, and risks. What we can best learn from such practices are, perhaps, the many ways selves and communities succeed in extracting sustenance from the objects of a culture—even of a culture whose avowed desire has often been not to sustain them" (150–51).

Projects approached reparatively, she says, attend to the significance of the local and contingent. Sedgwick also observes that the primary motive that drives reparative practice is seeking and giving pleasure. It appears, therefore, that the reparative writer or critic does not strive to restore the past or stabilize the present, but rather to perform repair in the moment and for the moment. The goal of reparative practice, she explains, is "to assemble and confer plenitude on an object that will then have resources to offer to an inchoate self" (149).

Touching Feeling is itself the expression of Sedgwick's reparative practices. Sedgwick's writing is generative, creative, and nondualistic, and she uses it to challenge the limits of her own thought. She describes reparative work in terms that clearly evoke her own project. It "is likeliest to occur," she explains, "near the boundary of what a writer can't figure out how to say readily, never mind prescribe to others, in the Jacoblike wrestling—or t'ai chi, as it may be—that confounds agency with passivity, the self with the book and the world, the ends of the work with its means, and, maybe most alarmingly, intelligence with stupidity" (2). By uniting the self, the book, and the world in *Touching Feeling*, Sedgwick links phenomenology and epistemology. Writing and reading are acts of discovery from which understanding emerges. She acknowledges the danger that her ideas will be seen as "sappy, aestheticizing, defensive, antiintellectual, or reactionary" (150), but insists that critics' previous failures to value the reparative are due to an insufficient theoretical vocabulary, not to her cognitive, affective, physical, and theoretical practice itself.

Sedgwick also makes no secret of the fact that the search for a reparative practice came about in part because of her cancer and in part because of the toll AIDS took among her friends and students. Living with the knowledge that breast cancer would shorten her life substantially, she needed to find a way for the experience of terminal illness to affect and express itself in her intellectual and artistic work. In the introduction to *Touching Feeling*, she explains that encounters with mortality and Buddhism loosened her strong sense of purpose as a professional critic, the vocational consciousness that had grounded her earlier books (2).[16] In fact, in the decade preceding the publication of *Touching Feeling*, she moved away from privileging criticism, or even writing, and experimented with alternative literary forms and nonlinguistic textile art that allowed her to connect being and doing. She collaborated on editorial projects and wrote in nonscholarly genres, among them poetry, cancer journalism, and a memoir, *A Dialogue on Love*. Much of the poetry and journalism focuses on her cancer, as does *A Dialogue on Love*, an illness narrative about both cancer and depression in which Sedgwick braids together journal entries, her ongoing dialogue with her therapist, the therapist's session notes, and haiku.[17] *Touching Feeling*, by contrast, is at once a collection of critical essays, an intellectual autobiography, and an illness narrative in which cancer is a motivating condition, rather than the subject.[18] When Sedgwick makes clear that the experience of cancer is a significant part of her turn to reparative practice, she also indicates that such practices may be particularly valuable for writers and readers of narratives about illness, not just critics.

Reparative Practice in The Diving Bell and the Butterfly

Whatever form reparative writing takes, Sedgwick suggests it will display openness, creativity, a responsiveness to affect—both positive and negative—and, ideally, interwoven ends and means. For a work in any genre to be reparative, one would also expect the writing to sustain the writer and, potentially, the reader. Narratives of illness do not necessarily display all these qualities, but many do, especially literary memoirs.

Jean-Dominique Bauby's illness memoir, *The Diving Bell and the Butterfly: A Memoir of Life in Death* demonstrates these reparative traits and more. Bauby composed his memoir while struggling with the effects of a "cerebrovascular accident"—a massive stroke that left him unable to speak or move. In an earlier era, he would certainly have died, but now, he explains, "improved resuscitation techniques have . . . prolonged and refined the agony. You survive, but you survive with what is so aptly known as 'locked-in syndrome.' Paralyzed from head to toe, the patient, his mind intact, is imprisoned inside his own body, unable to speak or move. In my case, blinking my left eyelid is my only means of communication" (4). Yet, somehow he writes a book. One could say that in doing so Bauby experiments with reparative reading and writing practices that help him make sense of death and dying. He does not seek to avoid suffering, surprise, humiliation, or other negative feeling, but he writes about these while also generating pleasure for himself and others. Writing allows him to explore the edges of his own understanding. It also keeps alive his connection to his past, to friends and family, to who he was, even to who he is.

To fully appreciate Bauby's memoir and to recognize how his writing is both a means to sustenance and an end in itself, one must take into account the circumstances in which he wrote, the acoustics of his own hall: he dictated his 132-page book using only his left eyelid. Lying in his hospital bed, he first composed his "bedridden travel notes" (5) in his mind, "churn[ing] over every sentence ten times, delet[ing] a word, add[ing] an adjective, and learn[ing his] text by heart, paragraph by paragraph" (6). To record his compact chapters, which offer a mosaic of reflections on fragments of experience, he had the help of a scribe and the tool of an ingenious alphabet—one arranged like a "hit parade in which each letter is placed according to the frequency of its use in the French language" (20). In order for Bauby to write, his assistant read through the alphabet until he signaled for her to stop at a particular letter by closing his eye. Through this laborious process, over a period of two months, Bauby composed his memoir letter by letter. *The Diving Bell and the Butterfly* was published in France two days after Bauby died of heart failure.

How does one respond to such a memoir—one that is remarkable for existing at all? Paranoid conventions bid one to be suspicious of the desire to spare this text a critical reading.[19] And the strong reading that would ensue would reveal the secrets in tension with the text's surface: Bauby's privileged past, his access to superior healthcare, his lifelong commitment to fashion over substance. (He was, before his stroke, the editor-in-chief of French *Elle*.) Stepping to the side of the paranoid stance and looking instead from a reparative one, readers are better positioned to see Bauby's efforts, borrowing Sedgwick's words, "to assemble and confer plenitude on an object"—the narrative of his life—"that will then have resources to offer to an inchoate self" (Sedgwick 149). This is, in other words, a text, written reparatively, and that is most rewarding when read from a reparative position.

Although confined in an inert body, Bauby's imagination returns again and again to nourishing thoughts about the sensual satisfactions of his past; he seeks pleasure through memory and imparts heartbreaking pleasure through his prose. He recalls and reinvents the smells and tastes, from a simple sausage to full banquets. When he is taken on an outing to the beach that he can see from the terrace of the hospital, his destination is not the seascape, but a food shack that emanates the "intoxicating" aroma of French fries (88). Such moments are occasions for both distress and repair. His bath, for instance, reminds him of sinking into a warm tub with "a cup of tea or Scotch, a good book or a pile of newspapers" (17). With such indulgences now lost to him, he clings to the satisfaction of wearing luxurious clothing. He explains that he "sees in the clothing a symbol of continuing life. And proof that I still want to be myself." "If I must drool," he concludes with a mixture of humor and pathos, "I may as well drool on cashmere" (17).

Ironic juxtapositions of tragic and comic define Bauby's voice, his approach to narrative, and his reparative view of life. Although irony might seem to distance him from his experience, he demonstrates that it also has a sustaining function. It allows him to accept experiences that are distressing, even maddening. For instance, he describes the morning when he woke to find the ophthalmologist sewing his right eyelid shut by simply noting, "I have known gentler awakenings" (53). He concludes another chapter—an account of a miserably long and empty Sunday during which the nurses are inattentive and he has no visitors—by observing a shelf of books that he cannot reach and describing the agony of having a black fly settle on his nose. With an appreciation for the absurdity of his situation, he notes that, "Olympic wrestling is child's play compared to this" (102). Here and throughout his memoir, Bauby delights in capturing in a scene or a sentence the surprising incongruities that emerge as he tries to understand and bridge the chasm between his past and present. He uses his sense of irony to puzzle through the relationship between despair and joy, which are no longer opposite emotions for him because he consistently encounters them within the same experiences. Irony, therefore, serves both as a rhetorical device for detaching himself from his misery and as a reparative strategy for reconnecting and living with loss.

His reliance on irony also calls into question the hyperbolic blurbs on the book's back cover that proclaim his story is "a celebration of the liberating power of consciousness"; "a triumphant book [that] allows us to follow the flight of an indomitable spirit and to share its exultation at its own survival"; "a testament to the freedom and vitality and delight of the human mind." These words, not Bauby's own, invite suspicion. Bauby is distinctly *not* exultant. Instead, he repeatedly sets melancholy beside pleasure and agony next to absurdity. One could say that this method of juxtaposition is his way of making sense of a world made so suddenly and completely strange. Thus, in line with Sedgwick's description of reparative practice, Bauby's approach to composing his narrative of illness "confounds agency with passivity . . . the ends of the work with its means" (Sedgwick, *Touching Feeling* 2). His example points to the motive of many illness narratives. Writers are pressed by circumstances to address how the experience of illness causes fixed ideas and narratives to fall away. Through the act of writing, these writers recreate, at least temporarily, a more coherent sense of themselves and their lives. When writers or readers hold both rupture and beauty in view at the same time, understanding them to exist in relationship, then they see from a reparative position.

Reparative Possibilities

Sedgwick's illness brought her to reparative practices. Whether such practices might serve as a meaningful, functional alternative to paranoid criticism for the field is a fair question. To address this question, I would like to return to the writing of Stephen Greenblatt. Earlier in this chapter, his epilogue to *Renaissance Self-Fashioning* served as an emblematic performance of paranoia, where the author displayed both a literal fear of death and an unshakable commitment to suspicious critical practices. Although there is little hint of the reparative in Greenblatt's epilogue, that does not mean the potential is not there.

By the time Greenblatt published *Hamlet in Purgatory* in 2001, it appeared, in fact, that his motives for writing had shifted from paranoid toward reparative.

In *Touching Feeling*, Sedgwick maintains that paranoid and reparative positions only *appear* to be in opposition. True, the reparative emphasizes happiness instead of fear, creativity over strong theory, the experience of pleasure rather than the avoidance of pain, and openness in contrast to knowingness. But Melanie Klein, who was Sedgwick's source for these key terms, sees the reparative and paranoid as having what Sedgwick calls an "oscillatory" relationship: both positions developed out of awareness and acknowledgment of suffering, loss, and political oppression (Sedgwick, *Touching Feeling* 128, 138).[20] Sedgwick, too, states that they exist beside one another and can, therefore, appear in works by a single writer and even within a particular work. She maintains that reparative elements can be found in otherwise paranoid arguments. In *The Novel and the Police*, for example, D. A. Miller makes his suspicion quite clear: "The novel has trained us to be nothing if not suspicious. Surprise—the recognition of what one 'never suspected'—is precisely what the paranoid seeks to eliminate. . . . He can never be paranoid enough" (164). Nevertheless, Sedgwick sees an abundance of reparative gestures in his artistry—his tone, creativity, humor, and style—all of which point to the pleasure he takes in writing and the enjoyment his prose gives readers.

One could argue that Greenblatt's epilogue contains elements of reparative practice, but that would be a stretch. Eighteen years later, however, he penned a parallel anecdote in the prologue to *Hamlet in Purgatory* that is unambiguously reparative. This story, like the one in *Renaissance Self-Fashioning*, addresses the interconnection of Greenblatt's scholarship and his preoccupation with death, and that is not the only parallel. He writes again about fathers and sons. A grieving son travels to Boston on a train, rather than a grieving father on a plane. An ailing man pleads for life, not death. A call for help is unfulfilled. But this time, pleasure and death exist beside one another. Despair does not exclude wonder and beauty.

In *Hamlet in Purgatory*, Greenblatt's critical project is to understand how Shakespeare made the ghost of Hamlet's father so vivid and compelling. He recognizes that his motive seems as simple as the desire to revel in the intensity of Shakespeare's play and that his book may therefore seem unserious. But he also understands the importance of the pleasures and passions that motivate critical work and is concerned that the profession "has become so oddly diffident and even phobic about literary power, so suspicious and tense, that it risks losing sight of—or at least failing to articulate—the whole reason anyone bothers with the enterprise in the first place" (4). Acknowledging the centrality of both reason and passion in his own work, Greenblatt is explicit about the personal origins of his interest in *Hamlet's* ghost: his father, his father's death, and his father's obsession with death. In addition, Greenblatt's curiosity is sparked after his father's death because his father's will contains a bequest to an organization that will arrange for the kaddish, the Aramaic prayer of mourning, to be said for him. In Jewish tradition, the mourner's kaddish is recited at funerals, and sons are expected to say the prayer for eleven months after the death of a parent. His father's assumption that his secular sons will not pray for him impelled Greenblatt to take on this task, even as he "scarcely knew how to pray" and did not know why Jews prayed for the dead (9). Questions about the origin of the kaddish moved Greenblatt from research into its history to questions about how it might be related to the Christian tradition of praying for souls in purgatory and ultimately to the ghost of Hamlet's father.

The reparative elements of Greenblatt's project in *Hamlet in Purgatory* become more fully apparent when the critic writes about his father's affective relationship to death—"a strange blend of wonder and denial" (6). His father witnessed death's horror from an early age. Among the events that haunted him was his failed effort to find a doctor to save his own father's life. When his father, Greenblatt's grandfather, was seriously ill, he took him from Boston to New York for medical help, but his father died there, clinging to his son and begging for help. The son then arranged to transport his father's coffin from New York back home to Boston by train. By chance, as he sat weeping in the train's club car, awaiting the trip home, a group of chorus girls from the Ziegfeld Follies boarded. Immediately, the women crowded around the mourning young man and coaxed him back into awareness of life's pleasures. When Greenblatt tells this story, as well as the related story about his motives for writing about Hamlet's father's ghost, he brings to the surface what Sedgwick would call the reparative quality of *Hamlet in Purgatory*. He recognizes, accepts, and even takes pleasure in the unresolvable tension between passion and reason in criticism. Thus, he develops a project that is epistemological *and* phenomenological, cognitive *and* affective, and both professionally *and* personally sustaining.[21]

While I have chosen to title this chapter "Theory's Aging Body," there is certainly no imperative for a critic's work to become reparative with age and experience. It was not inevitable that Greenblatt wrote reparatively as he grew older. Theorists age in many different ways, and their work may remain untouched by illness, aging, or loss. And yet, it is significant that Greenblatt tells a story that links his work so evocatively with Sedgwick's *Touching Feeling*. He writes about mortality and purgatory. She writes from her own middle realm between terminal diagnosis and death. Both seek a criticism that is affectively rich and personally resonant. Both accept the complex forces at play in the world, literature, and criticism without trying to resolve them. Neither seeks to banish suspicion from criticism but, at the same time, both recognize that critics need different critical practices to address aging, suffering, and death. The later work of Greenblatt and Sedgwick is a reminder of criticism's potential for pluralism. No matter how ubiquitous paranoid critique may be, there is room for a range of critical motives and projects. No critical practice, however, is more urgent than attending to the complex ways writing and reading sustain individuals, communities, and cultures.

Reparative Reading

IN PREVIOUS CHAPTERS, I discussed the challenges to expression posed by experiences of risk, pain, suffering, and even sympathy, and examined how personal narratives about illness present problems for dominant literary critical practices that are based in hermeneutics of suspicion. In her final book, *Touching Feeling*, Eve Kosofsky Sedgwick labels interpretive approaches that seek to expose secrets, errors, and manipulation "paranoid practices." She points out a truth that is hard to see from within the world of criticism: "paranoia knows some things well and others poorly" (130). Among the things that paranoia does not know well are personal accounts of embodied suffering and life's fragility. Sedgwick and other theorists and critics of the late twentieth- and early twenty-first centuries have proposed a range of alternative practices—both creative and critical—that are not solely driven by suspicion, but also by the desire to give sustenance to individuals, communities, and cultures. Out of experiences of aging, illness, and mourning, scholars such as Bruno Latour, Veena Das, Susan Sontag, and Michel Foucault, as well as Sedgwick, have explored approaches that attend to matters of concern, acknowledge stories of suffering, educate readers about the complexity of sympathy, reconceive the care of the self, or imagine art and criticism as performing repair.

Since aging, illness, and loss appear to have brought paranoid practices into question, it may seem that alternative reading, writing, and living practices are only accessible as a result of such experiences. If that were true, however, a broad readership would not find critics' complaints of fatigue with the goals of interrogation, exposure, subversion, and disruption so compelling or provocative. We can add to the list of critics who express such concerns Rita Felski, who writes in *Uses of Literature* that to "defin[e] literature as ideology is to have decided ahead of time that literary works can be objects of knowledge but never sources of knowledge" (7). She does not mean that critics should decline to ask political questions of literature, but she is concerned about criticism that dismisses the possibility "that a literary text could know as much, or more, than a theory" (7). In contemplating an alternative to dominant practices, Felski encourages the profession to develop a more phenomenological criticism in which "everyday attitudes are neither invalidated (as they are in poststructuralism and much political criticism) nor are they taken as self-explanatory (as in humanist criticism, with its unexamined use of terms such as 'self' or 'value'); rather they become worthy of investigation in all their many-sidedness" (17). Such an approach would allow for an interested and affectively rich criticism that is not governed by trust or suspicion. The question remains, however, can such attentive—perhaps even reparative—practices be taught? If so, *how* can they be taught?

To answer these questions, I would like to turn to the complicated reception history of Anne Fadiman's *The Spirit Catches You and You Fall Down,* which provides a valuable case study of the limits of teaching either what Felski calls self-explanatory, humanist practices or what Sedgwick calls paranoid practices. Fadiman's book is an ethnographic narrative about a medical disaster that occurred because of failed cross-cultural communication between doctors and a patient's family. It won the National Book Critics Circle Award for general nonfiction in 1997 and quickly took a prominent place in pre-med, medical school, and anthropology syllabi. In these separate realms, however, it has inspired diametrically opposite readings. In medical education, *The Spirit Catches You* is frequently used to teach what might appear to be an alternative to suspicion. Some educators trust Fadiman's perspective and her narrative and use the book as an unquestioned *source* of knowledge to teach empathy and "cultural competence." By contrast, anthropologists who have written about *The Spirit Catches You* express suspicions regarding errors and distortions in Fadiman's representation of Hmong culture. They suggest the book is not useful in the classroom except as the object of critique. These cultural critics hold different, yet still troubling, pedagogical assumptions. Their arguments suggest that literature should serve knowledge and affirm the lesson or theory at hand. The underlying premise here is that it is more valuable for undergraduates to know what experts say about culture than for them to participate in it by reading literature, posing questions, exploring ideas, and making meaning.

There are alternatives, however, to these two ways of reading *The Spirit Catches You*. Although Sedgwick never wrote directly about *The Spirit Catches You*, the reparative pedagogy she develops in the final chapter of *Touching Feeling*, "Pedagogy of Buddhism," reveals more about Fadiman's project than any of the critics who have addressed it directly. While living in the limbo between her terminal cancer diagnosis and death, Sedgwick became interested in a kind of learning that seeks meaningful ways to live with both not-knowing and the prospect of not-being. Like Sedgwick, Fadiman asks her readers to consider illness, mourning, and loss and to let their experience as readers bring them to the edge of their own understanding. *The Spirit Catches You*, like many of the texts considered in *Illness as Narrative*, is "a literary text [that knows] as much, or more, than a theory" (Felski 7).

The Book Catches You

The Spirit Catches You is a nonfiction narrative about illness and the challenges of cross-cultural medical treatment. In *The Spirit Catches You*, Fadiman interweaves ethnographies of the Hmong community in Merced, California, and the biomedical culture of the Merced Community Medical Center. Where these cultures intersect, she finds the story of Lia Lee, a young Hmong child of immigrant parents who has severe epilepsy and who, at the age of four, suffers a massive seizure after which she is pronounced "brain dead." Within a morass of cultural differences, misunderstandings, and conflicts surrounding Lia's treatment, Fadiman's goal is to construct an understanding of her illness and treatment that could not have been composed by those who were involved in the events at the time, and that is not predetermined by any strong theory.

Fadiman approaches her narrative about Lia's case by carefully moving back and forth between the Hmong community and that of the healthcare professionals, providing a nuanced account of how these groups define the body, identity, medical treatment, and healing in radically different ways. While Lia's American doctors are certain that the child has a neurological disorder in which brain cells rapidly and chaotically transmit neural impulses, Lia's family uses the term "the spirit catches you and you fall down" to name her condition. They understand that Lia has seizures because a spirit frightened her soul from her body and her soul is now lost. They also believe that she will be healed if her soul can be called back to her body. Lia's story unfolds in the space between these two interpretations.

In Fadiman's hands, *The Spirit Catches You* is not a simple story of cause and effect or error and blame. Lia, who was first diagnosed as having epilepsy at eight months old, was surrounded by people who loved and cared for her, but who nevertheless failed to save her from life in a coma. Her pediatricians,

Peggy Philps and Neil Ernst—who are married and share a practice—pre-scribed a series of treatments, searching for a drug or a combination of drugs that would control her frequent seizures. Over the next four years, Lia's par-ents were directed to give her fifteen different medications in various dosages and combinations, according to constantly shifting daily schedules. Because the Lees had such a different conception of illness and treatment, they either did not understand or did not accept the logic of the drug regimes. Even if they wanted to cooperate with the medical instructions—and it remains unclear to what degree they did—it would not have been easy for them. They could not read the English instructions on medicine labels or the markings on drop-pers and measuring spoons. Even when the directions were orally translated, the Lees could not record them because they were unable to read or write in Hmong. Lia continued to have seizures, apparently because she was not getting sufficient medication. When the doctors eventually realized that her parents were not following the prescribed treatment, they were baffled. Were the Lees confused, resistant, or, as Dr. Philps once wondered, insane? (Fadiman 47). Soon after Lia turned two years old and developmental delays became apparent, Dr. Ernst decided that "poor parental compliance" regarding the medication constituted child neglect and filed a report with Child Protective Services (58). As a consequence, Lia was removed from her parents' custody and placed in foster care for ten months.

When Lia was returned to her parents, her prescriptions were simplified and her parents began, to use the medical jargon, to "comply" with her treat-ment. Things nevertheless continued to go wrong. On the one hand, American medicine failed her with delayed and incorrect diagnoses, inconsistent treat-ment, and inadequate communication with and education for her parents; on the other, Lia presented a nearly impossible case for an array of biological as well as cultural reasons. Fadiman also makes clear that the choices Lia's par-ents made about her care, well-intentioned as they were, probably allowed her epilepsy to become less treatable by Western drugs. When Fadiman enters the scene after Lia's final seizure, she discovers that no one can offer sufficient an-swers to the questions "What went wrong?"; "Who is responsible?"; and "How could this have been prevented?"

Humanist Trust

The narrative of The Spirit Catches You has made it easy for medical edu-cators to use the book as a case study in cross-cultural communication.[1] For the past few decades, many teachers in the medical humanities, who typically teach in medical schools, have advocated using literary and patient narratives as tools for teaching empathy, self-reflection, and communication to medical students and other practitioners.[2] These scholars and teachers maintain that deep engagement with the interior lives of characters, attention to how language and narratives function, and practice reflecting on the ambiguities and uncertainties of other minds and lives will encourage doctors and other practitioners to be more empathic, and thus more effective in treating patients. In recent years, if medical students were assigned any book other than a textbook during the initial four years of professional education, it was likely to be Fadiman's.[3] In medical settings students typically encounter the book as a lesson in the importance of "cultural competence." This term is generally understood to refer to the professional capacity to work within the context of the "language, thoughts, communications, actions, customs, beliefs, values, and institutions of [patients'] racial, ethnic, religious, or social groups" (Cross 3). That Fadiman's book has been so widely used to teach medical students about cultural difference and communication is partly a consequence of timing. It was published in 1997, just before new requirements that medical students receive training about patients' diverse cultures—especially concepts of health, illness, and disease—and learn to apply that knowledge in professional practice.[4]

To skeptical literary scholars, this didactic use of literature and the idea that "cultural competence" could be taught through one book or one class sounds overly simplistic and too trusting of Fadiman's text. Actually, it is quite common in college English departments for teachers to assign works that they think will broaden students' understanding of human experience, with the goal of developing empathy for people very different from themselves. There is also a surprising level of agreement *outside* the academy that reading literature makes readers more empathic and broadens understanding across lines of difference. Consider the popularity and influence of talk show host Oprah Winfrey's book club. Between 1996 and 2010, Winfrey regularly selected contemporary books, generally fiction, for her viewers to read and explicitly encouraged them to read therapeutically—to "value novels they can take personally, novels that can speak to, challenge or transform their lives, novels that entertain them with lively stories or call them into political or social awareness, even action" (Harker and Farr 2).

Beliefs about the ethical (but not therapeutic) value of literature surface elsewhere in the academy, including in the work of philosophers Martha Nussbaum and Richard Rorty (discussed briefly in chapter 4), who both argue that literature helps to cultivate the imagination and thus to create a more compassionate society. Nussbaum writes that narrative and empathic imagination, which is exercised in reading novels, is "an invaluable way of extending our ethical awareness and of understanding the human meaning of events and policies" (*Upheavals of Thought* 14). She explains, "Narrative imagination is an essential preparation for moral interaction. Habits of empathy and conjecture conduce to a certain type of citizenship and a certain form of community: one that cultivates a sympathetic responsiveness to another's needs, and understands the way circumstances shape those needs, while respecting separateness and privacy" (*Cultivating Humanity* 90). According to Nussbaum, empathy should not be understood as a spontaneous reaction, but a habitual practice, cultivated and elevated to the service of citizenship and community. Like Nussbaum, Richard Rorty maintains in *Contingency, Irony, and Solidarity* that reading literature can train the imagination to find connections with others despite our differences. In a previous era, he writes, people would have turned to "the sermon and the treatise" as "the principal vehicles of moral change and progress" (xvi). He argues that currently "it is the disciplines which specialize in thick description of the private and idiosyncratic which are assigned this job. In particular, novels and ethnographies which sensitize one to the pain of those who do not speak our language must do the job which demonstrations of a common human nature were supposed to do" (94). In other words, the social solidarity generated by novels and narratives is not the old humanism in disguise. "It is to be achieved," Rorty maintains, "not by inquiry but by imagination, the imaginative ability to see strange people as fellow sufferers" (xvi).

What remains unclear after reviewing these arguments is *how* cultural competence, compassion, solidarity, or empathy emerge from reading literature. The assumption seems to be that reading naturally stimulates emotionally generous and kind imaginative engagement, which then leads seamlessly to ethical interaction with others. There is little evidence, however, that reading literature has such effects. In *Empathy and the Novel,* Suzanne Keen finds no significant research in psychology, cognitive science, neuroscience, or reading practices to support the claim that the private experience of reading and the generation of what she calls "narrative empathy" makes people more altruistic in everyday life. In practice, readers do not regularly choose reading material that cuts across social and cultural boundaries, so empathic imagining is generally a form of identification, not an affective understanding of difference. In addition, because reading is a private transaction between a reader and a book, readerly empathy differs profoundly from social empathy. When reading for pleasure, we are released from social obligations and need not put up the protective barriers of suspicion or skepticism (Keen 88).

It is important to note, however, that the complications to which Keen draws attention do not preclude the possibility that *teachers* could, and perhaps do, use literature to engender empathetic feeling and compassionate behavior in their students. Keen's study underscores two fundamental problems. We do not yet have compelling evidence that teaching empathy through literature is possible. And, assuming it *is* possible, we do not yet know how to teach the transfer from reading to empathy to action. At the moment, therefore, fostering empathy through reading is a goal in search of an effective pedagogy.

Anthropological Distrust

Cultural competence, like empathy, may seem to be a desirable pedagogical goal, but for anthropologists, in particular, the effort to categorize and summarize cultural differences so that they can be contained in clinical protocols can appear so reductive that it threatens to be counterproductive.[5] In addition, the idea that *The Spirit Catches You* might be medical students' only encounter with ethnography is troubling for many reasons. The most common critique of Fadiman's book among anthropologists is that she accepts and reifies simplified and romanticized explanations for Hmong beliefs and behavior. In a review, Mai Na M. Lee outlines evidence of Fadiman's tendency to accept stereotypes and myths. She objects, for instance, to the repetition of a number of false claims: that the Hmong are obstinate and resistant to authorities outside their community; that they generally believe epilepsy to be a disease of distinction; and that they are "differently ethical"—willing to lie and cheat to serve the group. In an article about media representations of Hmong–white relations, anthropologists Louisa Schein and Va-Megn Thog maintain that even when a representation of the Hmong appears to be sympathetic—such as Fadiman's portrait of Lia Lee's parents turning to their culture's traditional healing practices—"the metamessage is that Hmong immigrants can never do anything but hold on to traditional culture" (1072).[6]

In "The Story Catches You and You Fall Down: Tragedy, Ethnography, and 'Cultural Competence,'" anthropologist Janelle S. Taylor offers a thoughtful critique that specifically focuses on how Fadiman's book is used in medical school curricula. Taylor recognizes that Fadiman employs some romanticized explanations for Hmong beliefs and behavior, and these are particularly troubling given the book's status as a primer for cultural competence.[7] For Taylor, like the reviewer Lee, Fadiman is too quick to believe and report what she is told about the Hmong, and her generalizations imply that their culture is rigid, essential, and unchanging. Fadiman thereby perpetuates what anthropologist Eric Wolf labels the "'billiard ball' model of culture"—a model in which culture seems like a hard object that collides with everything in its way and then bounces away, unbroken, undamaged, unchanged (Taylor 166). If one adopts this way of thinking about culture, then Lia Lee's fate is inevitable: there is no possibility for negotiation or change when her parents encounter the American physicians. But the world is not "a global pool hall in which the entities spin off each other like so many hard and round billiard balls" (Wolf 6). As an anthropologist, Taylor understands culture to consist of many competing conventions and practices (Taylor 166). From this perspective, when cultures meet, they interact, intersect, and change, even when they are as different as biomedical and Hmong cultures. Taylor also claims that *The Spirit Catches You* is both persuasive and troubling as an ethnography because it adheres to the conventions of tragedy (162). In her view, when Fadiman presents Lia's story as tragic, she communicates to readers that the child's fate is inevitable, a dangerous conclusion given how the book is used in clinical training.[8]

Taylor also expresses deep concerns regarding the instrumentalist medical pedagogy of "cultural competence." She discusses the obvious problem that, if learning about cultural difference is limited to reading *The Spirit Catches You*, or limited to one course in four years of medical school, students will develop little actual competence in addressing the challenges of cultural difference in clinical practice. The goal of "cultural competence" is also undermined if teachers or readers believe that Fadiman's text provides a recipe for patient-doctor relationships. If what readers absorb from Fadiman's book, she speculates, "is a set of stereotypes about what 'they' think, or a bunch of rules about how to deal with 'them,' like so many specialized tools to be stashed in a briefcase and trotted out each time one of 'them' shows up, then we will certainly fail to keep alive the empathetic curiosity that allows one to be thoughtfully alert to difference" (Taylor 179). Even with increased attention to cultural difference in medical school curricula, Taylor notes that medical students are unlikely to see cultural competence lessons as important if the rest of their training indicates that *real* medical competence is something else entirely (178). In other words, physicians-in-training will only be committed to learning about patients' cultural differences if the medical profession redefines medical competence *as a whole* to include such knowledge.

While skepticism is certainly warranted if medical educators—or any educators—use Fadiman's book as a model for thinking about cultural difference, at moments Taylor extends her criticism of the book too far. Particularly disturbing from a literary perspective is Taylor's assumption that Fadiman constructs *The Spirit Catches You* as a tragedy in the Aristotelian tradition. This preconception ultimately leads her to a striking misrepresentation of Fadiman's narrative. She initiates her critique of Fadiman's use of tragic conventions with the observation that, "a story that *ends* with a small child slipping into an irreversible coma is among the saddest that it is possible to tell" (163; emphasis mine), and asserts that the plot structure leads readers to see the story as leading inevitably to catastrophe (163–64). While Taylor's general point is valid—that the conventional structure of tragedy distorts events in nonfiction narratives, she appears to overlook two important points. *All* narrative structures distort the events they describe. More specifically, Fadiman's text does not, in fact, *end* with Lia falling into a coma. This event occurs in the middle of the book. One could say that Taylor's misstatement regarding the narrative's organization actually lends support to her general argument that traditional stories and genres can blind us to the complexities of their subjects; she, after all, is so familiar with the conventions of ancient tragedy that she misremembers or misrepresents the timing of Lia's final seizure. Her misstatement even more strongly demonstrates that her paranoid practices obscure from her view some elements of Fadiman's complex reparative project. Fadiman's choice to position the story's "ending" in its center complicates readers' responses to Lia Lee's fate and disrupts assumptions about the relationship of individuals to families and communities, the meaning of embodied existence, and what constitutes health, illness, and healing. To the extent that Fadiman engages tragic conventions, it is to demonstrate how they do *not* apply to this story, which avoids closure and does not end with Lia's death.[9] Instead, Fadiman recognizes tales told and retold and rituals performed and repeated as part of the family's and community's way of living with loss.

After reviewing the errors and inadequacies in *The Spirit Catches You* and the problems with how it has been used in classrooms, it is worth asking whether this book should be taught at all in medical schools or anthropology classrooms. If the book is, in itself, expected to teach cultural competence and empathy or to transmit knowledge about Hmong culture or cultural conflicts, then it will fail. But the problem is not really the book, or literature more generally. The problem is pedagogy.

Taylor's Recuperative Pedagogy

In her essay about *The Spirit Catches You,* Taylor reflects upon pedagogical quandaries regarding *The Spirit Catches You*—in particular the idea that one should *not* assign the book because its presentation of an extraordinarily complex case of cultural conflict does not model the best anthropological practices. While it seems that she marshals evidence throughout her article to justify excluding the book from course syllabi in anthropology, by the end of her essay she shifts her perspective. She remembers what she gained from falling in love with the book when she first read it and wonders what her students will lose if they are not allowed the pleasure of getting "caught" by this and other stories. Recalling her own history as a reader, Taylor realizes that an engaging story engenders an affective and embodied experience that can motivate curiosity and learning. Taylor does not share the language Felski uses in *Uses of Literature,* but her project echoes Felski's insights (via Ricoeur) that "narrative [is] a staple of our cultural grammar, an indispensable means of connecting persons, things, and coordinates of space and time" (Felski 85). "To be sure,"

Felski acknowledges, "we can question the politics built into certain storylines. . . . but our conceptions of politics, literature, human relations, the interaction between social structures and human agency, remain deeply beholden to the logic of narrative" (85).

Although Taylor remembers how much she enjoyed getting caught by the "irresistible narrative drive" and the "shamanic" power of Fadiman's storytelling, she reports that she has hesitated to use narratives in teaching because her professional training in theory has altered what she values as a reader (160, 173–74). She admires scholarly works that "articulate a more complicated, processual, performative understanding of 'culture,'" and she recognizes that these texts "purposely tweak and disrupt the flow of narrative" (160). Academic arguments attend to the breaks, silences, and complications that render simple narratives insufficient. As rewarding as such reading may be for experts, Taylor recognizes that it is a mistake to serve students a uniform diet of dense theoretical texts that send the message that "culture" is too hard to understand. Taylor's meditations on reading and writing ultimately lead her toward Sedgwick's critical insight that "paranoia knows some things well and others poorly" (*Touching Feeling* 130). Critique of Fadiman's text as an object of knowledge has value, but experience of it as a source of knowledge is also valuable. Students, she argues, should have the time and place to fall in love with books and to allow themselves to be swept away, to be *caught,* by a story; medical students, too, should be given time to experience "the curative effects of reading" (174). They, in particular, need such experiences because, too often, "prov[ing] one's competence as a doctor . . . demands that one steel oneself *against* being caught by 'the story of the person'" (175). Thus, she concludes, "Books such as *The Spirit Catches You* and courses such as those offered in 'cultural competence' curricula (as well as articles such as this one) assume their proper place when we take them not as solid lumps of congealed truth, but as goads to curiosity, invitations to make meaning, moments in the ongoing process that *is* culture" (179).

In the classroom, Taylor says, Fadiman's text has the potential to give rise to "empathetic curiosity," cognitive and affective interest that remains attentive to difference (179). The term "empathetic curiosity" suggests that an emotional connection to others serves students and scholars best when it motivates habitual behavior of intellectual openness and questioning. A course that invites students to be curious about Fadiman's text—to explore without being compelled to pursue one particular line of questioning or another—provides an opportunity for students to contend with culture in ways that do not skirt conflict or conceal tensions. Thus, Taylor suggests that members of her profession should resist the temptation to withhold texts about which they have misgivings from nonexpert readers. To do so, she suggests, is to deny students engagement with the subject they are studying: "'Culture' is not a 'thing,' somewhere 'out there,' that books are 'about.' It is a process of making meanings, making social relations, and making the world that we inhabit, in which all of us are engaged—when we read and teach, or when we diagnose and treat, no less than when we embroider *nyas*[10] and conduct sacrifices" (179). A liberal education, Taylor confirms, entails more than mastery of a body of knowledge. Students need practice to become ever more thoughtful and complex makers of meaning.

There is a great deal to admire in Taylor's recuperative reading of *The Spirit Catches You* and her willingness to let go of some of her suspicion in order to be more responsive to her students. Her purpose in writing her article extends beyond her own experience and Fadiman's book to pose a challenge to her field to write and teach more engagingly by using the power of narrative. While I was "caught" by Taylor's essay with its narrative reflections and willingness to reconsider how to engage students in learning, I also find myself wishing that she had extended her thoughts about pedagogy beyond Fadiman's text and her own field. Taylor's discussion of *The Spirit Catches You* and teaching anthropology hints that pedagogy in the academy should value everyday motives for reading and use them to actively promote curiosity. She moves away from a theory-centered classroom where there are no surprises and toward a practice-centered classroom where students actively explore the not-yet-known. For a fuller discussion of this implicitly reparative pedagogy, however—one that reaches beyond concern with *The Spirit Catches You* and any particular course or field—we need to return to Sedgwick's *Touching Feeling*.

Sedgwick's Pedagogy of the Bardo

In the final chapter of *Touching Feeling*, "Pedagogy of Buddhism," Sedgwick writes about pedagogy because she, like Taylor, has experienced a discontinuity in teaching. The experience of living with terminal cancer and the evolution of her ideas about reparative reading and writing have altered her practice as a teacher. In "Pedagogy of Buddhism," she writes from the transitional state between her diagnosis with cancer and her death. She claims this intermediate realm as a privileged scene of learning and teaching, like the Buddhist "bardo" between death and the next life. Even as she reveals herself to have learned from her unenviable circumstances, however, she does not emphasize her individual experience as an English professor who has breast cancer. Instead, she bases her transformation in Buddhism, which has a two-thousand-year pedagogical history. Sedgwick's work in "Pedagogy of Buddhism" thus returns us to the question of whether reparative practices can be taught. If Buddhist practices can, then Sedgwick's reparative practices can, too—even to students who may not have experienced the disintegration of meaning that can result from illness, mourning, and recognition of mortality.

Although spirituality may be integral to her own experience, Sedgwick does not impose it on her readers, but rather shows how Buddhist traditions inform her approach to teaching. In Buddhism, Sedgwick finds a respect for ways of learning and knowing that are not typically recognized in the academy. In her bardo, illness and death can be a means to a further end—perhaps to rebirth, but also to the deep, embodied knowledge that she calls "recognition" and "realization" (167–68). "Perhaps nothing," she writes, "dramatizes the distance between knowledge and realization as efficiently as diagnosis with a fatal disease. As advertised, it does concentrate the mind wonderfully (even if by shattering it) and makes inescapably vivid the distance between *knowing* that one will die and *realizing* it" (173–74).[11] Sedgwick acknowledges that the words "realizing" and "recognizing" suggest relearning what one knows already; this sounds tautological and therefore either pointless or simple. But if one differentiates "being exposed to a given idea" from "catching on to it, taking it seriously, having it sink in, and wrapping your mind around it," then there is no tautology (167). These terms indicate different types and degrees of understanding, all of which are at work in our lives and our classrooms.

In *Uses of Literature*, Rita Felski uses the term "recognition" in a manner that resonates with and extends Sedgwick's use of the same term. For Felski, it denotes one of four common modes of textual engagement—the experience a reader has when something vaguely sensed emerges from the fog and becomes clear and known. Paranoid critics tend to see "recognition" as a self-deception that is superficial or ideological, but in Felski's words, "the literary field offers endless illustrations of its complexity as an experiential mode and an analytical concept" (46). Like Sedgwick, she seeks to demonstrate that recognition is not necessarily false or trivial: "[it] is about knowing, but also about the limits of knowing and knowability, and about how self-perception is mediated by the other, and the perception of otherness by the self" (49). Felski's account of recognition clarifies the relevance of Sedgwick's ideas to literary study: readers engage in these ways of knowing when they read literature.

While Sedgwick values recognition, "Pedagogy of Buddhism" emphasizes a different kind of learning altogether. In the bardo of prognosis, she is especially interested in a type of learning that "proceed[s] in the absence of spontaneous recognition," especially in experiences of negation, misrecognition, and cognitive or affective frustration (*Touching Feeling*, 169). Such learning is approached in Buddhist pedagogy through koans, paradoxical statements, stories, or questions that serve as objects of reflection and that "dramatiz[e] . . . the impossibility of methodical learning" (172). Koans disrupt the dualism between teacher and student, between the authority of text and experiential realization, between the knowable and the unknowable. Sedgwick therefore uses the koan as a model for narratives that unsettle teaching, learning, and the relationship between them. She structures her essay around a series of koanlike anecdotes that depict failed or "near-miss" pedagogical moments.

Sedgwick begins "Pedagogy of Buddhism," for instance, with what seems like an inconsequential anecdote about cats: "What does it mean when our cats bring small, wounded animals into the house?" (*Touching Feeling* 153). She turns to anthropologist Elizabeth Marshall Thomas for an answer. Thomas acknowledges the widespread belief that when cats bring still-living prey indoors they are offering gifts, but her analysis of what she calls cat culture suggests instead that they are instead trying to train us to kill, just as a mother cat will train her kittens by giving them practice with a wounded animal.[12] If we accept that Thomas's interpretation of cat behavior has some validity, as Sedgwick does, it is humbling to realize how badly we have misread this pedagogical scene. Humans are not figures of authority, but students, and poor students at that, who have not even recognized they are being trained. For Sedgwick's readers, it may be equally humbling to recognize that what they thought was simply an amusing opening gambit about a cat is, in fact, a deeper puzzle about teaching and learning. Sedgwick has offered this story in order to teach them what to do with it. She disrupts assumptions about when and how they are learning and raises the question: if we do not know whether we are teachers or students in encounters with cats, how many similar misperceptions about teaching and learning are occurring in our own classrooms?

Sedgwick brings up her cat again later to demonstrate a pedagogical paradox about what it means to know. She begins: "Whenever I want my cat to look at something instructive—a full moon, say, or a photograph of herself—a predictable choreography ensues. I point at the thing I want her to look at, and she, roused to curiosity, fixes her attention on the tip of my extended index finger and begins to explore it with delicate sniffs" (168). "Every time this scene of failed pedagogy gets enacted," Sedgwick continues, "(and it's frequent, because I am no better at learning not to point than my cat is at learning not to sniff) the two of us are caught in a pedagogical problematic that has fascinated teachers of Buddhism since Sakyamuni" (168).[13] In Buddhist writing, she explains, the problem illustrated by the story of her cat is referred to as "pointing at the moon." It is a scene of failed teaching that can be read as an admonition not to adhere too closely to a text or an authority. Sedgwick's lesson about the finger pointing at the moon directs attention (that is, points) to an element of the pedagogy of koans that is also at work in Fadiman's book: the search to know something reveals what one does not and perhaps cannot know. The pointing finger indicates the human "attraction to phenomena in all their immeasurable, inarticulable specificity" (171); it expresses our desire to know the moon for *what it is*. At the same time, however, the whole of the experience reveals the moon's "ineffability, ungraspability, and indeed emptiness of self-nature" (170).

Sedgwick's chapter, "Pedagogy of Buddhism," functions like this koan. She encourages readers to recognize her text as a pointing finger, and also to see that fully understanding her embodied, affective, and cognitive experience in the bardo remains beyond our reach. Playfully, she also draws attention to her koanlike approach as a writer by inserting small icons of pointing hands throughout her text. Each chapter in *Touching Feeling* begins with the image of two hands pointing at each other and, in this final chapter, icons of single pointing hands appear at the beginning of each new section, in lieu of subtitles. Sedgwick displays a willingness to learn, unlearn, and relearn, not by making an argument for a particular theory or methodology, but by experimenting with ideas and performance. There will be critics who therefore decide that *Touching Feeling*, particularly the chapter on "Pedagogy of Buddhism," lacks sufficient theory or method.[14] In seeking to pin down her logic, such readers may look at the pointing finger of her text—at its language and sources—and miss that she is pointing elsewhere. What might we see if we look beyond the pointing finger? Sedgwick's work raises questions about what Latour would call her "matters of concern"—why and how we read and write, why and how we teach and learn—all of which are connected to how we approach living and dying.

While Sedgwick's writing performs her reparative pedagogy—and this reminds us that all academic writing performs a pedagogy of one kind or another—her chapter does not reveal details about her practice in the classroom. The only time she published an account of her teaching was, perhaps surprisingly, not about a class in theory or literature, but about a *writing* class. "Teaching 'Experimental Critical Writing'" appeared in 1998, during the period when she was working on the chapters collected in *Touching Feeling*. In it, she describes a course in which she sought "to trouble and interrupt" students' sense of academic writing so that they "[would] not lose touch with their own writerly energies" (104). Why does she teach reparative practices through writing rather than reading, at least in this instance? Writing is a practice that results in a published performance so that students learn to attend to how their writing *acts* in the world and to what writing *does* for readers, as well as for the writer, the subject of the text, and critical practice in general. Although Sedgwick's focus is on writing, one effect of her writing pedagogy is to make the private act of reading public.

The assignments for Sedgwick's experimental writing class ask her students to think about how their work meaningfully participates in culture in ways that are not contained by the usual boundaries of criticism. Sedgwick generally assigned a short piece of writing every week, "organized around very specific formal choices and/or constraints" (105). Her assignments focused on performative utterances, often narrowing students' attention to rhetorical elements of everyday address—voice, pronouns, quotation—that also resonate personally, philosophically, spiritually, bodily, artistically, and politically. For example, she asked them to write a piece in which the grammatical person changes at least once ("I" becomes "you" or "they" becomes "he") and to reflect on how that grammatical person functions as "a heuristic" (108). Students also defined keywords, attending to how definitions employ a range of genres— historical narrative, ethnographic description, differentiation, and prescription (108). In response to her assignment on "Truth Effects," they wrote short essays that used a specific rhetorical gesture that is familiar in critical essays: "In short, we have been telling ourselves some lies" (109). This assignment, like the others, urged students to slow down and thoughtfully consider their prose and its relationships to the audience, the writer, and the world.

The assignment that speaks most directly to the question of how to teach less suspicious reading practices concerns "the Obituary Imperative" (110). Sedgwick did not explicitly define what she meant by "the Obituary Imperative," but she instructed her students to "Write a . . . piece that pays some attention to, or makes some use of, the issues of representation and address that attach to the processes of loss and mourning" (110). She told them, as well, to think about how "obituary issues and impulses may already be part of such everyday practices as historical or textual scholarship; sexuality and genderedness; activism; urban, domestic, and landscape space; advertising and the media, etc." (110). Then she asked, "What do such usages do, and what could they?" (110). This is a very open assignment, one that leaves to the students the task of figuring out what imperatives impinge on expressions of loss and where the force of convention limits what it is possible to say and think about the dying and dead.

Sedgwick offers readers no examples of what her students produced, but elsewhere in her own works—*Dialogue on Love,* her cancer journalism, and throughout *Touching Feeling*—there is ample evidence of her commitment to experimenting with how mourning and loss can be represented and addressed. In fact, Sedgwick used the phrase "obituary imperative" once before, in a published talk entitled "White Glasses," where she speaks about a dying friend, the gay activist and poet Michael Lynch. When she began writing "White Glasses," Lynch appeared to be about to die of AIDS, so she planned to write a memorial essay. As she wrote, however, his health rallied while she was diagnosed with breast cancer. The subject and object of her memorial became unstable. She could not write about her friend's approaching death without also contemplating her own. Against this uncertainty, Sedgwick defines the obituary imperative—as represented in the AIDS Names Project Quilt—as a "ravenously denuding, homogenizing, relentlessly anthropomorphizing and yet relentlessly disorienting . . . format of memorial relation and address" (265). She abhors these rhetorical constraints on the performance of memorializing, but she also knows she cannot ignore conventions and expectations as she writes for and about a beloved friend.

Watching Lynch approach death, Sedgwick wonders, in words that anticipate the final chapter of *Touching Feeling*, "out of what spaces I may speak of it, or be spoken for" (266).[15] This is a question that every autobiographer and every writer of an illness memoir must consider. Sedgwick's request that her students think carefully about how they both speak and are spoken for also has implications for criticism. If her students learn to read as attentively as they write, then they are more likely to be thoughtful about other writers' choices and constraints. If they step aside from the paranoid imperative and recognize evidence of a writer's intentions and agency in the realm of composing, they have the opportunity to see not just the text's authority, but also where the text and author are pointing.

Illness as Many Narratives

Sedgwick's pedagogy of the bardo ultimately suggests an approach to rereading Fadiman's *The Spirit Catches You and You Fall Down*. Readers who look at the text as an expression of Fadiman's authority are inclined to see it as self-explanatory or suspicious, and thus do not see what she is pointing at. As I see it, Fadiman's book points at knowledge itself—how to learn, how to think in new ways, how to encounter the unknown, how to communicate what one knows to others and how to acknowledge what one does not know. I am struck by a paragraph in Fadiman's preface, where she writes that she is most interested in where edges meet, like "shorelines, weather fronts, international borders" (xiii). She explains, "there are interesting frictions and incongruities in these places, and often, if you stand at the point of tangency, you can see both sides better than if you were in the middle of either one" (xiii). With her book, she is pointing toward such a realm of instability and uncertainty.

Fadiman puts her readers on an edge in *The Spirit Catches You* and keeps them there by interleaving chapters about the Lees and their American doctors, ancient Hmong history and an account of how the Hmong were used—and later discarded—by the United States during the Vietnam War, ethnographic portraits of Merced's Hmong community and the biomedical culture of its medical center. In the context of these intersecting narratives that reach across time and space, it is clearer than ever that Lia's medical diagnosis was just one narrative among many, not a preeminent truth. Fadiman draws attention to the cultural aspects of biomedical practice and thus positions her readers to question the *completeness* of Western medicine, even as she never questions that Lia has epilepsy or that it is best controlled with Western medicine. Readers may sense, if not fully understand, the significance of the Hmong worldview, which holds that the body, soul, and world are one, that illness indicates a world out of balance, and that any alteration of the body, whether from surgery, blood sampling, or medication, may threaten the eternal soul for all future lifetimes. Fadiman's gathering of these different pieces suggests how many stories one needs to accumulate to gain even a limited understanding of the life of one small girl. No story or combination of stories provides a complete picture of what happened or why. Fadiman may appear to seek final answers to the questions posed by Lia's case, but ultimately she asks readers to recognize not what they know, but what they do not know and perhaps cannot know.

With her narrative about the borderland where cultures meet, Fadiman draws attention to the complexity of knowledge, as well as the difficulty of her literary project. In the book's second chapter, for instance, she tells the story of an intermediate French class at the local community college. The teacher assigned a five-minute oral presentation, and a Hmong student chose to explain how to make *la soupe de poisson*: "To prepare Fish Soup, he said, you must have a fish, and in order to have a fish, you have to go fishing. In order to go fishing, you need a hook, and in order to choose the right hook, you need to know whether the fish you are fishing for lives in fresh or salt water, how big it is, and what shape its mouth is" (12). Fadiman observes that, "continuing in this vein for forty-five minutes, the student filled the black-board with a complexly branching tree of factors and options, a sort of piscatory flowchart, written in French with an overlay of Hmong" (12). This approach to storytelling, Fadiman explains, "is often used at the beginning of [a Hmong] oral narrative as a way of reminding the listeners that the world is full of things that may not seem to be connected but actually are; that no event occurs in isolation; that you can miss a lot by sticking to the point; and that the storyteller is likely to be rather long-winded" (13).

If Fadiman were Hmong, she tells her readers, she might have begun to tell Lia's story by recounting "the *first* beginning of the world" but, since she is not, she will "go back only a few hundred generations" (13). Fadiman adopts this narrative strategy when she finds herself surrounded by hundreds of pages of notes, photocopies, and clippings and realizes that she has no idea how to categorize them all. The same page might belong in folders about medicine, mental health, animism, shamanism, social structure, or the body/mind/soul continuum. Amid a sea of paper, she realizes she "was suspended in a large bowl of Fish Soup. Medicine *was* religion. Religion was society. Society was medicine. Even economics were mixed up in there somewhere" (60). To tell Lia's story, therefore, Fadiman sets information about cultures, practices, and beliefs—as well as different sections and versions of Lia's story—beside one another. She tries to avoid positioning these fragments in hierarchical relation. It is clear, however, that the stories that inform her understanding of Lia's experience are fundamentally more compelling than the stories of the doctors, and Fadiman makes no secret about how much she has grown to love the Lee family. Still, she does not attempt to resolve or even explain the asymmetries and tensions between of the two main versions of Lia's story—those of her parents and doctors.

At the end of the penultimate chapter, Fadiman writes of a dinner to which she invited a physician and a psychotherapist who should have had a lot in common. Both were Peace Corps veterans and both had been involved in Lia's case. Sitting beside each other, however, they cannot agree on the basic principles of treatment because they do not share the same worldview. The physician is certain that the ethical course of action in Lia's case was to protect the child's life even if her parents opposed treatment. "If the child dies," he argues, "she won't get the chance to decide twenty years down the road if she wants to accept her parents' beliefs or if she wants to reject them" (277). The therapist, on the other hand sees that attitude as "tyranny." If the family believes the illness has a spiritual cause, and altering the body with surgery might bring about eternal damnation, "death might not seem so important." "Which is more important," she asks, "the life or the soul?" (277). They cannot agree, and Fadiman, having led readers to a point where they can *acknowledge* both positions, if not understand them equally, leaves them in this quandary. She places them and herself in a location that evokes Sedgwick's description of the reparative position, "near the boundary of what a writer can't figure out how to say readily, never mind prescribe to others" (2). Even though the question about the life or the soul urgently needs an answer, no single answer will ever suffice.

Fadiman then faces the challenge of ending her narrative in a way that provides a satisfying conclusion, but that does not falsely resolve any of the conflicts that have made Lia's case so difficult. How can she conclude in a manner that preserves reparative potential and does not encourage readers to focus on the pointing finger rather than the ineffable? The final chapter of *The Spirit Catches You*, "Sacrifice," describes an elaborate healing ceremony performed for Lia and her family in which a shaman sacrifices two pigs, a small one to protect the health of the family, and a larger one whose soul is released in the hopes that Lia's soul might finally return. In this chapter, Fadiman recounts the experience of being physically inside the shaman's strange and powerful narrative. In Taylor's discussion of Fadiman's book, she observes that shamans function through a particular form of narrative performance and that narratives themselves may function as a "form of shamanic activity" (173). In this last chapter, Fadiman is in the process of handing over her position as narrator-shaman so that the story can continue without her.

Fadiman, like many of her readers, one might presume, enters the ritual skeptically. There is something comic about an ancient ceremony being performed in a cramped apartment where the altar is covered with the sports section of the *Merced Star,* holy water is poured into Styrofoam cups, the winged horse that will carry the shaman through a door in the sky is a crude bench, and the shaman himself casually spends his time before the ceremony watching Winnie the Pooh cartoons on television. After the first sacrifice, however, she can sense that the shaman "shrugged all the American incongruities off his outer aspect, and his inner aspect . . . now shone through, bright and hard" (283). He enters a trance, his soul leaves his body, and he risks his life to help the Lees. At this point, Fadiman narrates her experience as a witness to the drama of Lia's soul-calling without irony, without skepticism. Like her reader, she is caught up physically and mentally in a story that she does not control. The book comes to a close not with her words, but with the chant of the soul-caller. Again and again he calls, "Come home." There is no closure or catharsis. The process of calling Lia's soul home is without end.

This is one version of a reparative reading of *The Spirit Catches You,* a reading that has developed out of my engagement with all of the other narratives I have discussed in this book. While I have learned from how others have written about Fadiman's text, in my own conclusion I have tried to attend to the moon toward which Fadiman's narrative points. In this narrative of illness, as in many others, the ailing body points to culture, pain points to philosophy, language points to consciousness, and all point to what is still to be learned about our fragility, our mortality, and how to live a meaningful life.

NOTES

Chapter 1. Illness Narratives and the Challenge to Criticism

1. See the following American histories of World War I, in which the influenza pandemic receives scant mention: Kennedy, *Over Here;* Zeiger, *America's Great War;* Keene, *Doughboys, the Great War, and the Remaking of America;* and Morrow, *The Great War.* For a view of the significance of influenza in World War I, see Byerly, *Fever of War.*

2. Belling speculates in "Overwhelming the Medium" that "perhaps the flu overwhelmed language in ways that war did not" (57). Belling's study focuses on fiction. Dolezal writes about the 1918 flu in Willa Cather's *One of Ours* in "'Waste in a Great Enterprise.'"

3. This literature, it should be noted, did not reflect the full spectrum of those who were sick or infected: the vast majority of memoirs and fiction that were published in the last decades of the twentieth century were by or about economically privileged gay men. Few published works appeared by intravenous drug users, the urban poor in the United States, or those from impoverished regions across the globe.

4. It is virtually impossible to track the total number of lay or literary texts published about particular diseases, but the searchable *Modern Language International Bibliography* provides rough data about the number of scholarly texts that have appeared about diseases such as influenza, cancer, and HIV/AIDS, as well as about disabilities. The *Bibliography* lists only 6 entries in English about influenza, 4 of which appeared between 2000 and 2007. There are 166 listings under "cancer": only 2 appeared before 1980, and the numbers have been steadily increasing, from 24 in the 1980s, to 54 in the 1990s, and 86 between 2000 and 2008. For HIV/AIDS, by contrast, there are 713 listings, with the earliest in 1984. While only 27 articles related to AIDS appeared in the 1980s, 435 texts were published in the 1990s, and 250 between 2000 and 2008. Recently, the number of texts about disability have surpassed the number about HIV/AIDS. In the 1980s, 79 texts about disability appeared, with the earliest listing in 1980. This was followed by 192 published texts in the 1990s, and 438 between 2000 and 2008.

5. For critical overviews of the literary response to HIV/AIDS, see Brophy, *Witnessing AIDS;* Chambers, *AIDS Writing* and *Facing It;* Couser, *Recovering Bodies;* Kruger, *AIDS Narratives;* Murphy and Poirier, *Writing AIDS;* Nelson, *AIDS;* Pastore, *Confronting AIDS.*

6. See Nelson's introduction to *AIDS,* in which he rejects comparisons to other literary traditions about suffering. Instead, he "insist[s] on the uniqueness of the literature of AIDS. AIDS writing is produced in response to a puzzling and unmanageable medical catastrophe, primarily by individuals on the sexual margins who have been most profoundly affected. It is a diverse body of literature that documents, disrupts, testifies, protests, even celebrates" (3).

7. Foundational texts about the importance of narratives about illness include: Brody, *Stories of Sickness;* Charon, *Narrative Medicine;* Frank, *The Wounded Storyteller;* A. H. Hawkins, *Reconstructing Illness;* Hunter, *Doctors' Stories;* Kleinman, *Illness Narratives;* Mattingly, *Healing Dramas and Clinical Plots.*

8. See, for instance, Harrington, *The Cure Within;* D. B. Morris's two books, *The Culture of Pain* and *Illness and Culture in the Postmodern Age;* Mukhergee, *The Emperor of All Maladies;* Wald, *Contagious.*

9. Only in professional healthcare journals, particularly nursing journals, could one find personal accounts of the epidemic. See, for example, G. R., "Experiences during the Influenza Epidemic," and Thorne, "Four Weeks of Influenza," both of which appeared in the *American Journal of Nursing.*

10. Thomas Mann's *The Magic Mountain,* published in German in 1924, would not appear in English translation for several years.

11. Examples include Bromberg, *The Mind of Man;* Ingram, "Encephalitis"; Aldrich, *The Story of Burns;* and Newsholme, *Fifty Years in Public Health.*

12. See Wilson, *Living with Polio,* which is based on 150 patient narratives, many of them book-length. Most of these were published in the 1950s through the early 1960s, following the worst years of the epidemic in the United States.

13. A representative sample of such texts includes Clarke, "Katherine Mansfield's Illness"; Keevil, "The Illness of Charles"; Waterlow, "Illness and Death of Mozart"; White, "The Last Illness of Major Walter Reed."

14. Editor John H. Knowles entitled his 1977 book about the ambiguous achievements of the American healthcare system *Doing Better and Feeling Worse.*

15. For a rhetorical and sociological exploration of the emergence and evolution of *Our Bodies, Ourselves,* see Wells, *"Our Bodies, Ourselves" and the Work of Writing.*

16. Sontag's argument notably pushed against the democratizing tendency of other studies of illness and health in her era, and yet her argument is the most enduring of them all.

17. For detailed discussions of AIDS activism, see Epstein, *Impure Science* and Chambre, *Fighting for Our Lives.*

18. I take the phrase "limits of autobiography" from the title of Gilmore's book.

19. See Berger, ed., *The Crisis of Criticism.* This anthology contains Croce's article "Discussing the Undiscussable" and a collection of responses, including Oates, "Confronting Head-On the Face of the Afflicted," originally published in the *New York Times,*

and Bhabha, "Dance This Diss Around," originally published in *Artforum*. Additional criticism of Croce includes Teachout, "Victim Art," as well as commentary by Goldstein from the *Village Voice*, Rich from the *New York Times*, and Kushner from the *New Yorker*.

20. Conway begins *Illness and the Limits of Expression* by repudiating Croce's article; Couser concludes *Recovering Bodies* by arguing that Croce's logic serves to intensify cultural stigmas against illness and disability (291); Diedrich begins and ends *Treatments* by both rejecting and working with elements of Croce's argument.

21. See Spelman, *Fruits of Sorrow*, which closes with a chapter about Croce and the "aesthetic usability of suffering" (133).

22. See Garber, "Compassion"; Ahmed, *The Cultural Politics of Emotion;* and Spelman, *Fruits of Sorrow*.

23. See also Berlant, "The Subject of True Feeling" and *The Female Complaint*.

24. See Berlant's own critique of compassion in her introduction to *Compassion,* "Compassion (and Withholding)," where she writes that compassion is "in operation . . . a term denoting privilege: the sufferer is *over there*" (4).

Chapter 2. Life Narratives in the Risk Society

1. For a history of the concept of risk and the efforts to master risk, see Bernstein, *Against the Gods*.

2. Beck's *Risk Society* was originally published in German in 1986 and was first published in English in 1992.

3. In this discussion, I have set aside one of Beck's central and unsupported claims, the theory that late-modern risks affect everyone equally, regardless of social status. For a critique from within sociology, see Tulloch and Lupton, "Risk, the Mass Media and Personal Biography." Tulloch and Lupton argue that Beck "over-emphasiz[es] both invisible risks and the emergence of a new public sphere" (25). They object that Beck denies the significance of history, class, and the politics of everyday life. In *Risk and Everyday Life,* Tulloch and Lupton also criticize Beck for his macrosociological perspective and his "overly rationalistic and individualistic model of the human actor and for his tendency to generalize, failing to pay sufficient attention to the roles played by gender, age, social class, ethnicity, nationality and so on in constructing differing risk knowledges and experiences" (6). For additional arguments against Beck's thesis, see Mythen's overview in "Reappraising the Risk Society Thesis" and Lupton's *Risk*.

4. A vast archive of scholarship on risk was published after Beck's *Risk Society.* In my research I have consulted the following texts: Beck, Giddens, and Lash, *Reflexive Modernization;* Beck and Beck-Gernsheim, *Individualization;* Giddens, *The Consequences of Modernity* and *Modernity and Self-Identity;* Douglas, *Risk and Blame;* Wilkinson, *Anxiety in a Risk Society*. Excellent overviews include Mythen, *Ulrich Beck* and "Reappraising the Risk Society Thesis"; Lupton, *Risk;* Mythen and Walklate, eds., *Beyond the Risk Society;* and Peterson and Wilkinson, eds., *Health, Risk and Vulnerability*. See also Hacking, *The Taming of Chance,* and Woodward, "Statistical Panic."

5. Couser's studies of life writing, *Recovering Bodies* and *Vulnerable Subjects,* offer accounts of disability narratives that are quite different from Davis's argument that the

novel enforces normalcy. Couser sees disability memoirs as reclaiming the body from social marginalization and medical discourse.

6. For a discussion of anxiety in response to risk, see Wilkinson, *Anxiety in a Risk Society*. See also the introduction to Peterson and Wilkinson, *Health, Risk and Vulnerability*. While information about health risks may be intended to offer patients the opportunity to take greater control over their lives, they write, "at the level of everyday experience it may serve more to heighten people's sense of vulnerability before the contingencies of life" (5).

7. Heise, "Toxins, Drugs, and Global Systems," shows how the theme of risk affects the narrative form of Don DeLillo's *White Noise* and Richard Powers's *Gain*. Heise finds that postmodern narratives suit the topic of risk. In these novels, she explains, "Many of the hyperboles and the simulations that have typically been interpreted as examples of postmodern inauthenticity become . . . manifestations of daily encounters with risks whose reality cannot be assessed with certainty" (757). See also Buell, "Toxic Discourse." Beyond literary theory, medical historian Allan Brandt, in "Behavior, Disease, and Health," analyzes the ways in which the American cultural obsession with controlling risk has translated into a medical narrative about blame in which disease becomes a sign of moral failure. Anthropologist Mary Douglas also discusses the relationship of blame to risk in *Risk and Blame*.

8. The claims about biography made by Beck, Beck-Gernscheim, and Giddens echo scholarship about the narrative identity thesis—the contention that, as Oliver Sacks has claimed, "each of us constructs and lives a 'narrative,' and that this narrative *is* us, our identities" (110) or, in the words of Paul John Eakin, that "narrative and identity are performed simultaneously" (*How Our Lives* 101). These risk society theorists do not, however, explicitly argue that narrative is constitutive of identity. For more on the debate about narrative identity, see Eakin, *Living Autobiographically,* and the debate in the journal *Narrative* in response to Eakin's "What Are We Reading." See, in particular, Phelan, "Who's Here?" and Butte, "I Know That I Know."

9. Jain, "Living in Prognosis," offers a risk narrative embedded in a work of criticism.

10. Gould died in 2002 of an unrelated cancer.

11. Herman, "Stories as a Tool for Thinking," argues for "the advantages of viewing narrative theory as a subdomain of cognitive science, broadly conceived." "From that perspective," he writes, "stories can be studied as a primary resource for building and updating models for understanding the world—and also for creating and sustaining the supra- or transindividual 'society of mind' . . . in which such intelligence consists" (185).

12. Rieff's writing generally focuses on large-scale brutality and suffering in places such as Iraq, Bosnia, and Rwanda and the complex moral issues at the heart of both military intervention and humanitarian aid. See *At the Point of a Gun, A Bed for the Night,* and *Slaughterhouse*.

13. "Cancer Free at 33" is part of a *New York Times* series, *The DNA Age,* for which reporter Amy Harmon won a Pulitzer Prize in 2008.

14. For current information about the risks posed by these gene mutations, see the National Cancer Institute's Web page on "Genetic Testing for BRCA1 and BRCA2."

15. Literary criticism has just begun to address how genomics are affecting what and how we write and read. See the special issue of *Literature and Medicine* on "Genomics in Literature, Visual Arts, and Culture," edited by Wald, Clayton, and Holloway.

16. There is a popular misconception that prophylactic surgery is an economic indulgence for women with BRCA1 or BRCA2, or an overexpenditure by insurance companies. While the operation is certainly costly, it is significantly less expensive than cancer treatment—which also often involves surgery, chemotherapy and/or radiation, all of which may be needed again if the cancer metastasizes. See Anderson et al., "Cost Effectiveness of Preventive Strategies."

17. See Couser's discussion of *Mapping Fate* in *Vulnerable Subjects*.

18. Susanne Antonetta is the pen name of Suzanne Paola.

19. In common usage, the terms "chance" and "risk" tend to be used interchangeably, although the outcome of chance is more often thought to be unanticipated and unpredictable.

20. Using more specific terms from narrative studies, Abbott writes that Darwin's concepts of natural selection and species are "not . . . narrative entities at all": they are "neither Propp's 'characters' . . . nor Greimas's 'actors' and 'actants,' . . . nor Chatman's 'existents'" (144).

21. For Abbott, the absence of agents, as well as cause and effect in the theory of natural selection explains the advantage of the creationist myth as a popular story. Because humans are cognitively predisposed to knowledge that can be explained in narrative, he asserts, the story of natural selection resists understanding (145–46). Thus, in the struggle for narrative survival—Darwin's explanation of natural selection versus the tale of creationism—creationism has "a distinct cognitive advantage" (153).

22. In Abbott's discussion of the narrative challenge posed by chance, he finds elements of postmodernism in Darwin's Victorian text: "In Darwin's scheme of gradual change by infinite variations, chance is not simply decisive but a matter of starting anew always and everywhere, throwing the dice over and over. In this regard, Darwin's was a dull masterplot, an incursion of postmodern discord into one of the great ages of narrative orthodoxy" (148).

23. An incomplete list of novels that address 9/11 or its aftermath includes: Kalfus, *A Disorder Peculiar to the Country;* Messud, *The Emperor's Children;* Foer, *Extremely Loud and Incredibly Close;* DeLillo, *Falling Man;* Hamid, *The Reluctant Fundamentalist;* Rushdie, *Shalimar, the Clown;* Updike, *Terrorist;* Schwartz, *The Writing on the Wall;* Walter, *The Zero.*

24. See news accounts from CNN and BBC: "European Protesters Fill Cities," "'Million' March against Iraq War," and "Millions Join Global Anti-War Protests."

25. I have adapted Deborah Lupton's term "cocoon of invulnerability," but use it differently than she does. In *Risk,* Lupton writes that *trust* "allows individuals to develop a cocoon of invulnerability which enables them to get on with life, to fend off their knowledge of the risks that await them at every turn" (82). McEwan's novel does not exclude trust, but rather emphasizes that people construct such protected spaces for creative work or sensual and aesthetic experience.

26. In the second volume of her biography of Darwin, Browne writes that Darwin's addition of "the Creator" to the second and subsequent editions was "a concession that he later regretted" (96).

Chapter 3. Responding to the Pain of Others

1. For a historical overview of pain, see Rey, *The History of Pain*. Additional pain narratives include Andrews, *Codeine Diary;* Kumin, *Inside the Halo and Beyond;* and Levy, *A Brain Wider than the Sky.* See also Biro, *The Language of Pain.*

2. A search of Google Books for the exact phrase "pain does not simply resist language but actively destroys it" locates 194 books that contain this line from *The Body in Pain* (29 June 2011). The same search in Google Scholar shows that Scarry's claim is quoted in nearly 200 academic articles about trauma and narrative—far too many to list. A few recent examples include Sweeney, "The Unmaking of the World"; DeMeester, "Trauma and Recovery"; and Hesford, "Reading *Rape Stories.*"

3. Scholarship that uses Scarry's theory of pain's unspeakability includes Schweizer, *Suffering and the Remedy of Art;* Stanley, "The Patient's Voice"; and Goldberg, "Exilic Effects of Illness and Pain." Other studies engage Scarry's work in order to qualify her assertions, among them Bending, "Approximation, Suggestion, and Analogy," and van Hooft, "Pain and Communication." References to Scarry's work also appear in texts about politics, anthropology, medical training, and more, including Kushner and Thomasma, *Ward Ethics,* and Biro's memoir, *One Hundred Days.*

4. Daudet's editor and translator, Julian Barnes, explains the reference to "the boot." It was "a form of torture which involved planks of wood being roped to the sides of the legs, and then the ropes tightened with wedges until the legs were crushed" (21).

5. For further discussion of Daudet's "varieties of pain," see Bending, "Approximation, Suggestion, and Analogy."

6. The International Association for the Study of Pain defines pain as "an unpleasant sensory and emotional experience associated with actual or potential tissue damage, or described in terms of such damage." Its definition also notes "the inability to communicate verbally does not negate the possibility that an individual is experiencing pain and is in need of appropriate pain-relieving treatment. Pain is always subjective. Each individual learns the application of the word through experiences related to injury in early life" ("IASP Pain Terminology"). This subtle explanation of pain emphasizes its subjective nature, and even draws attention to the fact that the language used to describe pain may be figurative.

7. A similar argument appears in the introduction to Kleinman, Brodwin, Good, and Good, *Pain as Human Experience.* Looking cross-culturally and historically at language and pain, they maintain that there has been a "relative weakening in the modern era of moral and religious vocabularies, both in collective representations and the language of experts," and that, "in the contemporary discourses on pain or other forms of suffering—expert and popular—the idea of suffering has been attenuated, sometimes trivialized, and at times expunged altogether, although it may remain resonant in the personal

and family encounter with suffering" (13–14). See also the interdisciplinary collection edited by Coakley and Shelemay, *Pain and Its Transformations.*

8. Morris further discusses the interconnection of biology and culture in Davis and Morris, "Biocultures Manifesto."

9. In making this argument, Morris extends scholarship that emphasizes the importance of narratives in medical settings. In medical anthropology these include Kleinman, *The Illness Narratives;* Mattingly, *Healing Dramas and Clinical Plots;* and Mattingly and Garro, eds., *Narrative and the Cultural Construction of Illness and Healing.* In the medical humanities, foundational texts about narrative and medicine include Brody, *Stories of Sickness;* Charon, *Narrative Medicine;* Frank, *The Wounded Storyteller;* Hunter, *Doctors' Stories;* and Greenhalgh and Hurwitz, eds., *Narrative Based Medicine.*

10. A search of the medical profession's primary research database, PubMed, for articles related to pain published in medical journals, reveals that 9,105 articles with this subject appeared between May 1990 and May 1991. The number of published articles on pain has increased by about one thousand articles a year since 1990. Between May 2009 and May 2010, 29,857 articles with the subject "pain" were published.

11. Scarry expresses hope for humane progress in medicine because of contributions such as the McGill Questionnaire.

12. In *Camp Pain,* Jackson notes similar problems with what she sees as the objectification of pain and the ambiguity of language in the McGill Pain Questionnaire (156).

13. In *The Culture of Pain,* Morris points out what has been missed by many: that the second half of Scarry's book offers a grand theory of "the origin and development of human culture" in which "pain [is] the unseen basis for every act of cultural creation, from a wool overcoat to Keats's 'Ode to Autumn'" (6).

14. The long list of critical articles that work with Scarry's discussion of pain and silence include Schweizer, "To Give Suffering a Language"; Boureau, "Pain and the Unmaking of Self"; and McKim, "Making Poetry of Pain."

15. In *The Language of Pain,* Biro redefines pain as "an all-consuming interior experience that threatens to destroy everything except itself *and can only be described through metaphor*" (75). Biro does not mean that we should strive to talk as Tolstoy or Joyce write, but rather that writers like these make visible "the range of the possible" with regard to the expression of pain (17). The paperback edition of *The Language of Pain* published in 2011 has a new title: *Listening to Pain.*

16. In *Reading Lolita in Tehran,* Nafisi also claims that literature can have transformative moral and political effects on readers in the least likely circumstances. For a very different assessment of the imagination, see Scarry, "The Difficulty of Imagining Other Persons."

17. The spelling of the name Sa'adat Hasan Manto varies according to the source. It is even spelled differently in two versions of Das's essay, "Language and Body." I use the spelling from Das's most recent version of the essay, published in her book *Life and Words.* The title of Manto's story has also been translated differently in various editions. Translator Khalid Hassan calls it "The Return" in a collection entitled *Mottled Dawn.*

18. Das works from Manto's untranslated text, and in this instance offers her own translation: "Open it." Khalid Hassan translates the doctor as saying, "Open the window" (14).

19. See Das and Nandy, "Violence, Victimhood and the Language of Silence."

Chapter 4. Sontag, Suffering, and the Work of Writing

1. *On Photography* and *Illness as Metaphor* have the rare status among books of criticism of having been best sellers. *On Photography* sold 40,000 copies in hardback and *Illness as Metaphor* performed "at least as well" (Foer). They have each remained in print for over thirty years.

2. Entering "illness is the night-side of life" into Google yields 20,000 results, an incomplete catalog of the occasions when Sontag's description of illness appears in epigrams, self-help Web pages, and articles (29 June 2011). The same search in Google Books locates 287 texts containing the phrase, and a search in Google Scholar finds 141 references in academic sources. In a memorial essay about Sontag, "Bearing Witness," Rita Charon acknowledges the exceptional influence of this passage: "It is the rare book in social medicine that does not cite Susan Sontag's opening sentence in *Illness as Metaphor*" (756).

3. In *Treatments*, Diedrich notes that, although readers who focus on the opening metaphor appear to have "misread" her work, the split in the reception of Sontag's text occurs because both her metaphor and her argument against metaphor are *useful* to those who are ill (29).

4. In "Against Interpretation," Sontag argues that theory comes between art and its audience. She calls instead for "an erotics of art," a direct, sensual aesthetic experience, unmediated by interpretation (14).

5. Sontag encountered these images two months after the Germans surrendered to Allied forces in early May 1945. Bergen-Belsen was liberated on 15 April 1945 and Dachau was liberated on 29 April 1945. It is a bit surprising that even American *Vogue* had photographer (and former model) Lee Miller accompany the troops and document the liberation of Buchenwald and Dachau. Miller's biographer, Carolyn Burke, describes the layout of the *Vogue* article, with text and photographs by Miller: the article was "punctuated by sets of juxtaposed images—'German children, well-fed, healthy' next to 'burned bones of starved prisoners'; 'orderly villages, patterned, quiet' opposite 'orderly furnaces to burn bodies'—then some of her most disturbing shots from the camps" (*Lee Miller*, 265). See also Zox-Weaver, "When the War Was in *Vogue*."

6. Sontag's chapter title, "In Plato's Cave," makes explicit the similarities between her text and the "Allegory of the Cave" from Plato's *Republic*. In the allegory, Plato, like Sontag, is concerned with the problem that unenlightened thinkers mistake appearance for reality.

7. When Sontag says that photographs "acknowledge," she defines what these images accomplish as lesser than *explanation;* she values knowledge over acknowledgment. Her use of the term could not be more different than that of Stanley Cavell, discussed in chapter 3 of this book. For Cavell, "acknowledgment" is a practice that solves the philo-

sophical problem of other minds— that we cannot *know* other people with certainty. In everyday social encounters, Cavell notes, we do not demand that all knowledge of others be confirmed. Even if we do not have full knowledge, we can acknowledge others by accepting the complexity, necessity, and meaningfulness of social engagement.

8. Butler, "Photography, War, Outrage," similarly observes that "something of a persistent split takes place for Sontag between being affected and being able to think and understand; this difference is represented in the differing effects of photography and prose" (824).

9. Sontag's son David Rieff stated that her essays on Barthes, Benjamin, and Canetti are the closest she has ever come to autobiography. See Rieff, "Remembering Susan Sontag."

10. Sontag discusses her efforts to achieve a unity of her personal self and writer-self in a short essay, "Singleness," first published in 1995.

11. A measure of Sontag's changing interests is evident in her shifting patterns of publication. Between 1972 and 1980, Sontag published sixteen lengthy articles in the *New York Review of Books*. From 1980 to 1990, by contrast, she published only one essay—an article-length version of *AIDS and Its Metaphors*. During that period, however, she was active in PEN and signed thirteen formal letters regarding violations of the rights of writers in Guatemala, Poland, Vietnam, Czechoslovakia, Turkey, India, Hungary, Korea, Cuba, and Sudan.

12. Sontag published two novels early in her career—*The Benefactor* in 1963 and *Death Kit* in 1967—and continued to write short fiction for the next two decades, some of which was collected in *I, etcetera* in 1978.

13. The radical transformation of Sontag's views on realist fiction were widely noted after she returned to writing novels. Acocella's essay "The Hunger Artist" contains Sontag's complaint about the "omnipotent author" who makes her "compassionate and tearful," as does Paulsen's interview with Rieff for Salon.com, "Susan Sontag's Final Wish."

14. For more on Nussbaum's theory of compassion, see *Upheavals of Thought*.

15. For more on "narrative emotions," see Nussbaum, "Narrative Emotions," which originally appeared in *Ethics* and was later reprinted in *Love's Knowledge*.

16. In 2000, Sontag won the National Book Award for *In America*, another realist love story, steeped in history and brimming with detail about nineteenth-century American immigration and theater.

17. See Williams, *England's Mistress*, as well as the film *That Hamilton Woman* (1941), by screenwriters Walter Reisch and R. C. Sherriff, which starred Vivian Leigh (as Emma) and Laurence Olivier (Lord Nelson).

18. Kakutani's review of *The Volcano Lover*, "Historical Novel," notes, "miniature versions of 'Don Giovanni' and 'Tosca' lie embedded, like jewels, in the main narrative."

19. Reviewer Jenkyns, "Eruptions," complains about both the overwhelming burden of facts in *The Volcano Lover* and Sontag's tendency to lecture her readers. "At moments," he says, "the lecturer turns into the schoolmarm, with a priggish shaking of the head ... and a superiority too easily won" (47). Banville, "By Lava Possessed," concurs that the novel is burdened by its "encyclopedic discursiveness" and observes that "it operates in

that broad but nebulous area between fiction and essay." In Kerr's review of *In America*, "Diva," she writes, "Stimulating ideas, as usual, lurk around every corner. But they tend to arrive pre-interpreted. So marked out are the themes in this book that within minutes of finishing I felt ready to conduct a seminar." Kakutani, "Love as a Distraction," differs in her assessment of *In America*. She maintains that the novel would have been better if Sontag "had employed the sort of confiding, erudite voice she'd used in *The Volcano Lover* . . . or if the narrative bristled with the sort of provocative asides and historical cameos that energized that earlier novel."

20. In a memorial tribute, "Perspicuous Consumption," Koestenbaum states that, for Sontag, "fiction was one escape ramp; she used it to flee the punitive confines of the essay. And she used essays to flee the connect-the-dot dreariness of fiction. Her essays behave like fictions (disguised, arch, upholstered with attitudes), while her fictions behave like essays (pontificating, pedagogic, discursive)."

21. Several books of Sontag's writing have been published since her death in 2004: *At the Same Time* and *Reborn*. *Regarding the Pain of Others* remains the final manuscript that she brought to completion.

22. In the years before she wrote *Regarding the Pain of Others*, Sontag was in a great deal of physical pain. After she was successfully treated for uterine sarcoma in 1998, the aftereffects of chemotherapy left her with such pain due to damaged nerves in her feet that she spent a year on powerful medication and could not walk without assistance (Acocella 437).

23. Sontag wrote several articles about Sarajevo and her experiences there. See "'There' and 'Here'"; "Waiting for Godot in Sarajevo"; and "Why Are We in Kosovo?" For an analysis of the critical and popular responses to Sontag's involvement in Sarajevo, see Robbins, *Feeling Global*. For Robbins, responses to Sontag's writing about Sarajevo provide case studies of ambivalence and resistance to internationalism. His discussion of Sontag raises questions about "internationalism . . . as a rhetorical and political enterprise—one that oddly joins ethical urgency with aesthetic and geocultural distance, normative pressure with emotional eccentricity, self-privileging with the impulse to expand the geography of democracy" (15).

24. Several reviews describe *Regarding the Pain of Others* as a revision of *On Photography*. See Kakutani, "A Writer," and Hampton, "Wishful Seeing."

25. Sontag published a short, controversial *New Yorker* "Talk of the Town" piece on government and media responses in the days after the terrorist attacks of 9/11. She again raises concerns about how representations distort reality: "The disconnect between last Tuesday's monstrous dose of reality and the self-righteous drivel and outright deceptions being peddled by public figures and TV commentators is startling, depressing. The voices licensed to follow the event seem to have joined together in a campaign to infantilize the public."

26. Butler expresses concern that Sontag does not address our "*inability* to see what we see." Butler points out that, "To learn to see the frame that blinds us to what we see is no easy matter" ("Photography" 826).

27. A different reading experience is available from an early version of *Regarding the*

Pain of Others entitled "Looking at War." This essay appeared in the *New Yorker* along with reproductions of many of the images Sontag discusses.

28. In 2004, Sontag published another essay on war photography, "Regarding the Torture of Others." In this article, which appeared in the *New York Times Magazine* on 24 May 2004, she discusses the photographs of U.S. soldiers torturing Iraqi prisoners in Abu Ghraib.

29. Cibachrome, now called Ilfochrome, is a process of color printing from transparencies, rather than negatives. Ilfochrome photography uses special dyes that are intensely saturated and sharp, as well as very stable (Schellenberg, Riolo, and Blaue). Wall produces his images on glossy transparencies, not paper, and displays them in light boxes, backlit by fluorescent lights. For a general discussion of Wall and his work, see Lubow, "The Luminist."

30. A digital reproduction of Wall, "Dead Troops Talk," is available online at Media Art Net.

31. Numerous reviews and articles criticized Leibovitz's decision to publish photographs of Sontag as exploitative, exhibitionist, and cruel. See, for instance, Karnasiewicz "Annie Leibovitz's Reckless Candor"; Thomson, "Death Kit"; and Weinberger, "Notes on Susan." Although Joyce Carol Oates praises Leibovitz's book in "Memoirs of the Artist," she, too, raises the question of whether Sontag was aware of the photographer's presence when the most "unsparing" pictures were taken and therefore whether Sontag had granted permission. In interviews, Leibovitz has stated that before publishing the photographs, she consulted a circle of Sontag's friends and that "there was controversy within the group, but in the end they supported a decision to publish" (Brockes).

32. See Scott, "From Annie Leibovitz," as well as Karnasiewicz, "Annie Leibovitz's Reckless Candor."

33. "We tell ourselves stories in order to live" is the first sentence of Didion's *The White Album*.

Chapter 5. Theory's Aging Body

1. See Berlant, "Poor Eliza," as well as her introduction to the anthology *Compassion*, "Compassion (and Withholding)."

2. Woodward, "Calculating Compassion," sharply summarizes Berlant's conclusion: "The sentimental narrative is deliciously consumable and cruelly ineffective" (71). Woodward echoes Raymond Williams's argument in *Culture and Society* that nineteenth-century industrial novels led to a "recognition of evil," but that "sympathy was transformed not into action, but into withdrawal" (109).

3. In the mid-1980s, Tompkins argued in *Sensational Designs* that American writers from 1790–1860 sought to evoke an emotional response from a broad audience. Tompkins's work valued the affective work of popular writers, many of whom were women, and thus shifted the terms of canon formation. The question that has since been asked of Tompkins's defense of sentimentalism is: what if such works "move readers to tears but not to action?" (Harrison 264).

4. See Pechter, "The New Historicism and Its Discontents"; Martin, "Inventing Sincerity, Refashioning Prudence"; and Gearhart, "The Taming of Michel Foucault."

5. In *Ariel and the Police: Michel Foucault, William James, Wallace Stevens*, Lentricchia critiques the three preeminent critical approaches of the time—new historicism, neopragmatism, and essentialist feminism—juxtaposing their critical orthodoxies with the distinctive imaginative work of the three writers named in the title. He maintains that these deeply flawed critical movements "police" writers and texts, flattening out their differences in order to advance critics' professional ambitions.

6. Foucault begins part 2 of *The Care of the Self* with a summary of "a whole attitude of severity . . . in the thinking of philosophers and physicians in the course of the first two centuries," which includes "a mistrust of pleasures, an emphasis on the consequences of their abuse for the body and the soul, a valorization of marriage and marital obligations, a disaffection with regard to the spiritual meanings imputed to the love of boys" (39).

7. See Rajchman, "Ethics after Foucault," in which he writes that Foucault's work in *The Care of the Self* is a "modern" ethics: "His was an ethic neither of prudence nor of duty. Rather, it was an ethic of who we are said to be, and, what, therefore, it is possible for us to become. The issues it raises are issues about the various means through which we come to be constituted as the subjects of our own experience" (166).

8. For an overview of the various "outbreak narratives" that arose around AIDS, see Wald's chapter, "The Columbus of AIDS: The Invention of 'Patient Zero,'" in *Contagious*.

9. According to James Miller, Foucault's partner, Daniel Defert, gave his "blessings" to an interview given by Jean Le Bitoux to the *Advocate* in which he stated that the organization Association AIDES was started by Foucault's friends in his memory because he had the syndrome (J. Miller 24). Numerous biographies discuss Foucault's illness, though there is no certain documentation that he was ever diagnosed with AIDS. See Eribon, *Michel Foucault;* Macey, *The Lives of Michel Foucault;* and J. Miller, *The Passion of Michel Foucault*. See also Halperin, *Saint Foucault,* and Carvalho, "Fact and Fiction." There is general consensus that in the roman à clef *To the Friend Who Did Not Save My Life,* Foucault's friend Hervé Guibert portrays Foucault in the character of Muzil, who develops AIDS.

10. Before Foucault left Berkeley for the last time, he told Paul Rabineau in an interview that his next project was to take care of himself (Foucault, "On the Genealogy of Ethics," 255).

11. In recent years, a cluster of scholarship about suffering has appeared in anthropology and sociology. See Kleinman, Das, and Lock, *Social Suffering;* Das, Kleinman, Lock, Ramphele, and Reynolds, *Remaking a World;* and Das, Kleinman, Ramphele, and Reynolds, *Violence and Subjectivity*. See also Frank, "Can We Research Suffering?" and Farmer, "An Anthropology of Structural Violence."

12. The wars in Iraq and Afghanistan provided Butler with the catalysts for two additional books: *Giving an Account of Oneself,* which explores the complexities of ethical responsibility to one's self and others, and *Frames of War*.

13. Sedgwick adapts the terms "paranoid" and "reparative" from the conceptual vocabulary of Melanie Klein, whose psychoanalytic theory describes the fluctuating relationship of paranoid and depressive positions. The paranoid position is defined by anxiety, fear of the self's annihilation, and defensiveness. Objects in the world appear all good or all bad. The depressive position, by contrast, is a more mature position in which others can be seen as complex wholes. Oppositions, such as good and bad, can be recognized as belonging to the same complex object. People in the depressive position are not released from anxiety, but it is experienced differently. They are aware they can harm others and are able to feel guilt and grief. Empathy is possible from this position, as is the desire to assemble, repair, and make things whole.

14. For reviews of *Touching Feeling*, see Harris in *Feminist Theory*; M. Morris in *Journal of the History of Sexuality*; Sember in *Literature and Medicine*.

15. Sedgwick's choice to use the term "reparative" rather than Melanie Klein's term, "depressive," suggests an effort to focus on the positive potential of reading and writing from this alternative position (*Touching Feeling*, 128). Sedgwick's selection of the key term "reparative" may be surprising to readers who know her primarily as one of the founders of queer theory. The term "reparative therapy" generally refers to psychological treatments intended to change a person's sexual orientation to the heterosexual norm. In selecting the term "reparative," Sedgwick reclaims and redefines the idea of human repair from this history. For a bibliography of current work on reparative therapy, see Zucker, "The Politics and Science of 'Reparative Therapy.'"

16. The collection of essays is influenced as well by queer theory, Buddhism, the practices of teaching and learning, a core set of four theoretical readings, and innumerable other personal and professional elements that remain unnamed and unknowable. The texts that serve as Sedgwick's constant intellectual resources are Austin, *How to Do Things with Words;* the first volume of Foucault, *History of Sexuality;* Butler, *Gender Trouble;* and the first three volumes of Tomkins, *Affect Imagery Consciousness.*

17. Hawkins, "Woven Spaces," uses Sedgwick's discussion of reparative practice to explore *Dialogue on Love* as a reparative performance and as a radically innovative illness narrative. Sedgwick wrote the memoir in the form of a *haibun*—a travelogue in a combination of prose and haiku.

18. Sedgwick's essay "White Glasses" is also a reflective narrative about her dying friend, the AIDS activist Michael Lynch, and her own discovery that she has breast cancer. Diedrich, *Treatments,* offers a reading of "White Glasses" as an illness narrative (46–48).

19. For an example of paranoid criticism that refuses to spare texts about illness, see the discussion in chapter 1 of dance critic Arlene Croce's article, "Discussing the Undiscussable."

20. Sedgwick omits Melanie Klein from her list of sources in *Touching Feeling.* In Sedgwick's 2007 essay, "Melanie Klein and the Difference Affect Makes," however, she cites Klein's discussion of the paranoid/schizoid and reparative positions in "Notes on Some Schizoid Mechanisms."

21. Since this chapter was completed, Greenblatt has published more reparative work

—the preface to *The Swerve* and a related article, "The Answer Man," about Lucretius's poem, "On the Nature of Things," Greenblatt's deceased mother's terrible fear of death, and his own aging. Greenblatt celebrates the influence of Lucretius's work on literary history and what it gave to him: "the means to elude the suffocating grasp of my mother's fears and the encouragement to take deep pleasure in my brief time on the shores of light" (33).

Chapter 6. Reparative Reading

1. In recent years, *The Spirit Catches You and You Fall Down* has been assigned at Columbia University in their clinical practice program and at the University of California, Irvine, in a course called "Patient, Doctor, and Society." Dartmouth Medical School has asked students to read it for their orientation, and students at Southern Illinois were assigned the text in their second-year course, Empathy 201. (Empathy 101 is in the first-year curriculum, while Empathy 301 and 401 round out the four-year program.) In 2009, the Yale School of Medicine mailed all entering students a copy of the book and several hours were set aside during orientation for discussion and a meeting with Fadiman. See Dougherty, "Providing Better Care through Cultural Understanding," about teaching at Columbia's College of Physician and Surgeons; "Patient, Doctor and Society" for the course description in the *UCI Course Offering Handbook;* "Orientation Class 2010" from Dartmouth Medical School; "Empathy 201" course description from Southern Illinois University School of Medicine; and "Mandatory Orientation Activities" from the Yale School of Medicine.

2. Among the many works that have contributed to the pedagogical scholarship in literature and medicine or narrative medicine are Charon, *Narrative Medicine;* Charon and Montello, *Stories Matter;* Charon, Banks, Jones, Montello, and Poirier, "Literature and Medicine"; A. H. Hawkins, *Reconstructing Illness;* Hunter, Charon, and Coulehan, "The Study of Literature in Medical Education"; McLellan and Jones, "Why Literature and Medicine?"; Shapiro, "Teaching Empathy to First Year Medical Students"; and Trautmann, *Healing Arts in Dialogue.* For a collection of more than forty syllabi for courses in literature and medicine, see "Medical Humanities Syllabi" on the Medical Humanities Web site of the New York University School of Medicine.

3. Tracy Kidder's book about Dr. Paul Farmer's work with Partners in Health, *Mountains beyond Mountains,* has gained prominence on reading lists, as has Farmer's own book, *Pathologies of Power.*

4. In 2000, the Association of American Medical Colleges' (AAMC) Liaison Committee on Medical Education introduced standards for cultural competence, thereby encouraging medical schools to add cultural education to their curricula. See the AAMC pamphlet, "Cultural Competence Education for Medical Students." In addition, four years after the publication of *The Spirit Catches You,* the U.S. Department of Health and Human Services Office of Minority Health published "National Standards for Culturally and Linguistically Appropriate Services in Health Care" in an effort to improve healthcare workers' communication with diverse populations of patients.

5. See Gregg and Saha, "Losing Culture on the Way to Competence"; Kleinman and Benson, "Anthropology in the Clinic"; and Taylor, "Confronting 'Culture'."

6. See also Chiu, "Medical, Racist, and Colonial Constructions of Power."

7. Taylor cites Robert D. Newman's endorsement of *The Spirit Catches You* as a "primer" for cultural competence (Taylor 177). In the *Archives of Pediatrics and Adolescent Medicine,* Newman states that, "for those [physicians] with no source of cross-cultural training, the book can be used as a primer of sorts" (Newman 1278).

8. Taylor's primary source for her statements about Aristotelian tragedy is A. Rorty, "The Psychology of Aristotelian Tragedy."

9. According to the Macmillan Web page for *The Spirit Catches You,* last updated in 2008, "Lia Lee is still alive and still lovingly cared for by her mother and siblings. Her medical condition has not changed. Her father, Nao Kao Lee, died in January of 2003" (Macmillan, "Updates").

10. In *The Spirit Catches You,* Fadiman describes Lia's mother embroidering cloth *nyias*—a variant spelling of *nyas*—which is a Hmong baby-carrier (88).

11. Sedgwick acknowledges the influence of Sogyol Rinpoche's *Tibetan Book of Living and Dying* on her thinking about the pedagogy of illness and dying. She also draws on lessons from the "conscious dying movement," especially the idea that when one works with the dying, one receives more than one gives. The conscious dying movement she refers to developed in the United States and the United Kingdom after 1980. In Sedgwick's view, this movement brought together the Tibetan diaspora, the AIDS pandemic, and the hospice movement (*Touching Feeling* 173).

12. Sedgwick's source for this interpretation of feline behavior is Thomas, *The Tribe of Tiger.*

13. Sakyamuni, born in northern India and Nepal in the fifth century BCE, is recognized as the founder of Buddhism (Doumoulin 3–12).

14. See, for instance, the brief assessment of Sedgwick's "new age" paradigm in O'Connor, "Preface to a Post-Postcolonial Criticism."

15. Sedgwick published the talk after Lynch's death in her book *Tendencies.* In a tiny font, separated physically and graphically from the words of Sedgwick's text, is the sentence: "Michael Lynch died of AIDS on 9 July 1991" (266).

WORKS CITED

Abbott, H. Porter. "Unnarratable Knowledge: The Difficulty of Understanding Evolution by Natural Selection." *Narrative Theory and the Cognitive Sciences*. Ed. David Herman. Stanford, CA: Center for the Study of Language and Information (CSLI), 2003. 143–62.

Acocella, Joan. "The Hunger Artist." *Twenty-Eight Artists and Two Saints*. New York: Pantheon, 2007. 437–57.

Adorno, Theodor W. "Late Style in Beethoven." *Essays on Music*. Ed. Richard Leppert. Trans. Susan H. Gillespie. Berkeley: University of California Press, 2002. 564–68.

Ahmed, Sarah. *The Cultural Politics of Emotion*. New York: Routledge, 2004.

Aldrich, Robert Henry. *The Story of Burns*. Boston: N.p., 1941.

Anderson, Kristin, Judith S. Jacobson, Daniel F. Heitjan, Joshua Graff Zivin, Dawn Hershman, Alfred Neugut, and Victor R. Grann. "Cost Effectiveness of Preventive Strategies for Women with a BRCA1 or a BRCA2 Mutation." *Annals of Internal Medicine* 144.6 (2006): 397–407.

Andrews, Tom. *Codeine Diary: True Confessions of a Reckless Hemophiliac*. San Diego: Harvest/Harcourt Brace, 1998.

Antonetta, Susanne. *Body Toxic: An Environmental Memoir*. Washington, DC: Counterpoint, 2001.

Arnold, Matthew. "Dover Beach." *The Norton Anthology of English Literature*. 4th ed. Vol. 1. Ed. M. H. Abrams et al. New York: Norton, 1979. 1378–79.

———. "The Function of Criticism at the Present Time." *Essays in Criticism*. 1865. London: George Routledge & Sons, 1907. 1–36. Google Books. Web. 28 June 2011.

Austin, J. L. *How to Do Things with Words*. 2nd ed. Ed. J. O. Urmson and Marina Sbisa. Cambridge, MA: Harvard University Press, 1975.

Avrahami, Einat. *The Invading Body: Reading Illness Autobiographies*. Charlottesville: University of Virginia Press, 2007.

Banville, John. "By Lava Possessed." Rev. of *The Volcano Lover: A Romance,* by Susan Sontag. *New York Times* 9 August 1992. Web. 23 Feb. 2009.

Barry, John M. *The Great Influenza: The Epic Story of the Deadliest Plague in History.* New York: Viking, 2004.

Barthes, Roland. *The Pleasure of the Text.* Trans. Richard Miller. New York: Farrar, Straus and Giroux, 1975.

Bauby, Jean-Dominique. *The Diving Bell and the Butterfly.* New York: Vintage, 1997.

Beck, Ulrich. *Risk Society: Towards a New Modernity.* Trans. Mark Ritter. 1982. London: Sage, 1992.

Beck, Ulrich, and Elizabeth Beck-Gernscheim. *Individualization: Institutionalized Individualism and Its Social and Political Consequences.* London: Sage, 2002.

Beck, Ulrich, Anthony Giddens, and Scott Lash. *Reflexive Modernization: Politics, Tradition, and Aesthetics in the Modern Social Order.* Stanford: Stanford University Press, 1994.

Belling, Catherine. "Overwhelming the Medium: Fiction and the Trauma of Pandemic Influenza in 1918." *Literature and Medicine* 28.1 (Spring 2009): 55–81.

Benbassat, Jochanan, and Reuben Baumal. "What Is Empathy, and How Can It Be Promoted during Clinical Clerkships?" *Academic Medicine* 79.9 (2004): 832–39.

Bending, Lucy. "Approximation, Suggestion, and Analogy: Translating Pain into Language." *Yearbook of English Studies* 36.1 (2006): 131–37.

Berger, Maurice, ed. *The Crisis of Criticism.* New York: New Press, 1998.

Berlant, Lauren. *The Female Complaint: The Unfinished Business of Sentimentality in American Culture.* Durham: Duke University Press, 2008.

———. "Introduction: Compassion (and Withholding)." Berlant, *Compassion* 1–13.

———. "Poor Eliza." *American Literature* 70.3 (1998): 635–68.

———. "The Subject of True Feeling: Pain, Privacy, and Politics." *Cultural Pluralism, Identity Politics, and the Law.* Ed. Austin Sarat and Thomas R. Kearns. Ann Arbor: University of Michigan Press, 1999. 49–84.

———. "Trauma and Ineloquence." *Cultural Values* 5.1 (Jan. 2001): 41–58.

Berlant, Lauren, ed. *Compassion: The Culture and Politics of an Emotion.* New York: Routledge, 2004.

Bernstein, Peter L. *Against the Gods: The Remarkable Story of Risk.* New York: John Wiley, 1996.

Bhabha, Homi. "Dance This Diss Around." *Artforum* (Apr. 1995). *BNet Business Forum.* Web. 3 Nov. 2008.

Bingley, A. F., E. McDermott, C. Thomas, S. Payne, J. E. Seymour, and D. Clark. "Making Sense of Dying: A Review of Narratives Written since 1950 by People Facing Death from Cancer and Other Diseases." *Palliative Medicine* 20.3 (2006): 183–95.

Biro, David. *The Language of Pain: Finding Words, Compassion, and Relief.* New York: Norton, 2010.

———. *One Hundred Days: My Unexpected Journey from Doctor to Patient*. New York: Vintage, 2001.

Boston Women's Health Collective. *Our Bodies, Ourselves: A Book by and for Women*. New York: Simon and Schuster, 1973.

Boureau, Kristin. "Pain and the Unmaking of Self in Toni Morrison's *Beloved*." *Contemporary Literature* 36.3 (1995): 447–65.

Brandt, Allan M. "Behavior, Disease, and Health in the Twentieth-Century United States: The Moral Valence of Individual Risk." Brandt and Rozin 53–77.

Brandt, Allan M., and Paul Rozin, eds. *Morality and Health: Interdisciplinary Perspectives*. New York: Routledge, 1997.

"Breast/Ovarian Cancer: BRAC1 & BRAC2." Memorial Sloan-Kettering Cancer Center. 5 Jan 2009. Web. 14 Apr. 2010.

Brockes, Emma. "My Time with Susan." *The Guardian* 7 Oct. 2006. Web. 20 Feb. 2009.

Brodkey, Harold. *This Wild Darkness: The Story of My Death*. New York: Henry Holt, 1996.

Brody, Howard. *Stories of Sickness*. 2nd ed. Oxford: Oxford University Press, 2003.

Bromberg, Walter. *The Mind of Man: The Story of Man's Conquest of Mental Illness*. New York: Harper, 1937.

Brophy, Sarah. *Witnessing AIDS: Writing, Testimony, and the Work of Mourning*. Toronto: University of Toronto Press, 2004.

Brottman, Mikita. "The Fascination of the Abomination: The Censored Images of 9/11." *Film and Television after 9/11*. Ed. Wheeler Winston Dixon. Carbondale: Southern Illinois University Press, 2004.

Brown, David. "Health-Care Sector Grew as Economy Contracted in 2009." *Washington Post* 4 Feb. 2010. Web. 11 Aug. 2010.

Browne, Janet. *The Power of Place*. Vol. 2 of *Charles Darwin: A Biography*. 2 vols. Princeton: Princeton University Press, 2002.

Broyard, Anatole. *Intoxicated by My Illness*. New York: Fawcett Columbine/Ballentine, 1992.

Buell, Lawrence. "Toxic Discourse." *Critical Inquiry* 24.3 (1998): 639–65.

Burke, Carolyn. *Lee Miller: A Life*. Chicago: University of Chicago Press, 2007.

Burney, Fanny. "Letter of 1812." *The Body in the Library: A Literary Anthology of Modern Medicine*. Ed. Iain Bamforth. London: Verso, 2003. 16–20.

Butler, Judith. *Frames of War: When Is Life Grievable?* London: Verso, 2009.

———. *Gender Trouble: Feminism and the Subversion of Identity*. New York: Routledge, 1990.

———. *Giving an Account of Oneself*. New York: Fordham University Press, 2005.

———. "Photography, War, Outrage." *PMLA* 120.3 (2005): 822–27.

———. *Precarious Life: The Powers of Mourning and Violence.* London: Verso, 2004.

Butte, George. "I Know That I Know That I Know: Reflections on Paul John Eakin's 'What Are We Reading When We Read Autobiography?'" *Narrative* 13.3 (2005): 299–306.

Byatt, A. S. "Love and Death in the Shadow of Vesuvius." Rev. of *The Volcano Lover: A Romance,* by Susan Sontag. *Washington Post Book World* 16 Aug. 1992. News Bank–Access World News Database. Web. 30 June 2010.

Byerly, Carol R. *Fever of War: The Influenza Epidemic in the U.S. Army during World War I.* New York: New York University Press, 2005.

Carvalho, John. "Fact and Fiction: Writing the Difference between Suicide and Death." *Contemporary Aesthetics* 20 Nov. 2006. Web. 18 June 2011.

Cather, Willa. *One of Ours.* 1922. New York: Vintage, 1991.

Cavell, Stanley. *Philosophy the Day after Tomorrow.* Cambridge, MA: Belknap/Harvard University Press, 2005.

Chambers, Ross. *AIDS Writing, Testimonial, and the Rhetoric of Haunting.* Ann Arbor: University of Michigan Press, 2004.

———. *Facing It: AIDS Diaries and the Death of the Author.* Ann Arbor: University of Michigan Press, 1998.

Chambre, Susan M. *Fighting for Our Lives: New York's AIDS Community and the Politics of Disease.* New Brunswick: Rutgers University Press, 2006.

Charon, Rita. "Bearing Witness: Sontag and the Body." *New England Journal of Medicine* 352.8 (2005): 756.

———. *Narrative Medicine: Honoring the Stories of Illness.* Oxford: Oxford University Press, 2006.

Charon, Rita, Joanne Trautmann Banks, Anne Hudson Jones, Martha Montello, and Suzanne Poirier. "Literature and Medicine: Contributions to Clinical Practice." *Annals of Internal Medicine* 122 (1995): 599–606.

Charon, Rita, and Martha Montello, eds. *Stories Matter: The Role of Narrative in Medical Ethics.* New York: Routledge, 2002.

Chiu, Monica. "Medical, Racist, and Colonial Constructions of Power: Creating the Asian American Patient and the Cultural Citizen in Anne Fadiman's *The Spirit Catches You and You Fall Down.*" *Hmong Studies Journal* 5 (2004–5): 1–36. Web. 15 June 2011.

Clarke, B. "Katherine Mansfield's Illness." *Proceedings of the Royal Society of Medicine* 48.12 (Dec. 1955): 1029–32.

Coakley, Sarah, and Kay Kaufman Shelemay, eds. *Pain and Its Transformations: The Interface of Biology and Culture.* Cambridge, MA: Harvard University Press, 2008.

Conway, Kathlyn. *Illness and the Limits of Expression.* Ann Arbor: University of Michigan Press, 2007.

Cott, Jonathan. "Susan Sontag: The Rolling Stone Interview." *Rolling Stone* 4 Oct. 1979: 46–53. Rpt. in *Conversations with Susan Sontag*. Ed. Leland Poague. Jackson: University of Mississippi Press, 1995.

Couser, G. Thomas. *Recovering Bodies: Illness, Disability, and Life Writing*. Madison: University of Wisconsin Press, 1997.

———. *Vulnerable Subjects: Ethics and Life Writing*. Ithaca: Cornell University Press, 2004.

Cousins, Norman. *Anatomy of an Illness as Perceived by the Patient: Reflections on Healing and Regeneration*. New York: Norton, 1979.

Croce, Arlene. "Discussing the Undiscussable." *New Yorker* 26 Dec. 1994–2 Jan. 1995: 54–60. Rpt. in Berger 15–29.

Cross, T. L., B. J. Bazron, K. W. Dennis, and M. R. Isaacs. *Towards a Culturally Competent System of Care: Monograph on Effective Services for Minority Children Who Are Severely Emotionally Disturbed*. Vol. 1. Washington, DC: National Technical Assistance Center for Children's Mental Health, Georgetown University Child Development Center, 1989.

"Cultural Competence Education for Medical Students." American Association of Medical Colleges. 2005. Web. 26 Mar. 2010.

Darwin, Charles. *On the Origin of Species*. 1st ed. "Online Variorum of Darwin's *Origin of Species*: First British Edition (1859)." *The Complete Work of Charles Darwin Online*. Web. 20 Apr. 2010.

Das, Veena. "Language and Body: Transactions in the Construction of Pain." *Social Suffering*. Ed. Arthur Kleinman, Veena Das, and Margaret Lock. Berkeley: University of California Press, 1997. 67–91.

———. *Life and Words: Violence and the Descent into the Ordinary*. Berkeley: University of California Press, 2006.

Das, Veena, Arthur Kleinman, Margaret Lock, Mamphela Ramphele, and Pamela Reynolds, eds. *Remaking a World: Violence, Social Suffering, and Recovery*. Berkeley: University of California Press, 2001.

Das, Veena, Arthur Kleinman, Mamphela Ramphele, and Pamela Reynolds, eds. *Violence and Subjectivity*. Berkeley: University of California Press, 2000.

Das, Veena, and Ashis Nandy. "Violence, Victimhood and the Language of Silence." *The Word and the World: Fantasy, Symbol, and Record*. Ed. Veena Das. Delhi: Sage, 1986.

Daudet, Alphonse. *In the Land of Pain*. Ed. and trans. Julian Barnes. New York: Borzoi/Knopf, 2002.

Davis, Lennard. *Enforcing Normalcy: Disability, Deafness, and the Body*. London: Verso, 1995.

Davis, Lennard, and David B. Morris. "Biocultures Manifesto." *New Literary History* 38.3 (2007): 411–18.

DeLillo, Don. *Falling Man*. New York: Scribner, 2001.

———. *White Noise*. New York: Viking, 1985.

DeMeester, Karen. "Trauma and Recovery in Virginia Woolf's *Mrs. Dalloway*." *Modern Fiction Studies* 44.3 (1998): 649–73.

Dennett, Daniel. *Darwin's Dangerous Idea: Evolution and the Meanings of Life*. New York: Simon and Schuster, 1995.

Dickinson, Emily. "Pain—has an Element of Blank." *The Complete Poems of Emily Dickinson*. Ed. Thomas H. Johnson. Boston: Little Brown, 1960. 323–24.

Didion, Joan. *The White Album*. New York: Simon and Schuster, 1979.

Diedrich, Lisa. *Treatments: Language, Politics, and the Culture of Illness*. Minneapolis: University of Minnesota Press, 2007.

Dolezal, Joshua. "'Waste in a Great Enterprise': Influenza, Modernism, and *One of Ours*." *Literature and Medicine* 28.1 (Spring 2009): 82–101.

Dougherty, Matthew. "Providing Better Care through Cultural Understanding." *P&S* 25.2 (2005). Columbia University College of Physicians and Surgeons. Web. 27 June 2011.

Douglas, Mary. *Risk and Blame: Essays in Cultural Theory*. New York: Routledge, 1992.

Doumoulin, Henrich. *Zen Buddhism: A History, India and China*. 2nd ed. 1988. Trans. James W. Heisig and Paul Knitter. Bloomington: World Wisdom, 2005.

Drew, Richard. "The Falling Man." 2001. Photograph. See Junod, "The Falling Man."

Eakin, Paul John. *How Our Lives Become Stories: Making Selves*. Ithaca: Cornell University Press, 1999.

———. *Living Autobiographically: How We Create Identity in Narrative*. Ithaca: Cornell University Press, 2008.

———. "What Are We Reading When We Read Autobiography?" *Narrative* 12.2 (2004): 121–32.

Edson, Margart. *W;t*. New York: Faber and Faber, 1993.

"Empathy 201." Southern Illinois University School of Medicine. Office of Education and Curriculum. Web. 21 May 2007.

Epstein, Steven. *Impure Science: AIDS, Activism, and the Politics of Knowledge*. Berkeley: University of California Press, 1996.

Eribon, Didier. *Michel Foucault*. Trans. Betsy Wing. Cambridge, MA: Harvard University Press, 1991.

"European Protesters Fill Cities." CNN.com/World. 15 Feb. 2003. Web. 5 July 2008.

Fadiman, Anne. *The Spirit Catches You and You Fall Down: A Hmong Child, Her American Doctors, and the Collision of Cultures*. New York: Farrar, Straus and Giroux, 1997.

Farmer, Paul. "An Anthropology of Structural Violence." *Cultural Anthropology* 45.3 (2004): 305–17.

————. *Pathologies of Power: Health, Human Rights, and the New War on the Poor.* Berkeley: University of California Press, 2003.

Felski, Rita. *Uses of Literature.* Blackwell Manifestos. Malden: Blackwell, 2008.

"Finding Fact from Fiction." *The Guardian* 27 May 2000. Web. 30 June 2010.

Flynn, Kevin, and Jim Dwyer. "Falling Bodies, a 9/11 Image Etched in Pain." *New York Times* 10 Sept. 2004. Web. 29 June 2010.

Foer, Franklin. "Susan Superstar." *New York Magazine* 21 May 2005. Web. 29 June 2010.

Foer, Jonathan Safran. *Extremely Loud and Incredibly Close.* New York: Houghton Mifflin, 2005.

Foucault, Michel. "About the Beginning of the Hermeneutics of the Self: Two Lectures at Dartmouth." Ed. Mark Blasius. Transcribed by Thomas Keenan. *Political Theory* 21.2 (1993): 198–227.

————. *Archaeology of Knowledge and the Discourse on Language.* Trans. A. M. Sheridan Smith. New York: Pantheon, 1972.

————. *The Care of the Self.* Vol. 3 of *The History of Sexuality* (1984). Trans. Robert Hurley (1986). New York: Vintage, 1988.

————. *An Introduction.* Vol. 1 of *The History of Sexuality.* Trans. Robert Hurley. New York: Vintage, 1978.

————. "On the Genealogy of Ethics: An Overview of Work in Progress." Interview with Paul Rabinow and Hubert Dreyfus. Rabinow, *Ethics* 253–80.

————. "Self Writing." Rabinow, *Ethics* 207–22.

————. "Technologies of the Self." Rabinow, *Ethics* 223–51.

————. "What Is an Author?" *The Foucault Reader.* Ed. Paul Rabinow. New York: Pantheon, 1984. 101–20.

Frank, Arthur. "Can We Research Suffering?" *Qualitative Health Research* 11.3 (2001): 353–62.

————. "Metaphors of Pain." *Literature and Medicine* 29.1 (2011): 182–96.

————. *The Wounded Storyteller: Body, Illness, Ethics.* Chicago: University of Chicago Press, 1995.

Freedgood, Elaine. *Victorian Writing about Risk: Imagining a Safe England in a Dangerous World.* Cambridge: Cambridge University Press, 2000.

G. R. "Experiences during the Influenza Epidemic." *American Journal of Nursing* 19.3 (Dec. 1918): 203–4.

Garber, Marjorie. "Compassion." Berlant, *Compassion* 15–27.

————. "Shakespeare as Fetish." *Shakespeare Quarterly* 41.2 (1990): 242–50.

Garis, Leslie. "Susan Sontag Finds Romance." *New York Times* 2 Aug. 1992. Web. 20 Feb. 2009.

Gearhart, Suzanne. "The Taming of Michel Foucault: New Historicism, Psychoanalysis, and the Subversion of Power." *New Literary History* 28.3 (1997): 457–80.

Geertz, Clifford. *Interpretation of Cultures*. New York: Basic Books, 1973.

Gibson, Robert M., and Charles R. Fisher. "National Health Expenditures, Fiscal Year 1977." *Social Security Bulletin* 41.7 (1978): 3–20.

Giddens, Anthony. *The Consequences of Modernity*. Stanford: Stanford University Press, 1990.

———. *Modernity and Self-Identity: Self and Society in the Late Modern Age*. Stanford: Stanford University Press, 1991.

Gilmore, Leigh. *The Limits of Autobiography: Trauma, Testimony, Theory*. Ithaca: Cornell University Press, 2001.

Goldberg, Daniel S. "Exilic Effects of Illness and Pain in Solzhenitsyn's *Cancer Ward*: How Sharpening the Moral Imagination Can Facilitate Repatriation." *Journal of Medical Humanities* 30.1 (2009): 29–42.

Goldstein, Richard. "The Croce Criterion." *Village Voice* 3 Jan. 1995: 8.

Good, Byron J. "A Body in Pain: The Making of a World of Chronic Pain." *Pain as Human Experience: An Anthropological Perspective*. Ed. Mary Jo DelVecchio Good, Paul E. Brodwin, Byron J. Good, and Arthur Kleinman. Berkeley: University of California Press, 1992. 29–48.

Gould, Stephen Jay. "The Median Isn't the Message." *Discover* June 1985: 40–42. Web. 2 July 2008.

Greenberg, Lynne. *The Body Broken: A Memoir*. New York: Random House, 2009.

Greenblatt, Stephen. "The Answer Man." *New Yorker* 8 Aug. 2011: 28–33.

———. *Hamlet in Purgatory*. Princeton: Princeton University Press, 2001.

———. *Renaissance Self-Fashioning: From More to Shakespeare*. Chicago: University of Chicago Press, 1983.

———. *Shakespearean Negotiations: The Circulation of Social Energy in Renaissance England*. Berkeley: University of California Press, 1989.

Greenhalgh, Trisha, and Brian Hurwitz, eds. *Narrative Based Medicine: Dialogue and Discourse in Clinical Practice*. London: BMJ, 1998.

Gregg, Jessica, and Somnath Saha. "Losing Culture on the Way to Competence: The Use and Misuse of Culture in Medical Education." *Academic Medicine* 81.6 (2006): 542–47.

Guibert, Hervé. *To the Friend Who Did Not Save My Life*. Trans. Linda Cloverdale. New York: Atheneum/Macmillan 1991.

Hacking, Ian. *The Taming of Chance*. New York: Cambridge University Press, 1990.

Halperin, David M. *Saint Foucault: Toward a Gay Hagiography*. Oxford: Oxford University Press, 1995.

Hamid, Mohsin. *The Reluctant Fundamentalist*. New York: Harcourt, 2007.

Hampton, Howard. "Wishful Seeing: On War-nography and Radical Willfulness." Rev. of *Regarding the Pain of Others,* by Susan Sontag. *The Village Voice* 16 Apr. 2003. Web. 23 Feb. 2009.

Harker, Jaime, and Cecelia Konchar Farr. Introduction. *The Oprah Affect: Critical Essays on Oprah's Book Club.* Ed. Cecilia Konchar Farr and Jaime Harker. Albany: State University of New York Press, 2008.

Harmon, Amy. "Cancer Free at Thirty-Three, but Weighing a Mastectomy." *New York Times* 16 Sept. 2007. Web. 5 July 2008.

Harmon, Amy, Alissa Krimsky, and Kassie Bracken. "The Story of a 'Previvor.'" Video. Sept. 2007. *New York Times Online.* 5 July 2008.

Harrington, Anne. *The Cure Within: A History of Mind-Body Medicine.* New York: Norton, 2008.

Harris, Geraldine. Rev. of *Touching Feeling: Affect, Pedagogy, Performativity,* by Eve Kosofsky Sedgwick. *Feminist Theory* 5.3 (2004): 361–62.

Harrison, Mary-Catherine. "The Paradox of Fiction and the Ethics of Empathy: Reconceiving Dickens's Realism." *Narrative* 16.3 (Oct. 2008): 256–78.

Hawkins, Anne Hunsaker. *Reconstructing Illness: Studies in Pathography.* 2nd ed. West Lafayette: Purdue University Press, 1999.

Hawkins, Katy. "Woven Spaces: Eve Kosofsy Sedgwick's *Dialogue on Love*." *Women and Performance: A Journal of Feminist Theory* 16.2 (2006): 251–67.

"Health Guide: Breast Cancer." *New York Times.* Web. 14 Apr. 2010.

Heise, Ursula K. "Toxins, Drugs, and Global Systems: Risk and Narrative in the Contemporary Novel." *American Literature* 74.4 (2002): 747–78.

Herman, David. "Stories as a Tool for Thinking." *Narrative Theory and the Cognitive Sciences.* Ed. David Herman. Stanford: Center for the Study of Language and Information (CSLI), 2003. 163–92.

Hesford, Wendy S. "Reading *Rape Stories:* Material Rhetoric and the Trauma of Representation." *College English* 62.2 (1999): 192–221.

Heshusius, Lous. *Inside Chronic Pain: An Intimate and Critical Account.* Ithaca: Cornell University Press, 2009.

Hitchens, Christopher. "Civilization and Its Malcontents." Rev. of *Saturday,* by Ian McEwan. *Atlantic* Apr. 2005. Web. 14 Apr. 2010.

Holmes, Martha Stoddard. *Fictions of Affliction: Physical Disability in Victorian Culture.* Ann Arbor: University of Michigan Press, 2004.

Holmes, Martha Stoddard, and Tod Chambers. "Thinking through Pain." *Literature and Medicine* 24.1 (2005): 127–41.

Hunter, Kathryn Montgomery. *Doctors' Stories: The Narrative Structure of Medical Knowledge.* Princeton: Princeton University Press, 1991.

Hunter, Kathryn Montgomery, Rita Charon, and John L. Coulehan. "The Study of Literature in Medical Education." *Academic Medicine* 70 (1995): 787–94.

"IASP Pain Terminology." Web page. International Association for the Study of Pain. Web. 31 Jan. 2009.

Illich, Ivan. *Medical Nemesis: The Expropriation of Health.* New York: Pantheon, 1976.

Illouz, Eva. *Saving the Modern Soul: Therapy, Emotions, and the Culture of Self-Help.* Berkeley: University of California Press, 2008.

Ingram, Madeleine E. "Encephalitis: Story of a Patient." *American Journal of Nursing* June 1936: 553.

Jackson, Jean E. *Camp Pain: Talking with Chronic Pain Patients.* Philadelphia: University of Pennsylvania Press, 2000.

Jain, Sarah Lochlann. "Living in Prognosis: Toward an Elegiac Politics." *Representations* 98 (2007): 77–92.

James, Alice. *The Diary of Alice James.* Ed. Leon Edel. 1964. Boston: Northeastern University Press, 1999.

Jenkyns, Richard. "Eruptions." Rev. of *The Volcano Lover: A Romance,* by Susan Sontag. *The New Republic* 7 Sept. 1992: 46–49.

Junod, Tom. "The Falling Man." *Esquire* Sept. 2003. Web. 29 June 2010.

Kakutani, Michiko. "Historical Novel Flavored with Passion and Ideas." Rev. of *The Volcano Lover: A Romance,* by Susan Sontag. *New York Times* 4 Aug. 1992. Web. 30 June 2010.

———. "Love as a Distraction that Gets in the Way of Art." Rev. of *In America: A Novel,* by Susan Sontag. *New York Times* 29 Feb. 2000. Web. 23 Feb. 2009.

———. "A Writer Who Begs to Differ . . . with Herself." Rev. of *Regarding the Pain of Others,* by Susan Sontag. *New York Times* 11 Mar. 2003. Web. 2 Sept. 2007.

Kalfus, Ken. *A Disorder Peculiar to the Country.* New York: HarperCollins, 2006.

Karnasiewicz, Sarah. "Annie Leibovitz's Reckless Candor." Rev. of *A Photographer's Life: 1990–2005,* by Annie Leibovitz. Salon.com 18 Nov. 2006. Web. 20 Feb. 2009.

Keen, Suzanne. *Empathy and the Novel.* Oxford: Oxford University Press, 2007.

Keene, Jennifer D. *Doughboys, the Great War, and the Remaking of America.* Baltimore: The Johns Hopkins University Press, 2001.

Keevil, J. J. "The Illness of Charles, Duke of Albany (Charles I), from 1600 to 1612: An Historical Case of Rickets." *Journal of the History of Medicine and Allied Sciences* 9.4 (Oct. 1954): 407–19.

Kennedy, David M. *Over Here: The First World War and American Society.* Oxford: Oxford University Press, 1980.

Kerr, Sarah. "Diva." Rev. of *In America: A Novel,* by Susan Sontag. *New York Times* 12 Mar. 2000. Web. 23 Feb. 2009.

Kidder, Tracy. *Mountains beyond Mountains.* New York: Random House, 2003.

Klein, Melanie. "Notes on Some Schizoid Mechanisms (1946)." *The Selected Melanie Klein.* Ed. Juliet Mitchell. New York: Free Press/Macmillan, 1986. 175–200.

Kleinman, Arthur. *The Illness Narratives: Suffering, Healing, and the Human Condition.* New York: Basic Books, 1988.

Kleinman, Arthur, and Peter Benson. "Anthropology in the Clinic: The Problem of Cultural Competency and How to Fix It." *PLOS Medicine* 3.10 (2006): 1673–76.

Kleinman, Arthur, Paul E. Brodwin, Byron J. Good, Mary-Jo DelVecchio Good. "Pain as Human Experience: An Introduction." *Pain as Human Experience: An Anthropological Perspective.* Ed. Mary-Jo DelVecchio Good, Paul E. Brodwin, Byron J. Good, and Arthur Kleinman. Berkeley: University of California Press, 1992. 1–28.

Kleinman, Arthur, Veena Das, and Margaret Lock, eds. *Social Suffering.* Berkeley: University of California Press, 1997.

Knowles, John H, ed. *Doing Better, Feeling Worse: Health in the United States.* New York: Norton, 1977.

Koestenbaum, Wayne. "Perspicuous Consumption." *Artforum International* 1 Mar. 2005. Web. 23 Feb. 2009.

Kolata, Gina. *Flu: The Story of the Great Influenza Pandemic of 1918 and the Search for the Virus that Caused It.* New York: Farrar, Straus and Giroux, 1999.

Kruger, Steven F. *AIDS Narratives: Gender and Sexuality, Fiction and Science.* New York: Garland, 1996.

Kübler-Ross, Elizabeth. *On Death and Dying.* New York: Scribner, 1969.

Kumin, Maxine. *Inside the Halo and Beyond: The Anatomy of a Recovery.* New York: Norton, 2000.

Kushner, Thomasine K., and David C. Thomasma. *Ward Ethics: Dilemmas for Medical Students and Doctors in Training.* Cambridge: Cambridge University Press, 2001.

Kushner, Tony. Letter. *New Yorker* 30 Jan. 1995: 11.

Latour, Bruno. "Why Has Critique Run Out of Steam? Matters of Fact to Matters of Concern." *Critical Inquiry* 30 (Winter 2004): 225–48.

Lee, Mai Na M. Rev. of *The Spirit Catches You and You Fall Down,* by Anne Fadiman. *WWW Hmong Homepage.* Web. 27 May 2007.

Leibovitz, Annie. *A Photographer's Life: 1990–2005.* New York: Random House, 2006.

Lentricchia, Frank. *Ariel and the Police: Michel Foucault, William James, Wallace Stevens.* Madison: University of Wisconsin Press, 1988.

Levy, Andrew. *A Brain Wider than the Sky: A Migraine Diary.* New York: Simon and Schuster, 2009.

Lorde, Audre. *The Cancer Journals.* 2nd ed. San Francisco: Aunt Lute Books, 1980.

Lubow, Arthur. "The Luminist." *New York Times* 25 Feb. 2007. Web. 20 Feb. 2009.

Lupton, Deborah. *Risk.* London: Routledge, 1999.

Macey, David. *The Lives of Michel Foucault.* New York: Pantheon Books, 1993.

"Mandatory Orientation Activities." *Yale School of Medicine.* Web. 8 July 2010.

Manguso, Sarah. *Two Kinds of Decay.* New York: Farrar, Straus and Giroux, 2008.

Manto, Saadat Hasan. "The Return." *Mottled Dawn: Fifty Sketches and Stories of Partition*. Trans. Khalid Hassan. New Delhi: Penguin, 1997. 11–14.

Martin, John. "Inventing Sincerity, Refashioning Prudence: The Discovery of the Individual in Renaissance Europe." *American Historical Review* 102.5 (1997): 1309–42.

Mattingly, Cheryl. *Healing Dramas and Clinical Plots: The Narrative Structure of Experience*. Cambridge: Cambridge University Press, 1998.

Mattingly, Cheryl, and Linda C. Garro, eds. *Narrative and the Cultural Construction of Illness and Healing*. Berkeley: University of California Press, 2000.

McCarthy, Mary. *Memories of a Catholic Girlhood*. New York: Berkeley, 1946.

McEwan, Ian. *Saturday*. New York: Doubleday, 2005.

McKim, A. Elizabeth. "Making Poetry of Pain: The Headache Poems of Jane Cave Winscom." *Literature and Medicine* 24.1 (2005): 93–108.

McLellan, M. Faith, and Anne Hudson Jones. "Why Literature and Medicine?" *Lancet* 348 (1996): 109–11.

"Medical Humanities Syllabi." Medical Humanities. New York University. Web. 23 Nov. 2010.

Melzack, Ronald. "The McGill Pain Questionnaire: Major Properties and Scoring Methods." *Pain* 1 (1975): 277–99.

Messud, Claire. *The Emperor's Children*. New York: Knopf, 2006.

Miller, D. A. *The Novel and the Police*. Berkeley: University of California Press, 1988.

Miller, James. *The Passion of Michel Foucault*. New York: Simon and Schuster, 1993.

Miller, Richard E. "The Nervous System." *Writing at the End of the World*. Pittsburgh: University of Pittsburgh Press, 2005. 28–50.

"'Million' March against Iraq War. *BBC News World Edition*. 16 Feb. 2003. Web. 5 July 2008.

"Millions Join Global Anti-War Protests." *BBC News World Edition*. 17 Feb. 2003. Web. 5 July 2008.

"Mission Statement." Program in Narrative Medicine. College of Physicians and Surgeons, Columbia University. Web. 6 Nov. 2008.

Mitchell, Emily. "Sick Days." Rev. of *Two Kinds of Decay*, by Sarah Manguso. *New York Times* 22 June 2008. Web. 31 Jan. 2010.

Morris, David B. *The Culture of Pain*. Berkeley: University of California Press, 1991.

———. "How to Read *The Body in Pain*." *Literature and Medicine* 6 (1987): 139–55.

———. *Illness and Culture in the Postmodern Age*. Berkeley: University of California Press, 1998.

Morris, Marla. Rev. of *Touching Feeling: Affect, Pedagogy, Performativity*, by Eve Kosofsky Sedgwick. *Journal of the History of Sexuality* 13.2 (2004): 263–66.

Morrow, John H., Jr. *The Great War: An Imperial History*. New York: Routledge, 2005.

Mukhergee, Siddhartha. *The Emperor of All Maladies: A Biography of Cancer.* New York: Scribner/Simon and Schuster, 2010.

Murphy, Timothy F., and Suzanne Poirier. *Writing AIDS: Gay Literature, Language, and Analysis.* New York: Columbia University Press, 1993.

Mythen, Gabe. "Reappraising the Risk Society Thesis: Telescopic Sight or Myopic Vision?" *Current Sociology* 55.6 (2007): 793–813.

———. *Ulrich Beck: A Critical Introduction to the Risk Society.* London: Pluto Press, 2004.

Mythen, Gabe, and Sandra Walklate, eds. *Beyond the Risk Society: Critical Reflections on Risk and Human Security.* London: Open University Press, 2006.

Nafisi, Azar. *Reading Lolita in Tehran: A Memoir in Books.* New York: Random House, 2003.

National Cancer Institute. "Genetic Testing for BRCA1 and BRCA2: It's Your Choice." 29 June 2008. U.S. National Institutes for Health. Web. 5 July 2008.

Nelson, Emmanuel S. *AIDS: The Literary Response.* New York: Twayne, 1992.

Newman, Robert D. Rev. of *The Spirit Catches You and You Fall Down: A Hmong Child, Her American Doctors, and the Collision of Two Cultures,* by Anne Fadiman. *Archives of Pediatrics and Adolescent Medicine* 154.12 (2000): 1277–78.

Newsholme, Arthur. *Fifty Years in Public Health: A Personal Narrative with Comments.* London: G. Allen and Unwin, 1935.

Nussbaum, Martha C. "Compassion: The Basic Social Emotion." *Social Philosophy and Policy* 13.1 (1996): 27–58.

———. *Cultivating Humanity: A Classical Defense of Reform in Liberal Education.* Cambridge, MA: Harvard University Press, 1997.

———. *Love's Knowledge: Essays on Philosophy and Literature.* Oxford: Oxford University Press, 1990.

———. "Narrative Emotions: Beckett's Genealogy of Love." *Ethics* 98.2 (1988): 225–54.

———. *Upheavals of Thought: The Intelligence of Emotions.* Cambridge: Cambridge University Press, 2001.

Oates, Joyce Carol. "Confronting Head-On the Face of the Afflicted." *New York Times* 19 Feb. 1995. Web. 3 Nov. 2008.

———. "Memoirs of the Artist." *New York Review of Books* 54.1 (2007). Web. 23 Feb. 2009.

Obama, Barack. "Obama Delivers Speech to DNC in Chicago." Speech transcript. *The Washington Post* 14 Apr. 2011. Web. 18 June 2011.

O'Connor, Erin. "Preface to a Post-Postcolonial Criticism." *Victorian Studies* 45.2 (2003): 217–46.

"Oophorectomy (Ovary Removal Surgery)." MayoClinic.com. 10 Apr. 2009. Web. 21 Apr. 2010.

"Orientation Class 2010." Dartmouth Medical School. Web. 25 May 2007.

"*Our Bodies, Ourselves* Timeline." Our Bodies, Ourselves. Web. 3 Nov. 2008.

Parsons, Talcott. *The Social System*. 1951. New York: Free Press/Macmillan, 1964.

Pastore, Judith Laurence. *Confronting AIDS through Literature: The Responsibilities of Representation*. Chicago: University of Illinois Press, 1993.

"Patient, Doctor and Society." *UCI Course Offering Handbook*. 24 Sept. 2004. Web. 26 May 2007.

Pechter, Edward. "The New Historicism and Its Discontents: Politicizing Renaissance Drama." *PMLA* 102.3 (1987): 292–303.

Pennebaker, James E. *Opening Up: The Healing Power of Expressing Emotions*. New York: Guilford Press, 1997.

———. *Writing to Heal: A Guided Journal for Recovering from Trauma and Emotional Upheaval*. Oakland: New Harbinger Press, 2004.

Peterson, Alan, and Iain Wilkinson. "Health, Risk and Vulnerability: An Introduction." *Health, Risk and Vulnerability*. London: Routledge, 2008. 1–15.

Peterson, Iver. "Little Reassurance for Toms River Residents about Causes of Cancer." *New York Times* 19 Dec. 2001. Web. 17 Nov. 2008.

Phelan, James. "Who's Here? Thoughts on Narrative Identity and Narrative Imperialism." *Narrative* 13.3 (2005): 205–10.

Pinner, Max, and Benjamin F. Miller, eds. *When Doctors Are Patients*. New York: Norton, 1952.

Plato. "Allegory of the Cave." *The Republic*. Book 7. Trans. R. E. Allen. New Haven: Yale University Press, 2006. 227–32.

Porter, Katherine Anne. "Pale Horse, Pale Rider." *Pale Horse, Pale Rider*. 1939. New York: Harcourt, 1990.

Porter, Roy. *The Greatest Benefit to Mankind: A Medical History of Humanity*. New York: Norton, 1997.

Powers, Richard. *Gain*. New York: Farrar, Straus and Giroux, 1998.

Price, Reynolds. *A Whole New Life: An Illness and a Healing*. 1994. New York: Scribner, 2003.

"Probability of Breast Cancer in American Women." National Cancer Institute. U.S. National Institutes of Health. Web. 14 Apr. 2010.

Rabinow, Paul, Ed. *Ethics: Subjectivity and Truth*. New York: New Press, 1994.

Rajchman, John. "Ethics after Foucault." *Social Text* 13/14 (1986): 165–83.

Ramsay, Paul. *The Patient as Person: Explorations in Medical Ethics*. New Haven: Yale University Press, 1970.

Reisch, Walter, and R. C. Sherriff. *That Hamilton Woman*. DVD. Dir. Alexander Korda, 1941. London: Alexander Korda Films, 2009.

Rey, Roselyne. *The History of Pain*. 1993. Trans. Louise Elliott Wallace, J. A. Cadden, and S. W. Cadden. Cambridge, MA: Harvard University Press, 1998.

Rich, Frank. "Journal: Dance of Death." *New York Times* 8 Jan. 1995. Web. 17 Nov. 2008.

Ricoeur, Paul. *Freud and Philosophy: An Essay on Interpretation.* Trans. Denis Savage. 1970. New Haven: Yale University Press, 1977.

Rieff, David. *At the Point of a Gun: Democratic Dreams and Armed Intervention.* New York: Simon and Schuster, 2005.

———. *A Bed for the Night: Humanitarianism in Crisis.* New York: Simon and Schuster, 2002.

———. "Illness Is More Than Metaphor." *New York Times* 4 Dec. 2005. Web. 20 Feb. 2009.

———. "Remembering Susan Sontag." *Virginia Quarterly Review* 83.1 (2007): 303–5. Web. 29 June 2010.

———. *Slaughterhouse: Bosnia and the Failure of the West.* New York: Simon and Schuster, 1995.

———. "Susan Sontag's Final Wish." Interview by Steve Paulsen. Salon.com. 13 Feb. 2008. Web. 23 Feb. 2009.

———. *Swimming in a Sea of Death: A Son's Memoir.* New York: Simon and Schuster, 2008.

———. "Why I Had to Lie to My Dying Mother." *Guardian Observer.* 18 May 2008. Web. 29 June 2008.

Rinpoche, Sogyol. *Tibetan Book of Living and Dying.* Ed. Patrick Gaffney and Andrew Harvey. San Francisco: HarperCollins, 2002.

Robbins, Bruce. "Internationalism in Distress." *Feeling Global: Internationalism in Distress.* New York: New York University Press, 1999. 11–37.

Rollyson, Carl, and Lisa Paddock. *Susan Sontag: The Making of an Icon.* New York: Norton, 2000.

Rorty, Amélie Oksenberg. "The Psychology of Aristotelian Tragedy." *Essays on Aristotelian Poetics.* Ed. Amélie Oksenberg Rorty. Princeton: Princeton University Press, 1992. 1–22.

Rorty, Richard. *Contingency, Irony, and Solidarity.* Cambridge: Cambridge University Press, 1989.

Rosenberg, Charles. "Banishing Risk: Continuity and Change in the Moral Management of Disease." Brandt and Rozin 35–51.

Rothman, Sheila M. *Living in the Shadow of Death: Tuberculosis and the Social Experience of Illness in American History.* New York: Basic Books, 1994.

Rothstein, Edward. "Twilight of His Idols." Rev. of *On Late Style: Music and Literature against the Grain,* by Edward Said. *New York Times* 16 July 2006. Web. 11 Aug. 2010.

Rushdie, Salman. *Shalimar, the Clown.* New York: Random House, 2005.

Sacks, Oliver. *The Man Who Mistook His Wife for a Hat: And Other Clinical Tales.* 1985. New York: Simon and Schuster, 1998.

Said, Edward. *On Late Style: Music and Literature against the Grain.* 2006. New York: Vintage, 2007.

Scarry, Elaine. *The Body in Pain: The Making and Unmaking of the World.* Oxford: Oxford University Press, 1985.

———. "The Difficulty of Imagining Other Persons." *The Handbook of Interethnic Coexistence.* Ed. Eugene Weiner. New York: Continuum, 1998. 40–62.

———. "Elaine Scarry: Using Art to Encourage Empathy." Interview by Harriet Rubin. MSNBC. 29 Feb. 2008. Web. 30 May 2010.

———. "The Ideas Interview: Elaine Scarry." Interview by John Sutherland. *The Guardian* 7 Nov. 2005. Web. 30 May 2010.

Schein, Louisa, and Va-Megn Thog. "Occult Racism: The Masking of Race in the Hmong Hunter Incident." *American Quarterly* 59.4 (2007): 1051–95.

Schellenberg, Matthias, Ernst Riolo, and Hartmut Blaue. "Silver Dye-Bleach Photography." *The Focal Encyclopedia of Photography.* 4th ed. Michael R. Peres. Oxford: Focal Press/Elsevier, 2007. 700–711.

Schwartz, Lynne Sharon. *The Writing on the Wall: A Novel.* New York: Counterpoint/ Perseus Books, 2005.

Schweizer, Harold. *Suffering and the Remedy of Art.* Albany: State University of New York Press, 1997.

———. "To Give Suffering a Language." *Literature and Medicine* 14.2 (1995): 210–21.

Scott, Janny. "From Annie Leibovitz: Life, and Death, Examined." *New York Times* 6 Oct. 2006. Web. 20 Feb. 2009.

Sedgwick, Eve Kosofsky. *A Dialogue on Love.* Boston: Beacon, 1999.

———. "Melanie Klein and the Difference Affect Makes." *South Atlantic Quarterly* 106.3 (2007): 625–42.

———. "Teaching 'Experimental Critical Writing.'" *The Ends of Performance.* Ed. Peggy Phelan and Jill Lane. New York: New York University Press, 1998. 104–15.

———. *Touching Feeling: Affect, Pedagogy, Performativity.* Durham: Duke University Press, 2003.

———. "White Glasses." *Tendencies.* Durham: Duke University Press, 1993. 252–66.

Sember, Robert. Rev. of *Touching Feeling: Affect, Pedagogy, Performativity,* by Eve Kosofsky Sedgwick. *Literature and Medicine* 23.2 (2004): 364–68.

Shapiro, Johanna. "Teaching Empathy to First Year Medical Students: Evaluation of an Elective Literature and Medicine Course." *Education for Health* 17.1 (2004): 73–84.

Sontag, Susan. "Against Interpretation." *Against Interpretation and Other Essays.* 1961. New York: Picador/Farrar, Straus and Giroux, 1966. 3–14.

———. *At the Same Time: Essays and Speeches.* Ed. Paolo Dilonardo and Anne Jump. New York: Farrar, Straus and Giroux, 2007.

———. *The Benefactor.* 1963. New York: Picador/Farrar, Straus and Giroux, 2002.

———. *Death Kit: A Novel.* 1967. New York: Picador/Farrar, Straus and Giroux, 2002.

———. "Desperately Seeking Susan: A 2000 Conversation with Susan Sontag."
Interview by James Marcus. Amazonia-book.com. Feb. 2000. Web. 23 Feb. 2009.

———. *I, etcetera: Stories.* 1978. New York: Picador/Farrar, Straus and Giroux, 2002.

———. *Illness as Metaphor* and *AIDS and Its Metaphors.* New York: Anchor/Doubleday,
1978, 1988.

———. *In America: A Novel.* New York: Farrar, Straus and Giroux, 2000.

———. "In Plato's Cave." Sontag, *On Photography* 3–24.

———. Interview with Bill Moyers. *Now: Arts and Culture.* Public Broadcasting
Service. 4 Apr. 2003. Web. 2 Sept. 2007.

———. "Looking at War." *New Yorker* 9 Dec. 2002: 82–98.

———. "Mind as Passion." *Under the Sign of Saturn.* 1980. New York: Picador/Farrar,
Straus and Giroux. 181–205.

———. "Nathalie Sarraute and the Novel." *Against Interpretation and Other Essays.*
1961. New York: Picador/Farrar, Straus and Giroux, 1966. 100–111.

———. *On Photography.* New York: Picador/Farrar Straus and Giroux, 1977.

———. *Reborn: Journals and Notebooks, 1947–1963.* Ed. David Rieff. New York: Farrar,
Straus and Giroux, 2008.

———. *Regarding the Pain of Others.* New York: Farrar, Straus and Giroux, 2003.

———. "Regarding the Torture of Others." *New York Times Magazine* 24 May 2004:
25.

———. "Singleness." Sontag, *Where the Stress Falls* 259–62.

———. "Talk of the Town." *New Yorker* 24 Sept. 2001: 30. Web. June 2010.

———. "'There' and 'Here.'" Sontag, *Where the Stress Falls* 323–29.

———. "The Truth of Fiction Evokes Our Common Humanity." Speech excerpt. Los
Angeles Public Library. 7 Apr. 2004. Rpt. in *Los Angeles Times* 28 Dec. 2004. Web.
20 Feb. 2009.

———. *Under the Sign of Saturn.* New York: Picador/Farrar, Straus and Giroux, 1980.

———. "'Victim Art'; Philistinism All Over Again." *New York Times* 5 Mar. 1995. Web.
17 Nov. 2008.

———. *The Volcano Lover: A Romance.* 1992. New York: Picador/Farrar, Straus and
Giroux, 2004.

———. "Waiting for Godot in Sarajevo." Sontag, *Where the Stress Falls* 299–322.

———. *Where the Stress Falls.* New York: Farrar, Straus and Giroux. 2001.

———. "Why Are We in Kosovo?" *New York Times* 2 May 1999. Web. 20 Feb. 2009.

———. "Writing Itself: On Roland Barthes." Sontag, *Where the Stress Falls* 63–88.

Spelman, Elizabeth V. *Fruits of Sorrow: Framing Our Attention to Suffering.* Boston:
Beacon, 1998.

Stanley, Patricia Haas. "The Patient's Voice: A Cry in Solitude or a Call for Community." *Literature and Medicine* 23.2 (2004): 346–63.

Stegner, Wallace. *The Big Rock Candy Mountain*. 1943. New York: Penguin, 1991.

Styron, William. *Darkness Visible: A Memoir of Madness*. 1990. New York: Vintage, 1992.

Sweeney, Carole. "The Unmaking of the World." *Atlantic Studies* 4.1 (2007): 51–66.

Taylor, Janelle S. "Confronting 'Culture' in Medicine's 'Culture of No Culture.'" *Academic Medicine* 78.6 (2003): 555–59.

———. "The Story Catches You and You Fall Down: Tragedy, Ethnography, and 'Cultural Competence.'" *Medical Anthropology Quarterly* 17.2 (2003): 159–81.

Teachout, Terry. "Victim Art." *Commentary*. Mar. 1995: 58–61.

Thernstrom, Melanie. *The Pain Chronicles: Cures, Myths, Mysteries, Prayers, Diaries, Brain Scans, Healing, and the Science of Suffering*. New York: Farrar, Straus and Giroux, 2010.

Thomas, Elizabeth Marshall. *The Tribe of Tiger: Cats and Their Culture*. New York: Simon and Schuster, 1994.

Thomson, David. "Death Kit." Rev. of *A Photographer's Life: 1990–2005*, by Annie Leibovitz. *New Republic* 22 Feb. 2007. Web. 20 Feb. 2009.

Thorne, Mamie Ellington. "Four Weeks of Influenza in a Mining Camp." *American Journal of Nursing* 21.3 (1920): 154–57.

Tomkins, Silvan. *Affect Imagery Consciousness*. 4 vols. New York: Springer, 1992.

Tompkins, Jane. *Sensational Designs: The Cultural Work of American Fiction, 1790–1860*. Oxford: Oxford University Press, 1985.

Trautmann, Joanne. *Healing Arts in Dialogue: Medicine and Literature*. Carbondale: Southern Illinois University Press, 1981.

Tulloch, John, and Deborah Lupton. "Risk, the Mass Media and Personal Biography: Revisiting Beck's 'Knowledge, Media, and Information Society.'" *European Journal of Cultural Studies*. 4.1 (2001): 5–27.

———. *Risk and Everyday Life*. London: Sage, 2003.

Macmillan. "Updates to *The Spirit Catches You and You Fall Down*." 2008. Web. 8 July 2010.

Updike, John. *Terrorist*. New York: Knopf, 2006.

U.S. Department of Health and Human Services Office of Minority Health. "National Standards for Culturally and Linguistically Appropriate Services in Health Care." Washington, DC. March 2001. Web. 8 July 2010.

———. Office of Minority Health. "What Is Cultural Competency?" 19 Oct. 2005. Web. 26 Mar. 2010.

van Hooft, Stan. "Pain and Communication." *Medicine, Health Care, and Philosophy* 6.3 (2003): 255–62.

Veyne, Paul. "The Final Foucault and His Ethics." Trans. Catherine Porter and Arnold I. Davidson. *Critical Inquiry* 20.1 (1993): 1–9.

Wald, Priscilla. *Contagious: Cultures, Carriers, and the Outbreak Narrative.* Durham: Duke University Press, 2008.

Wald, Priscilla, Jay Clayton, and Karla F. C. Holloway, eds. Special issue on "Genomics in Literature, Visual Arts, and Culture." *Literature and Medicine* 26.1 (2007).

Wall, Jeff. "Dead Troops Talk: A Vision after an Ambush of a Red Army Patrol Near Moquor, Afghanistan, Winter 1986." 1992. Photograph reproduction. Media Art Net. Web. 20 Feb. 2009.

Walter, Jess. *The Zero: A Novel.* New York: HarperCollins, 2006.

Waterlow, W. G. "Illness and Death of Mozart." *Medical Journal of Australia* 44.21 (May 1957): 741–42.

Weinberger, Eliot. "Notes on Susan." *New York Review of Books* 54.13 (2007). Web. 23 Feb. 2009.

Wells, Susan. *"Our Bodies, Ourselves" and the Work of Writing.* Stanford: Stanford University Press, 2010.

Wexler, Alice. *Mapping Fate: A Memoir of Family, Risk, and Genetic Research.* Berkeley: University of California Press, 1996.

White, C. S. "The Last Illness of Major Walter Reed." *Medical Annals of the District of Columbia* 24.8 (Aug. 1955): 396–98.

Wilkinson, Iain. *Anxiety in a Risk Society.* London: Routledge, 2001.

Williams, Kate. *England's Mistress: The Infamous Life of Emma Hamilton.* New York: Ballantine/Random House, 2006.

Williams, Raymond. *Culture and Society.* New York: Columbia University Press, 1958.

Wilson, Daniel J. *Living with Polio: The Epidemic and Its Survivors.* Chicago: University of Chicago Press, 2005.

Wolf, Eric R. *Europe and the People without History.* Berkeley: University of California Press, 1982.

Wolfe, Thomas. *Look Homeward, Angel.* 1929. New York: Scribner, 1995.

Woodward, Kathleen. "Calculating Compassion." Berlant, *Compassion* 59–85.

——. "Statistical Panic." *Differences: A Journal of Feminist Cultural Studies* 11.2 (1999): 177–203.

Woolf, Virginia. *On Being Ill.* 1930. Ashfield: Paris Press, 2002.

Zeiger, Robert. *America's Great War: World War I and the American Experience.* New York: Rowman and Littlefield, 2000.

Zox-Weaver, Annalisa. "When the War Was in *Vogue:* Lee Miller's War Reports." *Women's Studies* 32.2 (2003): 131–63.

Zucker, Kenneth J. "The Politics and Science of 'Reparative Therapy.'" Editorial. *Archives of Sexual Behavior* 32.5 (2003): 399–402.

INDEX